*Getting Started in* —

# Tax
# Consulting

# The Getting Started in Series

# *Getting Started in*
# Tax
# Consulting

## Gary W. Carter, CPA

John Wiley & Sons, Inc.
New York • Chichester • Weinheim • Brisbane • Singapore • Toronto

Copyright © 2001 by Gary W. Carter. All rights reserved.

Published by John Wiley & Sons, Inc.

Published simultaneously in Canada.

This publication is designed to provide accurate and authoritative information in regard to the subject matter covered. It is sold with the understanding that the publisher is not engaged in rendering professional services. If professional advice or other expert assistance is required, the services of a competent professional person should be sought.

*Library of Congress Cataloging-in-Publication Data:*
Carter, Gary W.
    Getting started in tax consulting / Gary W. Carter.
      p.  cm.—(The getting started in series)
    Includes index.
    ISBN 0-471-38454-2 (pbk. : alk. paper)
    1. Tax consultants.  2. Tax accounting.  I. Title.  II. Getting started in.
HJ2351.8 .C37 2001
343.7304'2—dc21                            00-051314

Printed in the United States of America.

10 9 8 7 6 5 4 3 2 1

# Contents

# *Acknowledgments*

I would thank the many people who were gracious enough to be interviewed for this book or otherwise provided valuable information to pass on to you. They include Rita Benassi, Deloitte & Touche, LLP; Frank Claymon, Frank E. Claymon, Ltd.; E. Burke Hinds, Messerli & Kramer, P.A.; Catherine Holtzclaw, Holtzclaw & Associates, LLC; Bill Horne, McGladrey & Pullen; Fred Jacobs, MBT Program, University of Minnesota; Bill Knight, Internal Revenue Service; Kevin Koehler, Lund Koehler Cox & Arkema LLP; Bob Lindgren, Bob Lindgren's Income Tax Service; Ben Ostfield, Property Tax Management Group Ltd.; Edward Pyle, Tax Wise Shop; Ed Ryan, Edward M. Ryan, CPA; James Tilsner, James Tilsner, CPA; Craig Wilson, Craig H. Wilson, CPA; Jay Zack, RSM McGladrey, Inc.

Thanks also to Paul Gutterman Esq., CPA and Steve Warren, CPA, who provided chapter reviews. I would especially like to thank my wife, Deanna Carlson, for being the copyeditor, transcriber and contributor of creative ideas. Thanks, above all, to you, the reader. I sincerely hope that this book will help you to discover your ideal career, tax or otherwise.

Best wishes.

—Gary W. Carter

P.S. If you have comments about this book, your feedback is invited. Please e-mail me directly at gwc@thetaxguy.com or visit my Web site at www.thetaxguy.com.

# Introduction

*Taxation, in reality, is life. If you know the position a person takes on taxes, you can tell their whole philosophy. The Tax Code, once you get to know it, embodies all the essence of life: greed, politics, power, goodness, charity.*

— Sheldon Cohen, former IRS Commissioner

## WERE YOU BORN TO BE A TAX CONSULTANT?

Fred Hoenes came home from the war in 1945 and used the GI Bill to get a bachelor's degree in accounting from Gonzaga University. He eventually opened a certified public accountancy practice in Phoenix, Arizona. For over 40 years he carefully guided the tax and financial affairs of hundreds of clients. In a conversation I had with Fred when he was close to retirement, I asked him why he decided to become an accountant. Several years before that I had chosen the same profession, though I had taken a somewhat different route. Fred was my uncle, but for some reason we had never discussed career choices before, I guess because we lived a distance apart. Anyway, Fred's answer was surprising.

He replied, "Mrs. Johnson, my third-grade teacher, told me I was good at arithmetic so I should become an accountant." I waited a moment to hear the rest, but there was no further explanation. So I said, "You mean that's *it*—that's how you made your choice?" The matter-of-fact response was simply "Yup."

Fred was a tall wiry redhead, bald on top, with a wry grin, a quick wit and a sharp mind. It was hard to believe he would devote his life to a career based solely on an off-the-cuff comment by his third-grade teacher. But then again, he fell naturally into the role of an accountant and thoroughly enjoyed it. It was hard to imagine him as anything else. So perhaps Fred's die was cast before Mrs. Johnson's suggestion. Maybe he was born to be an accountant and was fortunate enough to be guided into his calling early in life.

Who's to say what forces conspire to place us in our life's work? Some are lucky enough to discover early what they are meant to do and live a life fulfilled. Others suffer through a few dry runs before their calling becomes apparent. Still others get trapped in an unhappy work life and never learn that getting up to go to work in the morning can be a joyful experience.

You might be a high school student contemplating a college degree, a young entrepreneur searching for a business opportunity, or someone mature in a nongratifying career who is seeking a new direction. Regardless of your current status in life, perhaps you are on the verge of discovery—you might be about to learn that you were born to be a tax consultant!

Tax consulting and return preparation is a fast-paced and dynamic industry. It is a well-respected, professional field requiring technical knowledge, but at the same time it can be entered at a basic level with relatively limited education and training. It carries the promise of high earning potential, can be entered either full or part-time, and is a perfect candidate for a home-based business. It has no barriers from entry based on age, sex, race, or religion. To the contrary, the demand for tax services is so universal that members of special groups can employ their status as an edge in establishing a niche in the market.

## WHAT YOU WILL LEARN FROM THIS BOOK

I presume that you opened this book to determine what it takes to be a tax consultant, what it is like to be a tax consultant, and how much money you can earn as a tax consultant. That is exactly what these pages reveal, and more. Here is a rundown of what you will find in each chapter.

Chapter 1 offers glimpses into the nature of the work of tax consultants, through an examination of the legal environment in which they operate and interview excerpts with several tax professionals. The typical roles played by unlicensed practitioners, enrolled agents, certified public accountants (CPAs), and tax attorneys are examined. You are invited to look in on the hypothetical Internal Revenue Service (IRS) audit of the tax return of an imaginary couple, Bubba and Bertha, and see how deftly their imaginary tax advisor, Leonard, handles the situation.

Chapter 2 provides an assessment of the current and future demand for tax consulting and offers assurance that the work of tax consultants will not become obsolete any time soon. Obsolescence is a legitimate concern for aspiring tax consultants, in view of the proposals by some politicians in recent years to design a greatly simplified flat tax or abandon the income tax and do away with the IRS. This chapter summarizes the consensus views of those who are knowledgeable about both the political process and the technical aspects of taxation.

Chapter 3 presents some thoughts on how to assess your personality fit within the tax profession. Tax consultants typically are not the introverted bean counters they are often perceived to be. Advice from tax professionals provides insight into the personality traits firms value the most and what it takes to become an entrepreneur in the tax profession. You are advised on how to break into the tax business and given the educational and certification requirements for the various designations within the field of tax consulting.

Chapter 4 describes how to formulate your business plan for starting a tax practice, emphasizing the importance of a solid business strategy before you begin. Aspects of starting your own practice independently or purchasing a franchise are compared, with information on available franchising opportunities provided. The comparative advantages of starting a practice from the ground up versus purchasing an existing practice are also discussed, and suggestions are made on how to determine the value of a practice. Operational considerations are examined, including finding a niche for your tax services, the location of your office, setting your fees, and marketing your services.

Chapters 5 and 6 focus on the business entity and tax issues that concern new and existing business owners. Chapter 5 compares the different forms of business organization that you and your clients might consider, including a sole proprietorship, a partnership, a C corporation, an S corporation, and a limited liability company (LLC). Features examined for these entities include their general tax treatment, tax accounting methods and periods, retirement plans, and liability for debts and claims. In Chapter 6 you will learn about state and local taxes, fees and permits, the home-office deduction, self-employment taxes, estimated tax payments, and employment taxes for employees. You will also get a few tips on keeping the books and record keeping.

Chapter 7 gives you a basic introduction to tax research, which is an essential skill of a tax professional. It also introduces you to tax information resources available from private and public sources, primarily over the Internet. You get a glimpse of the tax planning and compliance software available and a brief overview of what these programs have to offer.

In Chapter 8 I describe my recent journey into the world of e-business in starting and running a part-time, Web-based tax service. The inspiration for my practice may be atypical, but the lessons I have learned along the way may provide a head start to anyone considering such a venture. I do not profess to be an expert in this area, so I include plenty of additional resources for starting a business online.

The Internal Revenue Service is the adversary of tax consultants at times but is also their partner and advisor. Chapter 9 offers insight into the workings of this ominous federal agency. Its restructuring, modernization efforts, and revised goals are examined.

In Chapter 10 you get the opportunity to sit in on conversations with six experienced tax professionals. One of the best ways to determine your compatibility with a new profession is to seek out people in the profession to share their thoughts and experiences with you. This chapter saves you the legwork. You can sit back and read the views of these veteran tax consultants on all aspects of the profession.

## FORMULA FOR SUCCESS

The path to a career in tax consulting is a five-step process consisting of:

1. Keeping the dream.
2. Gathering the information.
3. Setting specific goals.
4. Developing the plan.
5. Taking action.

It starts with a dream—imagining yourself in the career. That is a necessary first step and will continue to be critical as you move toward your goal. Successful people never quit dreaming. The dream will become more and more specific as you acquire information about the various opportunities in tax consulting.

Gathering information is important to realistically assess your aptitude for the profession and to consider the role you would like to play. Open your eyes and ears and take in all you can. Then make your decisions with knowledge and consideration of all factors.

Learning critical information by completing this book will enable you to begin setting specific goals. Only specific goals, based on accurate information, are obtainable. Vague, unrealistic goals without a specific plan of action can never be achieved.

Once your goal is set, develop the plan. The plan must detail each step toward your goal, and how and when it can be completed. Plan what you know you can achieve and what you are honestly willing to do. Be sincere in your estimate of the time, effort, and expense each step will entail. The plan might require revisions along the way—there will be setbacks. But if it is a sound and realistic plan, you will have the confidence to press on.

The final step is the most critical and is the one on which most people stumble. Regardless of all the dreaming, goal setting, and planning you do, failure to take action assures you of failure. On the other hand, implementing your plan, one step at a time, guarantees your success. This is where the dream becomes reality. Let it happen. Keep the dream, focus on your goal, and don't quit until you have achieved it.

# Chapter 1

# The Role of a Tax Consultant

*Everything today is taxes. . . . What better seat on the grandstand of life can I offer you than that of tax counsel? . . . Who is the figure behind every great man, the individual who knows his ultimate secrets? A father confessor? Hell no, the tax expert.*

—Louis Auchincloss

## DISCOVERING OPPORTUNITIES FOR CLIENTS

It was 1980. I was a lowly staff accountant with one of the Big Eight (now Big Five) certified public accounting (CPA) firms in Denver. One day the tax partner came by my cubicle and invited me to lunch. He said he had a client he wanted me to meet. On the way to the restaurant I learned that the person we were to have lunch with was the multimillionaire owner of a local cable TV company. I will call him Mr. X. I also learned that I would

**Big Five:** Through mergers of the Big Eight, the five largest international CPA firms are now PricewaterhouseCoopers, KPMG, Arthur Andersen, Deloitte & Touche, and Ernst & Young. These are the premier employers for young CPAs entering public practice.

be preparing Mr. and Mrs. X's tax return that year and handling any tax planning needs they might have.

This news made my mouth go dry. Our firm did the audit for Mr. X's cable company, and I had heard about Mr. X from one of the auditors. Word had it that he was so aloof that none of the audit staff had ever seen him. The audit partner on the job dealt with the company's chief financial officer but never Mr. X. It seemed to me that someone so rich, powerful, and haughty would be difficult to work with.

We met Mr. X and Mrs. X at an upscale restaurant. I was surprised to discover that they were both charming and we hit it off. Mr. X did not talk to auditors because he had no interest in auditing. He did, however, have an interest in taxes and liked to talk about taxes a lot. After that day, my audit friends became quite jealous when Mr. X would call me in my little cubicle and talk for long periods. The audit partner in the big corner office was not even allowed to meet him.

**Auditors:** Those certified public accountants in public practice who audit the books of clients and issue reports to attest the fairness of financial statements. Tax and audit are the two major umbrellas in the public accounting profession.

I did some pretty routine tax planning for Mr. and Mrs. X and showed them how to save a bundle of taxes on their investment transactions. For this Mr. X was very grateful. It was a rush for me. I was making $19,000 a year then. Mr. X had more than that withheld from his biweekly paycheck to pay his taxes. It was fun to have this wealthy business owner look to me for advice and counsel.

I was the personal tax advisor for Mr. X, who had more money withheld from his biweekly paycheck to pay his taxes than I made in an entire year.

Today I am a tax educator. For several years I have been the coordinator of a volunteer income tax assistance (VITA) site on the University of Minnesota campus to help international students and scholars. In this position I often get inquiries about taxes from nonresidents. Last week I got an e-mail from a desperate international student from the Czech Republic whom I have never met. She had prepared her return herself and instead of getting the $300 refund she had expected, she got a bill from the IRS for $500. She was not living in my area but had heard about me from a friend and wondered if I could help.

**Internal Revenue Service (IRS):** The federal administration and enforcement agency of the U.S. tax system.

I asked her to fax me her tax return and the letter from the IRS. It turned out the IRS was correct—she had screwed up the return. I asked her a few questions, though, and found that she was eligible for a $5,000 exemption that she was unaware of (and that the IRS failed to tell her about), under the U.S./Czech tax treaty. Instead of having to make the $500 payment, she was still due a refund of about $200. Her e-mail back to me said "Thank you, thank you, thank you, thank you!" She even sent me one of those Web greeting cards. Guess what it said. "Thank you!" This free advice was easy for me to do and took less than a half hour of my time, but it was just as rewarding as helping Mr. X.

This is the essence of the tax profession. You get to help individuals and businesses save money that they would otherwise have to give to the IRS. What could be more gratifying? There are many ways of doing this in various capacities. This chapter offers glimpses into the nature of the work of tax consultants and the legal environment in which they operate. It examines the typical roles played by unlicensed practitioners, enrolled agents, certified public accountants (CPAs), and tax attorneys.

The essence of the tax profession is helping individuals and businesses save money that would otherwise go to the IRS.

## TAX CONSULTING VERSUS TAX COMPLIANCE

Throughout this book I use the term "consultant" interchangeably with "professional," "practitioner," and "advisor." In other words, I lump together all of the services of individuals who offer their tax expertise to clients on a fee basis. Within the industry, services are classified as tax return preparation (compliance) and tax consulting. Tax compliance is the process of reporting past transactions, while tax consulting generally involves planning for future transactions. These two functions are often intertwined, with tax professionals discovering consulting work in the process of return preparation and doing compliance work while engaged in tax consulting. Although the term "consultant" sparks a more professional and attractive image, most tax professionals, except perhaps for attorneys, begin their careers preparing tax returns. Many spend the majority of their time throughout their careers in compliance work.

> Tax compliance is the process of filling out tax forms while tax consulting is advising clients on how to save taxes in future transactions.

Both compliance and consulting require the same level of technical expertise. Jay Zack, a tax partner with RSM McGladrey, Inc., said, "We believe that you learn tax consulting best by doing compliance." The way most tax practitioners become very familiar with the rules for a particular transaction is by working through the IRS forms and instructions in order to report the transaction. Additional details might be learned by reading court cases, IRS regulations and rulings, and expert commentary. Tax consulting often draws from knowledge learned in this manner. It is extremely difficult for tax professionals to consult properly with a client in an area in which they are not familiar with the reporting requirements. Therefore, tax consulting generally grows from a tax compliance background.

> Tax compliance work usually precedes tax consulting in a typical career path and teaches a tax advisor how to be a good consultant.

Small practitioners rarely get approached for consulting prior to doing compliance work for a client, unless they have established a reputation in a specialized area. Once a small practitioner gains experience and proficiency in a particular area and establishes a reputation for proficiency, pure consulting opportunities become available. Most small and sole practitioners remain actively engaged in compliance throughout their careers, however, because compliance is generally the bread and butter of a small tax practice.

Still, compliance work presents the best opportunities to discover the consulting needs of a client. During the very busy tax season, getting the forms filled out and filed are the primary responsibilities of a small practitioner. In the process of doing so, the practitioner must review and analyze all of the client's financial dealings. This is the best time to take note of a client's potential consulting needs, which can be addressed later during the not-so-busy season. Like a doctor who discovers the health needs of patients during their annual physical, practitioners should be scrutinizing clients' consulting needs when they are financially naked at tax time.

**Tax season:** The time when most individual tax returns are filed—between January 15 and April 15. Many accountants are busy with tax return extensions and fiscal year filing deadlines throughout the year.

Ed Ryan, president of Edward M. Ryan, CPA, in Minneapolis, began his career in a two-member CPA firm doing primarily compliance work for individuals. Ed was eager to do more on the planning and business side, so he attended school at night to obtain a Master's of Business Taxation degree from the University of Minnesota's Carlson School of Management. After obtaining his master's degree, Ed started his own firm, which has grown to about 15 members.

"The fun is in the planning," said Ed, who now spends about 90 percent of his chargeable time doing consulting. "You have a target that you have to hit, but it is a lot more fun because there is a lot more reward that you are able to share with your clients. Families so often look for opportunities that will assist them in managing not only their business but their personal finances, and tax planning provides great opportunities to assist them in their financial affairs. So it is very self-fulfilling because you can see the results and they are reoccurring. It is really education. They are educating me about their family lifestyle and I am educating them about tax and planning opportunities. That is very rewarding—it's the reason you get up every day."

Working for a larger firm presents more opportunities for initial consulting engagements with clients. Managers and senior managers of larger firms (those with six to 10 years of experience) sometimes spend the majority of their time on consulting engagements while at the same time supervising lower-level personnel. Partners with larger firms generally neither prepare nor review tax returns; these chores are left to lower-level personnel. Many partners in large firms are involved with tax consulting, but often only by supervising work done by managers.

In larger CPA firms, entry-level professionals do compliance work while managers and partners do consulting.

The next section provides a glimpse of the working environment of a tax professional.

## FERTILE GROUNDS OF THE U.S. TAX SYSTEM

Some people think it is the IRS that determines how much we pay in federal taxes. Actually the Congress, with the consent of the President, writes federal tax laws. State tax laws are enacted by the various state governments. All federal tax laws are contained in Title 26 of the United States Code, commonly called the Internal Revenue Code (or the Code). The IRS is charged with administering, enforcing, and interpreting the Code, while state revenue departments administer state statutes. Determinations by the enforcement agencies, however, are not the final authority. A knowledgeable tax consultant is a taxpayer's best friend when faced with an IRS or state audit. Although most IRS agents are fair, honest, and ethical individuals, disagreements may arise between the IRS and taxpayers regarding both factual issues and the proper interpretation of the Code. On occasion, a taxpayer is faced with an IRS that is overbearing, abusive, or simply wrong. At such times, the advocacy of a tax professional is invaluable.

The Internal Revenue Code is the primary authority for our federal tax laws, not the IRS.

## *Specialization Is Essential*

Our federal tax system is complex and in a continuous state of change. There are no "tax experts" in the generic sense. The Internal Revenue Code is such a vast body of law that no one person can master it all. Additionally, each state has a different set of rules to follow. That is why tax consultants are compelled to specialize in particular areas of the law or in specific industries.

> A tax practitioner must specialize in a particular area of the law to truly be a tax expert.

There are those who specialize in corporate tax, in the taxation of passthrough entities, in individual tax, in the taxation of international businesses and individuals working overseas, in state and local taxation, in the taxation of estates and gifts, or in trust taxation, to name a few. Each of these areas is extensive enough to keep a person busy learning about it for an entire career.

Certain industries are subject to unique tax rules that require special knowledge. Banks and insurance companies come to mind. I once worked almost exclusively with oil and gas independent producers. Many of their transactions are so peculiar that they are not even described in the Internal Revenue Code. It was necessary to look to court decisions (called "case law") to find the answers. That brings us to a discussion of our judicial system—another component of the tax system that requires the special skill and knowledge of a tax consultant.

## *Our Territorial Judicial System*

In the tax world, the role of the judicial system is to settle disputes between the IRS and taxpayers that the parties were not able to resolve through negotiation. Disputes could involve either factual or legal arguments. A factual dispute might deal with whether a business expense was actually paid by the taxpayer or the value of a work of art given to a charitable organization. A legal dispute, on the other hand, involves the proper interpretation of an IRS ruling or regulation or of a particular section of the Internal Revenue Code. Judicial rulings on legal arguments provide support, for either the IRS or taxpayers, when the same issue comes up again.

Judicial rulings also create gray areas, however, because they tend to have only limited authority. Although the laws are written without regard to where taxpayers live, most of the federal appellate courts that decide tax issues have only regional jurisdiction. One appellate court is not required to follow decisions of other appellate courts. It might, therefore, rule in favor of the taxpayer, after another appellate court has ruled in favor of the IRS on the same issue involving a different taxpayer. All appellate courts must follow decisions of the Supreme Court, but the Supreme Court is often reluctant to hear tax cases, so few tax disputes are settled there.

Most tax disputes never go higher than a regional appellate court because the Supreme Court is reluctant to hear tax issues. This causes uncertainty because of the limited authority of the appellate courts.

### Do Not Try This at Home

The fractured and ever-changing nature of the judicial system, along with the overwhelming complexity of the tax code, give the IRS an immense advantage when dealing directly with the typical layperson about a tax matter. To a knowledgeable tax advisor, however, these are fertile grounds, ripe with opportunities.

The IRS has an immense advantage when dealing directly with the typical layperson.

Opportunities have their limits, however. As tax consultants are advocates for taxpayers, the IRS is an advocate for the federal government. Both tax advisors and the IRS are restricted by law from becoming overzealous. Some of these rules are discussed next.

## LEGAL RESPONSIBILITIES OF TAX CONSULTANTS

Besides the common-law rules relating to the relationship between a principal and an agent, strict standards must be followed when a tax advisor is dealing with the IRS on behalf of a client. The director of practice of the IRS is responsible for enforcing the rules governing practice before the IRS. These rules are published by the government as "Treasury Department Circular 230." Responsibilities of the director of practice include deciding who gets to practice before the IRS and conducting disciplinary proceedings relating to those who are allowed to practice.

**Treasury Department Circular 230:** Contains the standards that must be followed by a tax advisor in dealing with the IRS on behalf of clients.

## Practice Before the Internal Revenue Service

The term "practice before the IRS," as used in Circular 230, refers to the performance of specific activities. They include only the following duties:

- ✔ Communicating with the IRS for a taxpayer regarding the taxpayer's rights, privileges, or liabilities under the laws and regulations administered by the IRS.
- ✔ Representing a taxpayer at conferences, hearings, or meetings with the IRS.
- ✔ Preparing and filing necessary documents with the IRS for a taxpayer.

Anything else that a tax consultant can do for a client is not within the scope of practicing before the IRS. For example, furnishing information at the request of the IRS, or appearing as a witness for the taxpayer, is not considered practicing before the IRS.

Only attorneys, certified public accountants, enrolled agents, and, for limited purposes, enrolled actuaries can practice before the IRS. Any time one of these individuals wants to represent a client, a written declaration must be filed with the IRS stating that he or she is qualified and

Only attorneys, CPAs, enrolled agents, and enrolled actuaries in good standing can practice before the IRS.

authorized to represent the client. This declaration is made on IRS Form 2848, "Power of Attorney and Declaration of Representative."[1]

You cannot practice before the IRS if you have been convicted of a criminal offense under the tax laws of the United States or of any offense involving dishonesty or breach of trust. You are also banned if you are under disbarment or suspension from practicing as an attorney, CPA, public accountant, or actuary.

Also, individuals who are authorized to practice before the IRS but who do not follow the rules can be suspended or disbarred from practice by the director of practice. For example, they must not refuse to submit records or information requested by IRS agents; they must not misappropriate, or fail to promptly remit, funds received from clients for payment of taxes; and they must not knowingly give false or misleading information to the IRS in connection with an audit of a client.

Anyone who prepares a tax return for someone else and is not authorized to practice before the IRS is considered an unenrolled return preparer. An unenrolled return preparer can represent a taxpayer only before the Examination Division of the IRS and only with respect to the tax liability for the year covered by the return. An unenrolled return preparer cannot represent clients before the appeals, collection, or any other division of the IRS. Unenrolled return preparers are subject to the IRS rules of practice with respect to their limited privileges.

## Civil and Criminal Penalties for Return Preparers

As indicated under the rules for practicing before the IRS, certain behavior in dealing with clients, and certain conduct toward the IRS on behalf of clients, will result in civil or criminal penalties. A penalty could result in a preparer being barred from practice before the IRS, a CPA losing his or her certification, or an attorney being disbarred. Penalties (either civil or criminal, or both) will be imposed when a tax practitioner has cheated or defrauded a client. This could result in jail time, depending on the level of deceit. A penalty might also apply when a tax preparer is simply overly aggressive on behalf of a client, although such cases are more difficult to call.

Penalties for negligent or illegal acts of tax return preparers range from a fine, to loss of license to practice, to a jail sentence.

For example, a $1,000 penalty is imposed on a preparer for willfully attempting to understate tax on a client's tax return or reckless disregard for the rules.[2] This penalty cannot be imposed if the return position that the preparer has taken has a "realistic possibility of success." Therein lies the rub. A realistic possibility of success has been interpreted in regulations to mean at least a one in three chance of winning the issue in court. This standard can never be applied precisely. It is based on personal opinion given the evidence at hand.

> Do not take on more than you can handle and always deal fairly with clients and the IRS, or suffer potentially dire consequences.

## Carl Was a Rising Star

I happened to meet a very personable former tax professional while doing research for this book. His story is interesting and is one that all aspiring tax consultants should hear. Carl (not his real name) began his college career as a history major in a private liberal arts school. His dad, who was a doctor, had died, and Carl was unsure of what he wanted to do with his life. After his first two years of college, Carl's uncle convinced him to study accounting. He transferred to a public university that had a business school and found a mentor in the chairman of the Accounting Department, who was a CPA and an attorney. Enthralled with the world of business, Carl graduated with a degree in accounting and went straight to law school. Graduating magna cum laude, Carl had his pick of employers and went with one of the Big Eight (now Big Five) CPA firms. He passed the CPA exam, rose quickly in the firm, and became a leader in the state society of CPAs. He came to be sought after as a speaker and was asked to teach taxation part time at the local university. During this time Carl had gotten married and was raising a family. After about six years at the large firm, Carl's entrepreneurial spirit beckoned. He quit the firm and opened his own CPA practice.

Things went well for Carl's business at first—perhaps too well. Carl soon became overwhelmed and could not keep up with the volume of tax returns he was asked to file for his clients. I did not probe into why he did not hire help or turn clients over to someone else. He simply offered that the situation got out of hand, his record keeping was "lousy," and the result was a couple of tax returns not being filed at all. These were returns that had money owing rather than refunds due. So the clients sent the money to Carl, but unbeknownst to the clients, he did not send it to the IRS.

Everything was fine until a couple of years later when the business of one of Carl's clients was audited and the IRS discovered that the client had not filed a personal income tax return for that year. Things went downhill quickly for Carl after that. "The IRS had no sense of humor about this at all," he said. Carl was convicted of a criminal offense that carried a heavy fine and a two-year prison sentence. He lost his business, his license to practice law, and his CPA certificate, and his wife divorced him.

Carl lost his business, his license to practice law, his CPA certificate, and his wife.

When asked what advice he might have for someone getting started in tax consulting, Carl smiled and said the obvious: "Don't do what I did." It appears that he has learned his lesson. He has been dealing honestly with clients in an unrelated business for the past 20 years. Representing clients in tax matters can be an enjoyable enterprise, but it is also serious business. Be straightforward and up front in your business dealings and you will sleep soundly at night and be successful.

As long as I am telling stories, here is one about my Uncle Fred. It was 1960. Fred and his partner, Clinton Joerding, had just started their CPA practice and were eager for any new business. They received a call to meet with some prospective audit clients at a warehouse in South Phoenix, down by the railroad tracks. They met with several men, one of whom told Fred he expected everything to be done on the "up and up." Fred took exception to this comment and proceeded to tell him in no uncertain terms, while shaking his finger at him, that their firm did only that kind of business. He noticed that the longer he talked about it, the more nervous his partner, Clinton, seemed to get. Clinton finally ended the meeting, saying it was getting late and they should be leaving. As they drove off, the color had drained from Clinton's face and he would not talk for two blocks. When Fred asked Clinton what the problem was, he learned that he had been shaking his finger in the face of Joe Bonano, Jr., the reputed Mafia boss.

# LIMITATIONS ON INTERNAL REVENUE SERVICE POWERS

We all have our own particular phobias. What scares one person silly, someone else can take in stride. Yet the one thing that strikes fear in the heart of every citizen who is required to file a tax return is the prospect of an IRS audit. Most taxpayers are not sure what to expect and are ill equipped to defeat a tax adjustment by an IRS agent. An experienced tax advisor knows the boundaries of IRS power and authority and can use this knowledge to save clients money and trepidation. Following is an example of how a skilled tax practitioner can serve a taxpayer during the unpleasant task of dealing with an IRS audit.

An experienced tax advisor saves clients money and the fear of an IRS audit.

## *Audit of Bubba and Bertha*

Permit me to introduce Bubba and Bertha. They are imaginary clients whose quandaries, questions, and concerns I have used as examples for my introductory tax classes over the years. Leonard is their astute tax advisor. He is a self-employed CPA with about 15 years of experience.

**Issues** In addition to his regular job, Bubba was in a paid donor program for blood plasma. Bubba's blood type was in sufficient demand to make the needles in the arm and the weekly trips to the plasma lab worth the money. He would travel about 20 miles to and from the lab approximately once a week, and incurred about $650 in transportation expenses during the year in question. He was also required to eat a high-protein diet to retain a proper concentration of iron, protein, and antibodies in his blood. When he went to the lab, his blood was tested for the right stuff, and if it was deficient the doctors would not allow him to give plasma that week. Bubba paid about $800 for protein and mineral supplements during the year.

An experienced tax advisor can find deductions in unusual circumstances.

Before Leonard prepared Bubba and Bertha's return, he considered the nature of Bubba's blood activity. Leonard determined that Bubba was actively engaged in the continual and regular process of producing and selling blood plasma to the lab for profit, which qualified as a business. Leonard was aware that, generally, commuting is not deductible as a business expense, and meals are generally only deductible for entertainment or away-from-home expenses. However, Leonard found a Tax Court case that was pretty much on point. The case of *Green v. Commissioner*, 74 TC 1229 (1980) involved a taxpayer who was in essentially the same situation as Bubba, and the Tax Court allowed all of that taxpayer's claimed expenses as business deductions on Schedule C ("Profit or Loss from Business").

**United States Tax Court:** A federal trial court of national jurisdiction in federal tax matters. Learn about the legal system and how to find court cases in Chapter 7.

Leonard made sure that Bubba had all of the receipts and records necessary to substantiate his deductions. He then prepared Schedule C for Bubba and Bertha's return, claiming deductions for the protein and mineral supplements and the transportation. He advised Bubba and Bertha that claiming these deductions was a fairly aggressive position, even though the Tax Court supported them. Bubba asked if the deductions would increase the risk of being audited. Bertha said they did not want to have to go to court to claim a few hundred dollars in deductions. Leonard explained that although the risk was increased, their chances of audit were still quite low. "The only way to know if these deductions will be allowed is to claim them," he argued. "If you are audited, I will help you settle the matter quickly with the IRS, win or lose, without going to court." Both Bubba and Bertha agreed that they should go for the deductions.

"The only way to know if these deductions will be allowed is to claim them," Leonard argued.

**The Letter** About a year after their tax return was filed, Bubba and Bertha were unfortunate enough to receive one of those menacing letters from the IRS. The letter requested that they go to the IRS office to see Chad, an IRS agent, and to bring their tax records for the year in question. Bubba called Leonard about the letter, and Leonard knew exactly what to do. Leonard had Bubba and Bertha sign a power of attorney giving Leonard the right to discuss their case with the IRS, and faxed the form to Chad. Leonard then called Chad and said that he would be representing Bubba and Bertha at the audit. Chad told Leonard that he was primarily concerned about some business expenses claimed on Bubba's Schedule C. Leonard gave Bubba and Bertha the option of going along or letting him handle it on his own. Bubba said he would like to go along. Leonard said, "That's okay, Bubba, but please allow me to do the talking. Remember, a closed mouth gathers no feet."

**Meeting with the Agent** Fast-forward to Leonard and Bubba sitting in Chad's office. Bubba's large posterior filled the chair in which he was sitting. Leonard was a slow-moving, lanky fellow who slumped in his chair, forcing his knees to protrude well beyond Bubba's. Chad was cordial and confident, and greeted them with a handshake before they sat down. He was a fit 30-something who seemed to enjoy his work. His desk was clean, with a computer monitor and a keyboard at one end. Chad studied Bubba and thought about chatting a little with him before they got started.

"So, Bubba, you look like a guy who likes to fish," Chad said with an inviting smile. Before Bubba could open his mouth, Leonard intervened.

Agents are trained to be chatty with their victims and encourage them to talk about themselves as much as possible. This is particularly helpful when a tax advisor does not accompany the taxpayer, and the agent believes there is a chance of discovering unclaimed income from what the taxpayer reveals. For example, the agent might ask a taxpayer if he likes to fish. The taxpayer, relieved that the agent is actually someone he can talk to, might say he loves to fish, and begin to talk about the new bass boat he has at home. The agent, who is now doing the fishing, might be wondering what other new toys the taxpayer has in his driveway and whether he has a lake cabin, and how he can afford all that stuff on a reported income of $30,000 a year.

IRS agents are trained to encourage taxpayers to talk about themselves, in hopes of causing the taxpayer to reveal unreported income.

"I know you're busy, Chad. I'm busy and Bubba's busy, so let's just talk about why you had us come down." Chad was put on notice that he was dealing with an experienced tax advisor in Leonard. He found that his fishing expedition for unreported income was not going anywhere. Besides, he thought, he already had this guy hooked for a sizable tax adjustment. It was simply a matter of getting him on board.

An IRS fishing expedition does not work with an experienced tax advisor present.

"Fine," said Chad, as he picked up Bubba's Schedule C and turned to Leonard. "I'm afraid I have a problem allowing any of these business expenses at all. I don't think what Bubba has here is a business. He is simply giving blood for some extra income, and he is claiming the cost of a high-protein diet and transportation to and from the lab as business expenses. Even if he was running a business, meals are not deductible unless you are entertaining, and commuting to and from work is not deductible. I am going to have to disallow all of these deductions."

While Chad was talking, Leonard was busily rummaging through his briefcase looking for something, and showing Chad that he was completely unconcerned. He finally pulled out a copy of *Green v. Commissioner* and handed it to Chad. "The Tax Court says you're wrong," Leonard said casually as he leaned back in his chair.

Chad looked skeptically at the papers Leonard had handed him. He had not even gone to the trouble of looking for a case with these oddball facts. He had simply jotted down some cases that said business expenses must be ordinary and necessary and not personal. He read the headnote of *Green* and was surprised to find that the case was remarkably similar to Bubba's situation. "Let me see what we have on this case," he said to Leonard. Turning to his computer, Chad dialed up the Internet tax database to which the IRS subscribed. He checked to see if the IRS had appealed the Tax Court decision, or nonacquiesced to it, and if other opinions by different courts had followed or disagreed with *Green*. He found that the Tax Court ruling was not appealed, the IRS did not nonacquiesce, and a couple of other cases mentioned *Green* favorably. Chad was beginning to develop a knot in his stomach.

"It looks to me like the IRS should have nonacquiesced in the *Green* case," he told Leonard. "Anyway, it is the position of the IRS that personal expenses, like groceries and commuting, are not ordinary and necessary business expenses."

"Why cause all of us a lot more work and trouble when we all know what the answer is going to be in the end?" Leonard argued. "The case is on point. If I have Bubba and Bertha file a petition in the Tax Court, the IRS is going to lose again on this." At this point Bubba began to fidget in his chair. Leonard had promised him they were not going to go to court.

"The Tax Court might see the light and change its mind," Chad suggested. He knew the IRS would not litigate this case. But he also suspected that Bubba and Bertha were not willing to take it that far either. "I'll tell you what. If we can agree that the protein supplements and transportation to and from the lab are not deductible, I will not bother to look at any of the rest of the return."

"I'm afraid we'll have to stick to our guns on this one, Chad," said Leonard. "Frankly, I believe it is an abuse of discretion on your part not to follow relevant judicial authority. I would like to take this up with your supervisor." He knew that the rest of Bubba's return was clean. Had there been questionable items elsewhere on the return, Leonard might have been ready to negotiate.

When the IRS nonacquiesces to a court decision that has gone in favor of the taxpayer, it is announcing to the world that it will refuse to follow that decision as precedent. That means, regardless of the fact that it lost the case, the IRS will continue to argue the same interpretation of the law that was rejected by the court. The IRS can legally nonacquiesce to a tax decision by any court other than the Supreme Court.

**Appeals Conference** Unfortunately, Chad's supervisor backed the agent up on the adjustment. They both thought that Chad's argument was correct on the merits of the case and that *Green* was an aberration. Besides, because of the small dollar amount involved, Bubba was more likely to settle with the appeals officer than to take the case to court. Consequently, Chad wrote up the adjustment and sent Bubba and Bertha a "Notice of Proposed Deficiency," commonly called a "30-day letter." This notice contained a copy of the examination report explaining

Chad's proposed changes, and told Bubba and Bertha about their right to appeal the proposed changes to the IRS Appeals Office within 30 days.

> **Notice of Proposed Deficiency:** Commonly called a 30-day letter, it details the proposed adjustment by the IRS and gives the taxpayer 30 days to schedule an appeals conference with an IRS appeals officer.

Several weeks after the notice arrived, Leonard and Bubba were sitting at the desk of the appeals officer. Leanne was a stocky woman who had been with the IRS for about 20 years and in appeals for 10 years. Leonard braced himself for battle as he slid down in his chair. He knew that he must convince Leanne that his case for Bubba's deductions was strong and that he was willing to test it in the Tax Court, even though he had promised Bubba and Bertha that their protest would end here.

"Interesting case," said Leanne, who was paging through Chad's report. "Our goal here is to settle cases so that neither of us has to spend the time and money going to court," She looked directly at Bubba and ignored Leonard.

"If the agent had been reasonable, we wouldn't even be here," Leonard chimed in with the first volley. It was not his nature to be combative, but he believed that might be the best approach with Leanne. He had warned Bubba before the meeting not to be alarmed by his tenacity with the appeals officer.

Leanne turned to Leonard with a concerned look. "The IRS does have the right to take issue with court decisions that it believes are incorrectly decided. Now, the *Green* case was decided by the Tax Court over 20 years ago, and the Tax Court has not been asked to decide a similar case since. Perhaps it's time to test this issue again in the Tax Court and see if we can get the precedent back on our side."

As he had done when Chad was trying to make a strong point, Leonard was busy fishing around for something in his briefcase during the entire time Leanne was addressing him and had not even looked at her. He finally found what he was looking for just as she finished.

"The Tax Court hasn't had this come up again because this is a pretty unusual business that Bubba is in," he said. "There has been no indication from recent cases that the Tax Court is unhappy with its ruling in *Green*, and if we went to court with this we would definitely win." Leonard sat looking at Leanne with a slight grin on his lips. The stack of papers he had pulled from his briefcase was dangling from the fingers of his right hand.

Leanne realized that Leonard was going for the dramatic pause effect. She asked a little impatiently, "Do you have something there to show me?"

"Oh, yes." Leonard passed the papers over the desk. "Are you familiar with *Yapp v. Commissioner*?[3] The IRS had nonacquiesced to a Tax Court decision that it had lost, then it went back in with the same argument with another taxpayer. The Tax Court judge said, 'We told you that you were wrong before, and you're still wrong.'" Leonard chuckled. "Then do you know what the Tax Court judge did? He told the taxpayers they should file for litigation costs under Section 7430, because this case was definitely not justified on the part of the IRS."

Section 7430 of the Internal Revenue Code allows the awarding of court costs, attorney's fees, and certain administrative costs to taxpayers by the government if it is determined that the IRS was not "substantially justified" in litigating an issue.

Leanne was familiar with the *Yapp* case. She was impressed with Leonard, because he was the only tax practitioner that she had faced who knew of the case. "It doesn't look like you're in a compromising mood," she said. "Let me study all of this and write up my report. You should have it in a couple of weeks."

Leanne already knew that she was going to issue a no-change report and close the file. She didn't want to give Leonard or Bubba the satisfaction of knowing that now, though. "Let them squirm for a couple of weeks," she thought. She believed that Bubba's expenses should not be allowed. Nevertheless, Tax Court precedent was against her, and Leonard had demonstrated that he knew the system and the law so well that the hazards of going forward with the case were unacceptable.

Leonard demonstrated to the hearing officer that he knew the system and the law so well that the best thing for the IRS to do was to concede the adjustment.

## New Customer-Oriented Internal Revenue Service

Aside from the limitations alluded to in the above example, there are many congressionally mandated controls on IRS practices and procedures.

Hearings before Congress in 1998 detailing IRS abuses resulted in the IRS Restructuring and Reform Act of 1998. This legislation expanded tax-payer protections in several areas.

One new provision permits a taxpayer to recover up to $100,000 in civil damages arising from an IRS officer's or employee's negligent disregard of any provision of the Internal Revenue Code or of the Treasury regulations in connection with the collection of tax from the taxpayer.[4] Additionally, a taxpayer who can prove that an IRS officer or employee has *recklessly or intentionally* disregarded the provisions of the Code or regulations can collect up to $1 million in civil damages.

When a taxpayer encounters a problem with the IRS that results in a "significant hardship" as a consequence of a completed or pending IRS action, there are now standard procedures to get help.[5] A taxpayer can get a release of a property lien or an order to cease any action by the IRS through the National Taxpayer Advocate. The taxpayer, or the taxpayer's tax advisor, can apply for relief by completing and filing the aptly numbered Form 911, "Application for Taxpayer Assistance Order to Relieve Hardship." For more information about the taxpayer advocate, see Chapter 9, under "Role of the Taxpayer Advocate" on page 247.

The IRS now states that its mission is to "provide America's taxpayers top-quality service by helping them understand and meet their tax responsibilities and by applying the tax law with integrity and fairness to all."[6] According to the IRS commissioner, Charles Rossotti, "Our goal is to provide the easiest and most efficient ways for you to get the information, service, and assistance you need not only during the tax filing season, but throughout the year." Still, the tax advisor's role is as vital as ever, because differences of opinion will always exist between taxpayers and the IRS, however honorable the intentions of both parties. See Chapter 9 for more information on dealing with the IRS.

The IRS Restructuring and Reform Act of 1998 expanded taxpayer protection in several areas, but the tax advisor's role is as vital as ever.

## VARIOUS FACES OF THE TAX CONSULTANT

The term "tax consultant" is generic, not limited to a single occupation or type of tax. The designations "unenrolled practitioner" and "enrolled agent" are not subsets of broader fields, although such individuals might sell insurance, do bookkeeping, or provide a variety of other services as well as tax return preparation and consulting. The designation "CPA," however, denotes a broad array of services that might be offered by such individuals. Tax consulting is just one specialization in which a CPA might be trained. Likewise, an attorney might specialize in any area of the law as well as in tax law. Additionally, although most tax consultants might share a common body of knowledge, specialization in specific areas of law or in specific industries requires special knowledge and training. Following are examples of typical services performed by tax consultants under the specific designations.

## Unenrolled Tax Practitioner

An unenrolled tax practitioner is anyone who prepares tax returns for someone else and is not authorized to practice before the IRS. In most states today, people actually can become unenrolled practitioners by preparing tax returns and advising clients, even if they have not graduated from high school yet. Except for residents of California and Oregon, there are virtually no minimum education or training requirements. Continuing education is vital, however, for anyone who hopes to survive and prosper in the tax business.

**Unenrolled tax practitioner:** Anyone who prepares tax returns for someone else and is not authorized to practice before the IRS.

One unenrolled tax practitioner who has built a very successful practice is Bob Lindgren of Bloomington, Minnesota. Bob specializes in tax return preparation for individuals and is able to charge as much for his services as many CPAs because he has developed a reputation of competency. "The first year I started in this business I did 55 returns all season," Bob told me. "But I spent 12 to 14 hours per day in the office. Those hours in the office, when I was not preparing returns, were spent poring over IRS publications and instructions." Today Bob prepares over 700 returns annually. He takes great pride in finding deductions that other practitioners might miss. He can do this only because he has learned the tax rules very well. "The hard work has paid off," he said. "Even people who don't like me come to me to have their taxes done because they know I can save them money."

Ben Ostfield of Property Tax Management Group Ltd. in Edina, Minnesota, is an unenrolled practitioner who works in a less conventional area of taxation. Ben saw an opportunity several years ago when real estate property values were on the decline. Ben is in the business of protesting property tax valuations for commercial real estate. "In the early 1980s commercial real estate values skyrocketed because of tax laws that were favorable to property development as tax shelters," Ben explained. "But the 1986 Tax Reform Act put an end to that, and property values soon began to plummet. When property values were on the rise, assessed values followed suit. But when prices plummeted, assessed values tended to remain substantially higher than the cash value of the properties." Ben said he has always been a strong negotiator, and he saw a niche to work on behalf of property owners to negotiate lower assessed values, hence lower property taxes. He did a considerable amount of research in the area, then, in 1990, began working exclusively in real estate tax reduction for commercial property owners.

Ben started by purchasing lists from local counties of properties with assessed values between $500,000 and $5 million. He targeted owners of properties with those values, because he believed that owners of higher-priced properties were more likely to deal with attorneys or large firms. Ben then developed a direct mailing campaign to market his services to those property owners.

Ben said, "Since my fees are simply a percentage of the tax reductions I negotiate, the first couple of years were pretty lean. But I stuck it out and have had some major successes in this business, while creating many satisfied clients. I took one guy a check for $10,000, and he said, 'You know, Ben, over the years I have had all kinds of people tell me how they could save me money, but you really did—you brought it to me.'" Ben is contemplating retirement now but will still have a steady stream of income for the next three years because all of his settlements have been negotiated on a three-year basis.

### Being an Enrolled Agent Opens More Doors

Unlicensed practitioners are somewhat limited in the services they can perform for clients. They cannot "practice before the IRS," which means they can only represent clients before the examination division of the IRS—not the appeals, collection, or any other division. Enrolled agents are admitted to practice before the IRS. They also have the advantage of documented tax proficiency. The designation "Enrolled Agent" is evidence that a tax professional has demonstrated technical competence in the field of taxation. This generally translates into higher fees for services.

 **Enrolled agent:** Currently the only nondegree designation for tax advisors that indicates proficiency in the field of taxation.

Enrolled agents are tax professionals who have been licensed by the IRS. The enrolled agent designation is earned either by passing a difficult two-day examination administered by the IRS covering major tax topics or by working for the IRS for a minimum of five years as a revenue agent.

Edward Pyle is an enrolled agent who owns the Tax Wise Shop in Bloomington, Minnesota. Ed entered the tax business full time in 1990, after what he described as "corporate cutbacks." He decided he did not want to go the CPA route because of the time required. However, he thought professional tax credentials would help his business, so he became an enrolled agent in 1993. Ed prepares mostly individual tax returns but also has some small businesses as clients, including self-employed individuals, partnerships, and S corporations. During the off-season (between April 15 and of the end of the year), Ed manages to keep quite busy with clients who have received notices from the IRS for various reasons, new clients who have neglected to file returns, and clients needing tax planning for future transactions. Ed's office is located in a modern strip mall on a busy street and has a large lighted sign in front saying "Tax Wise Shop," which attracts a significant number of walk-in clients.

## *Various Roles of a CPA*

Certified public accountants (CPAs) are qualified to audit businesses and attest to their financial well-being. They are well-respected strategic business advisors and decision makers. CPAs who specialize in taxation advise both individuals and businesses on all aspects of compliance with the tax laws.

Becoming a CPA is not a simple matter. You must meet the minimum requirements of the state in which you wish to practice. That generally means completing a program of study in accounting at a college

CPAs are qualified to work in many different capacities involving a client's financial affairs.

or university of at least 150 credit hours. You then must pass the uniform CPA Examination, which is developed and graded by the American Institute of Certified Public Accountants (AICPA). This rigorous two-day exam consists of four sections: Business Law and Professional Responsibilities; Auditing; Accounting and Reporting—Taxation, Managerial, Governmental and Not-for-Profit Organizations; and Financial Accounting and Reporting—Business Enterprises.

To become a CPA, you must complete 150 hours of college course work and pass a rigorous two-day exam.

Rita Benassi is a CPA with the international accounting firm of Deloitte & Touche. She came up through the ranks in the tax department of the Minneapolis office and has been a partner for several years. Rita is a generalist in corporate tax and often acts as a quarterback when bringing teams of corporate tax specialists together for a project.

"I have loved this job from the day I started," said Rita. "I have a real passion for it. There is a lot of authority and responsibility. When I am really busy and under stress and the adrenaline is pumping—that is a real rush for me. "I think it's a very powerful position to be able to advise, in my case, from a corporate tax perspective, some of the top companies in the world."

## Law Degree Provides Many Options

The broad-based education and training of attorneys gives them the basic tools to work in any area of legal, business, or financial consulting. Law school preparation is general rather than vocational, however. To obtain on-the-job training in taxation, many attorneys begin their careers in the tax department of a CPA firm. Some go on to law firms to specialize in a particular area of taxation or to practice litigation, or they go into private industry. Others, however, stay with a CPA firm after learning that the work there is similar to what they would do in a law firm. Many attorneys who wish to specialize in taxation obtain an advanced degree in taxation, either an LLM (master of laws) in taxation from a law school or a master's in taxation degree from a business school.

Many attorneys specializing in taxation begin their careers with a CPA firm to gain tax experience. Some remain with CPA firms while others go on to practice law.

E. Burke Hinds is an attorney practicing in estate planning for the law firm of Messerli & Kramer, P.A., in Minneapolis. Burke determined early that he had a facility for numbers, so he went to business school at the University of Nebraska to get a degree in accounting. He was fascinated by a senior tax course that he took and decided to concentrate in taxation. Burke took the CPA exam while finishing his undergraduate degree and passed all four parts, then went on to law school. When Burke was looking around for a summer clerking position after his first year in law school, he got an opportunity to work as an intern for a large CPA firm, which happened to pay much more than a clerking position. After law school he accepted a position with the CPA firm and was exposed to various areas of taxation. After a couple of years with the CPA firm, Burke moved to a law firm to specialize in estate planning. "As my clients grew, my estate planning sophistication grew," Burke told me, "largely because of a mentor who urged me to get additional training in the area. That's how my practice has grown over time. So now I market myself to entrepreneurs who are high-net-worth individuals." Burke's clients generally have a net worth between $10 million and $200 million.

When asked what he likes about his work, Burke said that trying to work through family-type issues in order to achieve estate-planning objectives can be a fascinating process. "This [family conflicts] is one of the strongest reasons why individuals do not do the estate planning that they should," said Burke. "It has nothing to do with the money, it is the psychological background." Burke also enjoys the puzzle making involved in putting incredibly diverse pieces together into a consolidated whole. His sophisticated practice is tailored to specific situations. "The diversity in the estate planning area is interesting because you play off the gift tax against the estate tax against the fiduciary tax against both the corporate and individual income tax," Burke explained, "and this draws on my broad-based background."

## CONCLUSION

The field of tax advising is a growing and vital component of the U.S. economy. Tax professionals are in high demand. Of course, just about everyone is in high demand in today's economy. What are the chances that things will change? Could the industry be destroyed by an act of Congress that repeals the income tax and shuts down the IRS? How likely is that to happen? Of course, no one knows for certain what the future holds, but Chapter 2 provides insight into the future of the tax industry, and the prospects for basic tax reform, by examining the past.

*Chapter*

# 2

# Enduring Demand for Tax Services

*Our Constitution is in actual operation; everything appears to promise that it will last; but nothing in this world is certain but death and taxes.*

—Benjamin Franklin

This chapter not only describes the expanding market for tax services under the current income tax system but also offers insight into the future of the tax industry, in light of the many calls for fundamental tax reform. Insight into the future is always enhanced by a clear understanding of the past. So before the potential impact on fundamental tax reform is addressed, you are provided with a brief history of our current system. As an aspiring tax consultant, you should be aware of our tax history anyway—it is good fodder for interviews. Proposed alternative systems are then described and analyzed for their impact on the tax profession. In the end, I believe you will agree that the future is very bright for the tax industry and the future demand for tax consultants.

The future is very bright for the tax industry and the future demand for tax consultants.

## DEMAND FOR TAX PROS IS GREATER THAN EVER

As Benjamin Franklin noted, taxes are pretty inescapable. Supreme Court Justice Oliver Wendell Holmes once said, "Taxes are what we pay for a civilized society." In today's society, while civility might be on the wane, what we are asked to pay for it keeps going up. Our tax system is also becoming more and more complex. Major tax legislation is hurled at us so frequently these days that it is impossible for anyone to keep up with it all. These factors, together with a healthy and expanding economy, make the demand for tax services very strong.

A recent article written for the *Wall Street Journal* Web site says that the demand for tax professionals is soaring and that candidates are in high demand at all levels.[1] Some of the hot areas are corporate, international, and state and local taxation. The hiring binge, says the article, has put upward pressure on salaries, causing pay for mid- to upper-level professionals to rise by 15 to 30 percent in the past two to three years. The demand is so great among national and international CPA firms that smaller firms are feeling the effects of rising salaries and a tight market. Some of the small firms are offering sign-on bonuses to get a better crack at new recruits on college campuses.

According to Fred Jacobs, director of the Master's of Business Taxation program at the University of Minnesota's Carlson School of Management, "We've had almost a frenzy of firms wanting to locate people in the tax field. There has probably been more activity in the last couple of years than at any time that I can remember in terms of the demand for tax people. Firms just need more qualified people and there aren't enough coming into the field."

Tax professionals agree that the future demand for tax services is strong.

All of the tax professionals with whom I spoke predicted a continuing strong demand for tax services. Bill Horne, the director of national recruiting for RSM McGladrey, Inc., sees the current hiring frenzy to continue well into the future. Rita Benassi, a partner with Deloitte & Touche, also believes employment opportunities for the next 10 years will be stronger than ever. She agrees that the areas of international tax and state and local taxation will continue to grow rapidly. Jay Zack, a tax partner with RSM McGladrey, Inc., echoes that opinion. "This is an ideas-driven industry," explained Rita Benassi. As business clients expand to other states and internationally, more and more opportunities for tax savings arise.

Kevin Koehler, a tax partner with Lund Koehler Cox & Arkema, a 60-member firm in Minnetonka, Minnesota, identified mergers and acquisitions as a hot tax consulting area because there's a lot of activity in the market. Kevin also named sales tax issues as an emerging area. "When I started in this business 20 years ago, I did very little out-of-state work. Clients used to be geographically located and operated only in that geographic area. Almost all of our clients now are in all states and are becoming international. With multistate businesses it is not so much the income tax that becomes the issue, because that's just a question of who gets a piece of the pie of among the states. But sales tax becomes a big issue because it is a question of whether a client has nexus in a particular state. If the client should have collected the tax but didn't, the tax becomes the liability of the client. This is an area that keeps me awake at night, because if the state auditor calls up and wonders why the tax was not collected it is my responsibility."

International tax, state and local taxation, corporate mergers and acquisitions, sales tax issues, and estate and trust taxation are hot areas.

Kevin identified several other areas that are expanding rapidly. "International is becoming a huge area in a lot of different ways. A lot of foreign individuals are being imported for talent, especially in the software industry, so we have the tax issues of alien taxpayers. And most of our clients are either selling or using talent outside the country, which creates tax issues that must be addressed. Obviously estate and trust is a growing practice area—certainly the stock market has been a big part of that. Long-term tax planning for high-net-worth clients is now a big area. Scheduling out the exercising of stock options—how we do that is becoming another attractive area." These are all great examples of how tax consultants use their creativity to produce opportunities for clients, which also increases the demand for qualified individuals.

## Income Potential of a Tax Professional

For someone working in the tax profession as a self-employed individual, potential income relates to one's activity level, technical and marketing expertise, and client base. In the Minneapolis area, in the summer of 2000 when this book was written, the popular billing rate seemed to range between $90 and $130 per hour for sole practitioners. Partners in larger firms can demand a much higher hourly rate and earn several hundred thousand dollars per year.

> A tax professional can make well into six figures, even in a local CPA firm.

Bill Horne says the low side for new recruits coming into the firm out of a four-year undergraduate program in accounting is around $30,000 if they are hired to work in a smaller community. The average goes up to around $38,500 in the Twin Cities and is in the low $40,000s in some of the larger metropolitan areas around the country. Within eight or nine years these people are making up to $120,000 per year as senior managers, according to Jay Zack. Jay said, "Average compensation for a partner is currently around $170,000 but could go up to over $250,000." Average compensation for staff and partners in Big Five firms is more.

Kevin Koehler said five-year people in local firms are making $60,000 to $75,000 in today's market. Compensation for partners in local firms, according to Kevin, ranges from $75,000 to $300,000 depending on the partnership. "It depends on how good of a partnership you are in—how much business you are bringing in and how good your partners are. But I can't imagine a tax partner making less than $150,000 if the firm is any size at all." All these figures must be viewed in light of the strong demand for tax services and the general increase in the cost of living.

## Nonmonetary Incentives

Both large and small firms desire to attract and retain qualified employees so strongly that more flexible work schedules are available today than a few years ago. Part-time and flexible work schedules are now available, even at Big Five CPA firms. Several years ago Deloitte & Touche started an initiative on the retention and advancement of women and has poured millions of dollars into the project, according to Rita Benassi. "That initiative has helped us retain more women and has also had a positive effect on our retention of men." The initiative has resulted in flexible work schedules and a more positive working environment. "That is proven by the fact that, for the third year in a row, we have made the 100-best-places-to-work list," said Rita.

More flexible work schedules are available today than a few years ago.

Kevin Koehler said his firm has a part-time partner who is juggling her career with family duties. "If we have a good employee," said Kevin, "we will be very flexible in order to retain that person, even if it is on a part-time basis." This sentiment was echoed by Bill Horne, who said that there are also part-time partners at RSM McGladrey.

Nevertheless, while the demand for tax services is growing, so is the dissatisfaction with our current tax system. In a recent survey of American taxpayers, the one government agency or institution chosen as most hated was the Internal Revenue Service. In fact, it was chosen over all other government agencies *combined*.[2] When people were asked which they would prefer, having their wallet or purse stolen or getting audited by the IRS, only 45 percent opted for the audit; 45 percent went for the mugging, and 10 percent said there was no difference! And when asked if Congress should support a complete overhaul of the federal tax system, including abolishing the IRS and replacing the current rates with a single rate, 59 percent said "Yessss!"

The dissatisfaction with the current system is increasing along with the demand for tax services.

## WILL TAX REFORM DESTROY THE TAX SERVICES INDUSTRY?

Most Americans believe the federal tax system is too complicated, and politicians are well aware of this sentiment. Almost every presidential candidate in the last two campaigns has offered some sort of tax simplification plan. Some have promised to reduce the distasteful task of tax return preparation to filling out a few lines on a postcard. When a politician wants to get an audience to sit up and bark these days, all he or she has to do is complain about the power of the IRS and the complexity of the tax code.

Doing so appears to be a great way to raise campaign contributions, even by those members of Congress who are most responsible for increasing the mess of the current system. The former chair of the House Ways and Means Committee, Congressman Bill Archer (R, TX), has two lines he uses just about every time he rises to his feet. "I want to tear the income tax out by its roots so that it can never grow back again. I want to get the IRS out of the individual lives of all Americans and eliminate all the loopholes in the tax code, creating a new, fairer system." This seems reminiscent of Dr. Frankenstein plotting with the villagers against the monster. During Mr. Archer's brief tenure as head tax writer in Congress, hundreds of pages were added to the Internal Revenue Code containing dozens of new deductions and credits. The tax writers in Congress, chief among them the chair of the Ways and Means Committee, can tame the beast only by action, not by rhetoric.

Current proposals to replace the income tax with something much simpler have great support. In fact, even organizations of tax professionals are very supportive of reform. In a recent joint press release with the American Bar Association Tax Section and the Tax Executives Institute, David Lifson of the American Institute of Certified Public Accountants (AICPA) said this:

> The AICPA has long been an advocate for tax law simplification. We are committed to helping make our tax system as simple and fair as possible. Unfortunately, we believe that the law's complexity in certain key areas may be strangling voluntary compliance. The lack of deliberation in the legislative process, the frequent law changes in recent years, and the increasing magnitude and complexity of the Internal Revenue Code are serious concerns for all tax professionals.

Still, in spite of the honest desire on the part of taxpayers and tax professionals to simplify the system and in spite of all of the hyperbole from politicians, federal tax laws continue to get more complex.

What are the prospects that fundamental tax reform will be enacted? If it is enacted, will the form of taxation in the United States continue to support a robust and expanding tax consulting industry? Or, after the great reform, will today's highly sought after tax professional end up selling TV sets for Sears? Perhaps, before tackling these questions head-on, it would be best to take a look at how, when, and why the current system evolved and at the political forces that created and feed this monstrous statute.

> Will the highly sought after tax professional of today end up selling TV sets for Sears?

## HAL THE ROOFER HAD IT WRONG

In order to perceive what the future might hold for our federal tax system, it is important to know its history. In fact, a little history lesson would not hurt anyone subject to the income tax, if only to clarify its place in the federal legal hierarchy.

A case in point. A few years ago I needed to have the roof on my home replaced. I called several contractors for bids. One gentleman, who went by the name of Hal, bid the job at a price substantially below the others. After being assured by a couple of Hal's references that he did quality work, I hired him. Hal had a crew of about seven men. With his crew toiling away on my roof, Hal usually barked orders from a lawn chair in my backyard while sipping from a glass of homemade carrot juice. Hal was a likable fellow, but I sensed he was somewhat of a nonconformist. I chatted with him for a few minutes each day before I went to work. In a conversation we had one morning he revealed how he managed to submit the lowest bid.

Somehow this day our talk turned to taxes, though I had not divulged my line of work. Hal blurted out, "I don't pay any income tax, state or federal. Neither do any of the guys up on the roof." I learned that Hal did not withhold or pay his crew's social security taxes either. Not paying taxes, of course, can really give a guy an edge over the competition. Hal was unaware that I was a former state revenue agent. I knew that the IRS offers rewards for information leading to the collection of tax from cheaters. So I said, "You know, Hal, you should be careful who you're talking to about that." Hal was unconcerned about where I worked or what I knew. He simply said, "It doesn't matter who I tell because the Supreme

Court has declared the income tax illegal. The only reason people pay it is because they are too stupid to know any better."

"[T]he Supreme Court has declared the income tax illegal. The only reason people pay it is because they are too stupid to know any better."

Well, I sensed this might be a good time to end our chat for the day. You might be surprised to learn, however, that Hal was right—the Supreme Court did in fact declare the income tax unconstitutional. Unfortunately, it happened in 1895, before the Constitution was amended to allow for an income tax, which was subsequently reenacted in 1913. The Supreme Court later approved the income tax in 1916. Hal, of course, had not heard the rest of the story. Had he known the history of our tax system, as you are about to learn, he would be a free man today! Oh, just kidding—Hal is free and still sipping his carrot juice. I don't plan to turn him in for the reward until the 20-year guarantee on my roof expires.

The Income Tax of 1894 was declared unconstitutional in 1895. The Sixteenth Amendment to the Constitution authorized it, and it was reenacted in 1913.

## A LOOK BACK

As you may have surmised from the Hal story, we did not always have an income tax in the United States. In fact, for most of our nation's first century, tariffs on imported goods were the primary source of federal revenue. Taxes on real and personal property were enacted in the 1790s, along with certain excise taxes, but most of those taxes were repealed soon after Thomas Jefferson became president in 1800.

**Excise tax:** A sales tax imposed on the value of specific goods or services.

For most of our nation's first century, tariffs on imported goods were the primary source of federal revenue.

Wars are expensive endeavors, so our country's wars and the income tax share a parallel history. During the War of 1812, the secretary of the treasury recommended an income tax. But the war ended soon thereafter and peacetime imports increased tariff revenue, making an income tax unnecessary.

### Our First National Income Tax

The first federal income tax did not make its debut until the Civil War, which was much more costly than the War of 1812. In 1862 an income tax was enacted under President Lincoln to finance the war effort. It was a very modest tax by today's standards. It taxed income up to $10,000 at 3 percent and income over $10,000 at 5 percent, with a $600 exemption. (The Confederate states had their own income tax, payable in Confederate money.) The rates were increased a couple of years later but were reduced again after the war ended as revenue needs declined. In 1872, when the federal government was enjoying large budget surpluses, the Income Tax of 1862 was completely repealed. (Can you imagine such a thing?) During this brief run of the income tax, less than 1 percent of the population was subject to the tax—the Civil War tax was a tax on the rich.

**Exemption:** An amount of income that is not taxed. Different from a deduction, which is generally an expenditure that is subtracted from gross income.

After repeal of the income tax in 1872, excise taxes adopted during the Civil War, primarily on liquor and tobacco, and tariffs financed the federal government for the next 40 years. But the American people had

The first federal income tax was enacted in 1862 to finance the Civil War. It was repealed 10 years later.

> **Progressive tax:** When the rate, either nominal or effective, increases with income.

seen how an income tax worked, and the idea was particularly appealing to the liberals of the day. Liberals, called "populists" back then, dominated the Democratic party. They were primarily farmers and laborers, residing in the southern and the western states.

The populists favored an income tax over various excise taxes for two important reasons. The first was a matter of equity—they argued that progressive taxes are more equitable than regressive taxes. That is, taxes that are proportional to a person's ability to pay (progressive) are better than taxes that are imposed equally on all, regardless of income level (regressive). For example, excise taxes on liquor and tobacco account for a proportionately higher percentage of the income of low-income consumers than of high-income consumers, given an equal propensity to imbibe and smoke. An income tax, on the other hand, is charged proportionately more to high-income taxpayers.

> **Regressive tax:** When the rate, either nominal or effective, decreases with income.
>     The liberals of the day argued that a progressive tax, such as the income tax, was more equitable than the regressive excise taxes.

The second notable reason the populists liked the idea of an income tax was simply that it would not be imposed on them. Most populists were of modest means, and the income tax they were familiar with was only for rich folks. The conservatives of the day were primarily wealthy easterners who dominated the Republican party. They, of course, opposed the idea of an income tax because they were the ones who would be paying it.

### Constitutional Question

In 1894 the Democrats finally gained enough strength in Congress to enact another income tax—the Income Tax of 1894. This was a 2 percent flat tax on individual and corporate net income with a $4,000 exemption for individuals. This tax was probably the most contentious political issue of the day. The conservatives considered it a move toward socialism and wanted it repealed.

The legality of the tax was soon challenged in the courts by taxpayers claiming that Congress lacked the authority to enact an income tax under the Constitution. In 1895 the case of *Pollock v. Farmer's Loan & Trust Co.*[3] reached the Supreme Court. The Court heard the case, even though it had previously held that the Income Tax of 1862 was constitutional. This time the Supreme Court ruled in favor of the taxpayer and declared the Income Tax of 1894 null and void because it violated the apportionment clause of the Constitution.

Here was the problem. Article I, Section 2 of the Constitution contains the apportionment clause, which says: "direct taxes shall be apportioned among the several States which may be included within this Union, according to their respective Numbers. . . ." In other words, direct taxes must be levied in amounts that directly correspond to the population of each state, rather than to the wealth or income of taxpayers. This clause was apparently inserted to prevent Congress from discriminating against the wealthier states with direct taxes, although the framers neglected to define what they considered to be a "direct" tax. The Supreme Court's decision in *Pollock v. Farmer's Loan & Trust Co.*, that an income tax fit the meaning of a direct tax, made the income tax unconstitutional by definition. So ended the federal government's experiment with an income tax for another few years. (Incidentally, this was also where my friend Hal's knowledge of the tax system abruptly ended.)

The Constitution of the United States did not originally authorize an income tax on individuals.

## Sixteenth Amendment

It was 1909 before the notion of an income tax again gained enough support in Congress to be reconsidered. Congress first enacted an income tax on the net income of corporations. This tax was held constitutional by the Supreme Court because it was not a direct tax on individuals. At the same time the corporate income tax was passed, Congress sanctioned a constitutional amendment, to be ratified by the states, that would nullify the Supreme Court decision in *Pollock v. Farmer's Loan & Trust Co.* and allow a personal income tax to be enacted. The Sixteenth Amendment was ratified by three-fourths of the state legislatures on February 25, 1913, and read as follows: "The Congress shall have the power to lay and collect taxes on incomes, from whatever source derived, without apportionment among the several States, and without regard to any census or enumeration."

Congress didn't waste much time after that. An individual income tax was enacted on October 3, 1913, and made retroactive to February 28, 1913. In *Brushaber v. Union Pacific Rail Road*,[4] the Supreme Court affirmed the constitutionality of the Income Tax of 1913, under the explicit power of the Sixteenth Amendment.

The original version of our modern income tax was enacted on October 3, 1913 and made retroactive to February 28, 1913.

## Income Tax of 1913

The 1913 act was the origin of our current income tax system. At about 14 pages long, it was a model of simplicity. The average citizen could read and substantially understand the entire document in less than an hour. It had a graduated rate structure with seven brackets for individuals. The rates ranged from 1 percent of net income up to $20,000, to 7 percent of net income in excess of $500,000. An exemption of $3,000 was allowed for individuals ($4,000 for married individuals). There was no standard deduction and there were no itemized deductions as we have today, but interest, taxes, casualty losses, and bad debts were allowed in arriving at net income.

Less than one-half of 1 percent of the population paid income tax in 1913.

In 1913, only about 425,000 of the nation's wealthiest citizens were income tax payers—less than one-half of 1 percent of the population. By 1939 the tax was still imposed on only about 6 percent of the population. It was not until World War II that the income tax engulfed middle-income Americans to finance the war effort. During the war, the highest rate for individuals reached 94 percent. There were 50 million taxpayers—over 74 percent of the population. It was also during World War II that employers were first required to withhold the tax on wages. With those high rates, it was unlikely that people would be willing to send their payments in on their own. The top rate would not fall below 70 percent again until 1981, when the "Reagan revolution" dropped the top rate to 50 percent.

> During World War II, the top rate for individuals reached 94 percent.

With refinement of the law came more and more complexity. Today there are over 100 tax forms for individual returns alone. The instructions for Form 1040, which took up only one page in 1913, now occupy 56 pages to explain just the first two pages of the form. Not only are there thousands of pages of tax code, there are even more pages of rulings and regulations to clarify the Code, plus thousands of court opinions to interpret the clarifications. It is, in a word, messy, and there is no shortage of opinions on how it got this way.

## HOW DID WE GET INTO THIS CONVOLUTED MESS?

The finger can be pointed in several different directions to account for the runaway chaos and confusion of our current tax system. Some think it is the desire on the part of our legislators to eliminate loopholes and prevent unintended abuses. Others say it is a belief by politicians that tax laws are not simply a means of raising revenue but also the best tool for social and economic engineering. Perhaps it is the desire by lawmakers to maximize fairness for the sake of simplicity. Then again, maybe it is a devious scheme, planned and promoted by politicians as a means of maximizing campaign contributions. Certainly the answer is not simple. That's why, as I contend later in the chapter, there is not a simple solution.

### *Is Loophole Closing the Culprit?*

In the early years, legitimate loophole-closing efforts demanded that the Code be spelled out in greater detail. Originally the word "loophole" meant an omission or ambiguity in the rules that created an unintended advantage to those who were smart enough to find it. Early tax writers often underestimated the ability of American taxpayers to creatively avoid paying taxes. Fixing these errors necessarily added some pages, but these pages clarified more than complicated the rules.

Incidentally, although tax writers in Congress have been quite good at covering their legal backsides for many years, politicians still consider themselves in the business of "loophole closing." With each major tax bill you still hear the term being tossed about. That is because today the work of closing loopholes is quite different from what it once was. Senator Russell Long (D, LA) once defined a loophole as "something that benefits the other guy. If it benefits you, it is tax reform." In other words, today when politicians talk about plugging loopholes, they are talking about getting rid of someone else's deductions, credits, or exclusions to generate revenue for their own agendas. This is not the correction of errors but the elimination of legitimate benefits. A variation of the modern term even has an official definition in *The Conservative Dictionary*: "Loophole: To liberals, any provision of the tax code that fails to claim money earned, inherited, saved, or otherwise pocketed by known taxpayers."

> Originally a "loophole" was an omission or ambiguity in the rules that created unintended benefits for those who were smart enough to find it. Today it means someone else's deduction.

## Are Overzealous Intentions the Key?

Rather than being brought about by the elimination of unintended results, complexity has evolved with a tax system that is constantly being asked to do too much. According to the General Accounting Office, "Tax systems can have multiple goals. For example, in addition to the common goal of raising revenue for the government, goals can also include redistributing income, stabilizing the economy, and achieving various other social and economic objectives through the use of preferences. Generally speaking, the greater the number of goals, the more complex is the tax system."[5] Bingo! This is precisely the problem, at least in part.

> Our tax system has many goals in addition to raising revenue, which makes the system more complex.

When the Income Tax of 1913 was enacted, the goal was to provide an efficient, equitable, and flexible means of generating revenue. For the first few decades this remained the key objective, and the rules remained manageable. Beginning in the 1960s, however, the tax code began to be looked at as the major governmental tool to promote social welfare and drive economic activity. That is when complexity began to get out of hand. As incentives were enacted to encourage certain activities, tax shelters began to emerge to take advantage of the incentives in unintended ways. This, of course, prompted legislation to discourage the tax shelters, which complicated things even more.

According to Michael Graetz, author of *The Decline and Fall of the Income Tax*, both political parties "now seem to regard the income tax as a magic elixir that can solve all the nation's economic and social difficulties. If the nation has a problem in access to education, child care affordability, health insurance coverage, or financing of long-term care, to name just a few, an income tax deduction or credit is the answer."[6] Complexity, therefore, has evolved to a large extent out of misguided reform efforts and excessive demands made on tax laws as the vehicle for implementing public policy.

## A Helping Hand or a Greased Palm?

It must also be remembered that the President and every member of Congress serve constituents, all of whom have interests involving the tax code that are at odds with the interests of someone else. There are conflicting interests between various regions of the country, between various industries, between young workers and retired ones, between labor and business, even between parent and child. A tax code that tries to accommodate a multitude of special interests can hardly be simple.

Every politician must balance the interests of constituents in a way that permits winning reelection. This goal, unfortunately, often means hearing the call of those constituents who speak the loudest. That is why the tax code is the single greatest source of lobbying activity in Washington.

Lobbyists promote tax changes that benefit their clients and oppose tax changes that harm their clients or help their clients' competitors. All of this activity is focused directly on members of Congress and the President of the United States. As a result, members of the tax-writing committees in Congress tend to get more campaign contributions than members who are not on these committees. The charge has been made by some that in tax law, complexity stems from greed taking cover in obscurity. According to a cynical Milton Friedman, "The political function of the income taxes, which is served by their being complex, is to provide a means whereby the members of Congress who have anything whatsoever to do with taxation can raise campaign funds. That is what supports the army of lobbyists in Washington who are seeking to produce changes in the income tax, to introduce special privileges or exemptions for their clients, or to have what they regard as special burdens on their clients removed."[7]

Be it greed, self-survival, or a genuine interest in helping their electorate, it is evident that tax writers are not generally concerned with the interests of taxpayers as a whole, and have not been for a very long time. If they were, the desired attributes of convenience, certainty, and economy would demand precedence over the complexity brought about by appeasing various factions. The attributes of a good tax system have been lost through the effects of the political process on the intrinsic deficiencies of individuals. The tax laws often favor cohabitation to marriage, institutional to family child care, indebtedness to parsimony, and are obstructive to capital formation. These are probably not the results that were sought. They are, however, the unpleasant side effects of counterbalancing interests having more political clout.

Counterbalancing influences on the political process have caused complexity along with less than desirable results.

## *Where Is the Political Will to Change the System?*

Notwithstanding all the problems with our current tax system, the big push for tax reform that energized the 1996 presidential campaign has all but fizzled. George W. Bush's income tax initiative in the 2000 campaign was large tax cuts for middle-income Americans. Al Gore's tax plan was small tax cuts for middle-income Americans. Neither side offered fundamental income tax reform. George Bush has talked about a plan for fundamental social security reform, which many consider more pressing. Presidential hopeful Steve Forbes's declaration of the death penalty for the tax code and the IRS that sparked the imagination of the electorate in 1996 did not sell in 2000. Even Bill Bradley, a major player in shaping the bipartisan tax reform of 1986, did not conceive a major tax reform proposal to attempt to save his failing presidential campaign.

In the House of Representatives during the closing years of Bill Clinton's presidency, no serious tax reform proposals were even debated. The Republicans passed "Scrap the Code" legislation in 1998 and again in 2000 in time for an April 14 press release. The latter bill set December 31,

No fundamental income tax reform proposals emerged from the 2000 presidential campaign.

2004, as the termination date of the Internal Revenue Code and required that Congress approve a replacement system no later than July 4, 2004. Never mind that they didn't even talk about what they were going to replace it with—that, they said, would come later. The bill would establish a National Commission on Tax Reform and Simplification to develop recommendations for Congress on fundamental reform and simplification of the Code. A few Democrats got up and said the bill would cause uncertainty in the business world and destabilize the stock market. The bill passed 229 to 187. The legislation did not make it through the Senate, but would have been vetoed if it had. Rather than working on fundamental income tax or social security reform, Bill Archer and the Ways and Means Committee spent the first half of 2000 working on a bill to end the estate and gift tax. This legislation passed both houses of Congress but, as expected, was vetoed by President Clinton. Also as expected, the bill's backers in Congress were unable to override the veto. At least the Republicans were busy doing something. The Democrats had no tax reform agenda whatsoever.

Still, even though our political representatives are not currently serious about tax reform, the public is. Recent opinion polls indicate that almost no one likes the current income tax system and that a flat tax is favored two to one.[8] Earnest reform proposals have been offered in the past and will be rolled out again when the mood strikes someone to take the lead in a reform agenda. Every aspiring tax consultant should be familiar with the plans that might be pulled from the closet when that happens.

## POPULAR TAX REFORM PROPOSALS

There are several candidates for replacing the income tax, chief among them the so-called flat tax and a national sales tax. Floated about more as a supplement to than a replacement of the income tax is the value-added tax (VAT). All of these proposals rely on a consumption base rather than the current income base. In other words, the taxes are levied on the amount one spends rather than on the amount one earns.

## Flat-Tax Proposals

Economists Robert Hall and Alvin Rabushka are credited for conceiving the flat tax in a book by the same name.[9] The name is really not descriptive of what the tax taxes, simply that it taxes it flatly. It is much different from the concept that most Americans have of a flat tax, which is a single rate tax on income. Representative Dick Armey (R, TX) and Steve Forbes, among others, have proposed the Hall/Rabushka tax in various forms.[10] It would impose a flat rate value-added tax on business income allowing for a deduction for wages, purchases of goods and services, capital equipment, structures, land, and contributions to employee retirement plans. At the individual level, there would be a flat tax on wages with a standard deduction and exemptions for dependents. The wage base would include pension benefits but exclude fringe benefits. All investment income—interest, dividends and capital gains—would be tax-free. Every itemized deduction and every credit would be gone. For example, you would get no benefit from mortgage interest, property taxes, state and local income taxes, charitable contributions, and medical expenses. Additionally, there would be no earned income credit. There would no longer be a tax benefit from investing in municipal bonds or any other tax-favored investments, because they would all be tax-free.

The flat tax is different from the concept that most Americans have, which is a single-rate tax on income. The flat tax is basically a tax on consumption.

A more progressive but complicated variation of the flat tax is the Unlimited Savings Account tax (USA tax), proposed in the Senate a few years ago by Senators Sam Nunn (D, GA) and Pete Domenici (R, NM).[11] This scheme would also impose a value-added tax on business income, with a few twists. There would be no deduction for wages, but businesses could deduct investments. All taxes paid by the business to a state or local government would be deductible, and employers would receive a credit against the business tax for their portion of the social security tax. Exports would be excluded from sales, and imports would be taxed. On the individual side, it would really not be a flat tax at all. There would be a progressive rate structure on taxable income computed by including wages, interest, dividends, distributions from noncorporate businesses, life insurance proceeds, annuity contracts, and the entire proceeds from asset sales. There would be personal exemptions, a standard deduction, plus deductions for mortgage interest, charitable contributions, and tuition for education. Additionally, there would be an unlimited deduction for amounts deposited in banks or invested. Withdrawals from banks or investments, however, would be taxed.

The USA tax is not a flat tax at all but a progressive consumption tax.

The allure of flat-tax proposals, for some, is the fact that investment income that is saved and accumulated rather than spent on consumer goods goes tax-free, thus eliminating the bias in the current system against saving and capital formation. Wages are taxed progressively, even with a single-rate Hall/Rabushka tax, because tax is excluded on a certain amount of income by the standard deduction and exemptions. The tax, however, is regressive in its business component, because it would be borne proportionately more by lower-income purchasers than upper-income consumers. Also, eliminating tax on investments benefits higher-income people more because they are the ones who generally make the investments. The plans would result in a tax cut for the wealthy and a tax increase for low- and middle-income Americans. This is something that would not fly with the American public. It would therefore not pass Congress or be signed by a president who hoped to be reelected.

So-called flat-tax plans that have been offered so far would result in a tax cut for the wealthy and a tax increase for low- and middle-income people.

Even if the distribution problem could be corrected, there is evidence that flat-tax schemes would ultimately be a hard sell to the American people. A recent Gallup poll reported that although most Americans would like to see major changes or a complete overhaul of the tax system, 56 percent also said they would be unwilling to give up any deductions to make the system simpler.[12]

## National Sales Tax

Representative Billy Tauzin (R, LA) wants to repeal the income tax, both personal and corporate, and the estate and gift tax, and replace them with a 15 percent national retail sales tax (NRST).[13] Oh yes, he also wants to abolish the Internal Revenue Service. The NRST would be imposed on the gross receipts from the sales of any taxable property or service sold, used, or consumed in the United States. There would be exemptions for any good or service purchased for resale, purchased to produce a good or service for retail, or exported from the United States. No income earned would be taxable until it is actually spent on something taxable. To ensure that the basic necessities of life remain tax-free, every wage earner would receive a refund equal to the sales tax rate times the poverty level (adjusted for the number of exemptions claimed) in every paycheck. Any business required to collect and remit the sales tax would be allowed to keep some of the tax receipts to offset compliance costs. There would be no need to file an individual tax return. In fact, there would not even be an IRS to send it to!

A national sales tax that completely replaces the income tax would provide a large tax cut to the wealthy and shift the tax burden to the middle class.

This plan sounds wonderful to the average Joe and Jane who struggle with an income tax return every year. And never again having to worry about a letter from the IRS—nirvana! It really sounds too good to be true—which, of course, it is. The main problem is that the rate would have to be flat. Neither individuals nor families would be taxable units under a sales tax, so the tax could not be imposed at a higher rate on the consumption of more affluent persons or households. A complete replacement of the income tax with a sales tax would therefore provide a large tax reduction for the country's wealthiest individuals and a huge shift of the tax burden to the middle class. Regardless of the merits of such a plan, it simply would not be politically feasible.

The income tax burden actually has been shifting more and more to upper-income individuals in recent years, to a point where a significant portion of the population now pays little or no income tax. According to the Congressional Budget Office, taxpayers in the top 5 percent of the income distribution pay close to 30 percent of all income taxes, and those in the top 20 percent pay about 80 percent.[14] More tax revenue from the rich has caused the effective tax rate on 99 percent of taxpayers to drop to 11.7 percent (in 1997) from 14.2 percent in 1981.[15] This means that Billy Tauzin's 15 percent sales tax would be a tax increase for about 99 percent of the population. Even the most diehard conservative legislators would not jeopardize their political careers by trying to increase taxes on 99 percent of their constituents. If a national sales tax is ever enacted it will be at a much lower rate, and it will merely supplement the income tax rather than supplant it.

Currently the top 20 percent of income earners pay about 80 percent of the income tax. The sales tax would mean a tax hike for about 99 percent of the population.

As far as eliminating the IRS is concerned, get real. A federal tax system without a federal enforcement agency would be a joke. Cheating would be out of hand. If noncompliance is a problem now, what would it be like if there were no IRS? Even with the IRS working hard, retailers would have huge opportunities to evade this tax. Detecting evasion under a retail sales tax is harder than under any other system. With an income tax, one taxpayer's deduction is another's income; there are automatic check procedures. Not so with a sales tax. Besides, Congress always has used the IRS as a scapegoat and will want to keep it around. When our law makers preach reform, they invariably refer to the dreaded "IRS code" as their target of abhorrence, knowing full well that it is the "Internal Revenue Code," a product of their own making. Without the IRS they would have no one to blame for future failings of the tax system but themselves.

## Value-Added Tax

A value-added tax is like a retail sales tax, except a portion of the tax is collected on each producer of a product, from raw material to finished product. The tax is imposed on only what that producer adds to the value of the product. It is a tax that increases the price of products but is not visible to purchasers because it is not all collected at the point of retail sale. This fact makes a VAT easier to administer and far more difficult to evade than a retail sales tax.

Most of our foreign trading partners have VATs, but they also have income taxes. The idea of replacing the income tax with a VAT suffers from the same fatal defect as the sales tax—it would cause a huge shift of the tax burden from the upper to the middle class. Another problem is that the VAT has proven politically fatal to at least one of its proponents. Al Ulman, a Democrat from Oregon, was the powerful chair of the House Ways and Means Committee in 1980. After 24 years in Congress, he lost his bid for reelection that year after proposing a VAT for the country. Whether the VAT suggestion was his undoing or not, these days politicians use the words "value-added tax" reluctantly. VAT proposals tend to be couched in different, more alluring terms. Those proposals labeled "flat tax" are really just VATs with some progressivity thrown in for wage earners.

The complete replacement of the income tax with a VAT would cause a shift in tax burden from the upper to the middle class.

## WILL TAX REFORM MEAN LESS COMPLEXITY?

Among the leaders in the call for tax simplification are organizations of tax professionals—the American Institute of Certified Public Accountants (AICPA), the Tax Section of the American Bar Association (ABA), and the Tax Executives Institute (TEI). This should serve notice that the health and wealth of the tax profession does not depend on overly complex tax laws. In fact, we could find plenty of work with half the gobbledygook that is in the Code now. Nevertheless, a would-be tax consultant might fear that fundamental tax reform would make entry into the profession more difficult. I believe such fears are unfounded, given the dim prospects for the enactment of a national sales tax or VAT as a replacement of the income tax. The flat-tax proposals that have surfaced so far are anything but simple. Even if a replacement system started out simple, it would not stay that way for long.

Most tax professionals could find plenty of work with half the gobbledygook that is now in the Code.

We've been through all this before, you know. In the mid-1980s tax shelters were a multibillion-dollar industry. There were cries that the system was so complex and inequitable that if it were not fixed, it would die from massive noncompliance. President Reagan was solidly behind the idea of fundamentally reforming the tax code. In fact, here is an excerpt from a Treasury Report that set the tone of the debate:

> Any tax inevitably discourages the type of activity that is taxed. An ideal tax system would, however, interfere with private decisions as little as possible. That is, it would not unnecessarily distort choices about how income is earned and how it is spent. It would not unduly favor leisure over work, or consumption over saving and investment. It would not needlessly cause business firms to modify their production techniques or their decisions on how to finance their activities. A neutral tax policy would not induce businesses to acquire other firms or to be acquired by them merely for tax considerations. It would not discourage risk-taking or the formation of new businesses. It would not discourage competition by granting special preferences only to one industry or one type of financial institution. In short, an ideal tax system would be as neutral as possible toward private decisions. Any deviation from this principle represents implicit endorsement of governmental intervention in the economy—an insidious form of industrial policy based on the belief that those responsible for tax policy can judge better than the marketplace what consumers want, how goods and services should be produced, and how business should be organized and financed.[16]

The goal was to level the playing field in a fair and simple manner. Long and heated debates resulted in landmark legislation—the Tax Reform Act of 1986. That act gave us one rate bracket for ordinary income and capital gains.

After the 1986 act was enacted, Congress erased from its memory the virtues of a level playing field and simplicity. Since then there have been major tax bills almost annually adding thousands of pages to the law. Ten years after the 1986 Act took effect, Congress passed the Taxpayer Relief Act of 1997. It contained complex tax breaks for parents and a multiple layer of capital gains rates. The only reason today's top rate bracket for individuals is not as high as it was before the 1986 Act is because of a complicated array of phase-outs for deductions and credits for high-income taxpayers. Any tax accountant with enough history will tell you that the Code is much more complex now than it was before the 1986 Act.

The temperament of politicians and the nature of our political process guarantees tinkering. If a fair and simple tax law were handed to Congress from above, kind of like the 10 Commandments, it would be a complete mess within a few short years. As skillfully explained by Michael Graetz, "Democrats are anxious to spend more money on social programs, but the ceilings on direct spending imposed by congressional budget laws block such action. Republicans want to cut taxes and seem never to have encountered a tax break they will vote against. So the bipartisan congressional consensus is to spend money on social programs through targeted tax cuts. And, despite the additional tax complexity, this strategy seems to please the public."[17]

The temperament of politicians and the nature of our political process indicate that tax laws will never be simple.

## FUTURE IS BRIGHT FOR TAX CONSULTANTS

Ben Franklin had it right about death and taxes. Actually, they're working on death, but taxes will be with us always. And as long as we maintain a representative form of government and a complex society, the tax legislative process will continue to be a competition among diverse interests that vigorously endeavor to minimize their current or proposed tax burdens. If the past is any indication of the future, taxation in the United States will never be a simple matter. The bottom line is that even in the unlikely case that fundamental tax reform is enacted, there will always be a demand for tax professionals to service the general public. In fact, legislative amendments are an important reason for the expansion of tax services.

There will be changes, of course, resulting not only from legislation but from technological advances and industry practices. There are always risks and uncertainties involved in entering a profession that is rapidly changing. It is necessary to take risks, however, in order to achieve your goals. Risk taking produces winners and losers, but one thing is certain: You will never win if you don't play the game.

The other day my wife, Deanna, and I went to a popular local art fair where close-in parking is always hard to find. I had zeroed in on a space, but some jerk made a U-turn in front of me and stole it. I then found a nice spot in a restaurant parking lot. The only problem was, above the place I chose was a sign that said "Customers only. No art fair parking. Violators will be towed." When Deanna protested leaving the car there, I tried to explain to her how it was sometimes necessary to take risks in life. "I know," she said, "I married you." Well, okay, so maybe some risks are not worth taking. Becoming a tax consultant is.

# Chapter 3

# Self-Assessment
# and Education

*This is too difficult for a mathematician. It takes a philosopher.*
—Albert Einstein, on preparing his tax return

## HAVE YOU GOT WHAT IT TAKES?

### *Listening and Communication Skills*

There is a consensus among tax professionals that key qualities of a successful tax consultant are good listening habits and effective communication skills. According to Rita Benassi, a partner with the accounting firm of Deloitte & Touche in San Francisco, you must be a good listener to be a successful tax consultant. "You need to really be able to understand what a client's needs are. If you don't sit back and listen to what the problems are, you will never be able to watch for solutions and opportunities for them."

It does not require a natural extrovert to be successful in tax consulting. In fact, many natural extroverts I know would make terrible tax consultants. Those who are aggressively outgoing and who like to dominate the conversation are not good candidates, because they are too busy talking to be listening. A client needs someone who knows when and how to listen.

It is equally important to be able to communicate the benefits of a particular tax service or technique to clients. Bill Horne, director of na-

> The key qualities of a successful tax consultant are good listening skills and good verbal and written communication skills. People who enjoy teaching are a good fit.

tional recruiting for RSM McGladrey, Inc., says the trait he looks for the most in candidates is verbal and written communication skills. "The communication thing is huge to me," Bill told me. "Nowadays tax accountants are not just preparing tax returns, they have a lot of interface with the clients. If they don't have those communication skills, I think they're almost doomed to fail."

Bob Lindgren, a tax preparer in Bloomington, Minnesota, worked several years as a high school teacher before entering the tax profession. Jay Zack, a CPA and partner in charge of the tax department at RSM McGladrey, Inc., in Minneapolis, also was a teacher before moving into the business world. Often the best consultants are people who enjoy teaching and are good at it. Teachers enjoy conveying difficult concepts in a way that others can understand. The qualities of a good teacher are skills that people of all personality types can acquire.

"When I started in this business in the late 1970s," said Jay, "the skill base that I brought from teaching school was so different than people who were coming out of accounting programs in those days had. Those were the green-eyeshade type of people who wanted something technical and enjoyed the technical work and enjoyed working by themselves. That was the beginning of the change for the accounting profession, when that is not what you would be expected to do in a career in public accounting. The people side of the business is much more prominent now. Today everybody must deal with clients and everybody must deal with building a team and working with your peers."

Listening and communication skills are also critical to being a good negotiator. The tax professional is often called on to negotiate, be it with a client, a purchaser or seller who is dealing with a client, an employee, a colleague, or the IRS. According to Herb Cohen, author of *You Can Negotiate Anything*, "Negotiation is a field of knowledge and endeavor that focuses on gaining favor of people from whom we want things."[1] One of the most important skills of negotiating is having the ability to listen to the other party. It is necessary to understand what the other party can offer and to assess the other party's desire to come to an agreement. It is also necessary to be able to communicate effectively what it is you want. Most negotiations take place with individuals with whom you will deal in the future, so it is necessary to establish a relationship with them that will be beneficial in future meetings. Although IRS negotiations may be adversarial, working for a win-win solution and establishing a positive relationship with IRS agents might be extremely important to your success in future negotiations.

### Desire to Learn

Teachers are also natural scholars and enjoy studying and learning new things. This is precisely what one must do in the tax business. Taxation is probably the most dynamic body of law we have, and to be effective it is necessary to update your knowledge constantly. Kevin Koehler, a tax partner with the CPA firm of Lund Koehler Cox & Arkema, LLP, in Minnetonka, Minnesota, says, "Taxes are really my hobby as well as my career. There is so much to know and to keep up with in this business that you really must enjoy doing it."

Being in the tax profession, whether it is primarily preparing returns or primarily consulting, means being in the business of research. It is impossible to know all the rules, even when specializing in a fairly narrow area. The Internal Revenue Code consists of thousands of pages, and for each page of the law there are dozens of pages of regulations, rulings, and court cases. Each of these sources of information might change on a daily basis. If you have no interest in learning new rules or learning what is new about old rules, you will not be successful as a tax professional. Failing to claim a deduction for a client because you missed a new ruling or court decision means losing a client to a more astute tax advisor.

The tax profession involves constantly learning something new.

### Ability to Comprehend Complex Tax Rules

Regardless of your ability to communicate effectively, you must first possess the talent to be able to interpret and apply complex rules of tax law. This is true whether your work is primarily tax consulting or primarily tax return preparation. This is not brain surgery or nuclear science, but it does involve an ability that comes naturally to some people and escapes others entirely.

The practice of taxation is not a precision discipline like accounting or mathematics. It often involves puzzle solving in creative ways. It is a combination of law, finance, philosophy, and politics. It involves discovering nuances of written words and sometimes requires reading between the lines. The most successful tax advisors do not entrust the interpretation of statutory and regulatory rules to others but have the confidence to rely on their own interpretation. If you are naturally curious and creative, and enjoy the challenge of deciphering what to others might appear as mere gobbledygook, you have a future in the tax business.

> The practice of taxation is not accounting or mathematics; it involves interpreting rules and having the confidence to rely on your own interpretation.

## Vigor of an Entrepreneur

If you are planning to develop an independent tax practice, you must assess whether you have the qualities of an entrepreneur. You must be prepared to accept the financial risks and uncertainties of such a venture, such as the lack of a steady paycheck. You must be a self-starter, innovative, and creative. You must be willing to work longer hours and to put in a sustained effort, especially during the tax-filing season. You must be confident in your ability to succeed and not be easily discouraged. You must be organized and detail oriented. If you plan to hire staff, you must have the temperament to be a good manager.

**Being Financially Prepared** Competition in the field of tax services is extremely stiff these days. The lag time between starting a practice and finding enough clients to support it is continually increasing. Unless you plan to continue in your current occupation and start part time with little capital, you must be certain that you have sufficient funds to cover business and personal expenses until you earn a profit. A wise time to make your move is not right after you have remodeled the house and signed your kid up for Harvard. See more on this in Chapter 4, where we talk about your business plan.

You should also consider the benefits you might be losing if you leave your employer. Health insurance, payroll taxes, continuing professional education, membership dues, and other fringe benefits could add up to several thousand dollars each year. All of these things are added costs when you go out on your own.

Finally, do not overlook the emotional stress on family members if financial sacrifices are necessary. If personal plans of family members must be altered, or if your spouse will be forced into full-time employment, you should have some serious family meetings before proceeding.

You must be prepared for the added financial burden, and prepare your family as well.

**Time Commitment** While an employee, you can focus on your given tasks. Owners or other employees handle the things for which you are not responsible. Running your own practice, however, means being responsible for everything. You must therefore be able to balance chargeable and nonchargeable time effectively.

Only chargeable time directly pays the bills, but you must reserve time for practice development and promotion, technical updating, firm administration, and anything else that might arise. It is always a struggle for a new business owner to find the time to do all of these things while working enough chargeable hours to survive and at the same time trying to meet family obligations.

Doing so is particularly challenging for the tax professional during filing season. The majority of your revenue must be generated in the three-month period between the middle of January and the middle of April. This time compression problem arises from the fact that nearly all individuals file their tax return on the calendar-year basis. It was made worse by the Tax Reform Act of 1986, when all partnerships, S corporations, and personal service corporations were required, with limited exceptions, to adopt the calendar year. In my days of public accounting, I worked many 80-hour weeks during this time of year. This is a fact of life that all tax professionals must endure. You and your family should be prepared.

**Marketing Skills** With your added responsibilities comes a necessary change in attitude. As an entrepreneur you are totally responsible for the success and welfare of your new business. You should consider nearly

You must reserve enough time for promotion, development, and administration while logging enough chargeable hours to survive.

everyone you meet a prospective client or source of referral. You may wish to increase your civic and social activities and spruce up your image as much as possible. In addition, if you never needed marketing skills in your past life, it will be time to try to develop some. "Business today is so different than when I started," explained Rita Benassi. "Companies don't call us anymore for the majority of our tax work. If we waited for companies to call we would be out of business. It is more than just prospecting; it is diagnosing and understanding enough about a company so that you see where their problems are that they did not know they had, and you not only bring up the problem but a solution for them."

**Other Key Traits** Consider the following key traits of the successful entrepreneur according to the American Institute of Certified Public Accountants:

✔ *Goal driven.* Staying focused on a clear goal—and keeping employees focused on that goal—is often one of the most difficult tasks of the entrepreneur. In fact, one of the most important lessons business owners learn early on is that their company can't be all things to all people. The more focused the company is on providing what it does best, the more likely it will succeed.

✔ *Client focused.* Without clients, you can't build a business. The successful entrepreneur spends time understanding the interests and needs of potential clients and views the company's services through the client's eyes.

✔ *Team oriented.* Most successful entrepreneurs recognize that they can't build or run their business alone. Delegating responsibilities to teams of employees or even outside consultants will not only allow the company to focus on its core competencies but also will improve the efficiency of its operations and provide avenues for creative ideas to filter their way up to management.

✔ *Skills oriented.* Each member of the team must have demonstrable skills that can contribute to the company's overall performance.

Astute entrepreneurs make sure that their team possesses a diverse skill base—one that complements their own skills and can create synergies in a team environment. And the entrepreneurs are committed to employees' maintaining their skills by providing ongoing educational opportunities.

✔ *Techno-knowledgeable.* Virtually every aspect of a business requires technological proficiency. Entrepreneurs must possess some knowledge about technology and take the initiative to hire individuals who can implement technology plans and programs.

✔ *Global thinking.* Today more and more businesses are going international. Operating in a global environment means that entrepreneurs must understand the trends and economic and legal issues that have an impact on international markets and products as well as local customs. But even if you do not anticipate expanding your business across continents, understanding how companies similar to yours operate in other parts of the world can provide valuable information that you can put to use in your own business.

✔ *Flexible minded.* Successful entrepreneurs are sensitive to the changing marketplace, competitor strategies, and client preferences, and adapt services accordingly.

✔ *Bottom-line oriented.* Making money—and profits—requires managing money successfully. Being financially astute, carefully managing vendors and suppliers, and hiring the right team of financial advisors can all help a business prosper.

✔ *Socially responsible.* Being socially responsible can also contribute to the company's success. In today's business and social climate, entrepreneurs who are looking to provide a social benefit by making a commitment to serve the economically disadvantaged, protecting the environment, or adopting some other social cause are more likely to be favorably perceived by end users of their services.

✔ *Future oriented.* Successful entrepreneurs don't get overwhelmed or consumed by day-to-day problems. They have a vision for the future of their company and make an effort to understand the trends and forces that will impact their ability to achieve that vision. Last, thanks to the impact of the World Wide Web, more and more clients are expecting businesses to be accessible 24 hours a day. For entrepreneurs, that means making a commitment of time, energy, and resources to be responsive to client demands and needs.

Here are a few more considerations, in the form of questions to ask yourself, to determine if you are right for the role of an independent tax advisor.

✔ Are you a problem solver?

✔ Do you enjoy technical puzzles?

✔ Are you comfortable working alone for long periods of time?

✔ Would you be uncomfortable not knowing what your income will be from one month to the next or one year to the next?

✔ Do you generally have a positive attitude and plenty of determination, or do you tend to get discouraged easily?

✔ Do you like helping people and are you easy to get along with?

✔ Are you a self-starter, comfortable working on your own without any supervision?

✔ Are you organized and detail oriented?

✔ Would you mind working long hours, including evenings and weekends, to make a business successful?

✔ Are you a good teacher and communicator?

✔ Do you think you can make complicated tax rules easy for others to understand?

✔ Are you constantly looking for better and more efficient ways to do things?

✔ Are you creative? Do you think you could take given information about tax rules and apply it creatively and advantageously to a client's situation?

✔ Do you read people well?

✔ Do you enjoy constantly studying and learning new things, or do you find it a burden?

If your answer to all or at least most of these questions is positive, you are on the right track. Let us press on to see if you really like the work and to examine the education and certification necessary to get started.

Self-Assessment Inventory: To facilitate being candid with yourself, write out the answers to these questions. Also write down your strengths and areas that need improvement.

# GETTING YOUR FEET WET

## *Start with Your Own Return*

The best way to determine if you actually like tax work is to jump right in and do it. This is one of the easiest professions in which to get practical experience because you have a tax return of your own to file every year. If you have opted to hire a tax professional in years past, your interest in the role might not be sufficient to make a career of it. That is not necessarily the case, however, if your return was complex and your time was limited. In any event, when tax season rolls around again, you will want to take charge of preparing your own return.

Do not try to do your return by hand. Doing so will lead to the pulling of hair and the gnashing of teeth. Go out and buy TurboTax or an equivalent software program. Tax software is fully appreciated only by those of us who remember preparing complex tax returns prior to the age of the computer. Tax software actually makes return preparation fun! If you do not have a computer, you will, of course, first need to get to one. A computer to a tax consultant is like a hammer to a carpenter, a truck to a trucker, a chisel to a sculptor, a cell phone to a soccer mom—you get my drift. You cannot be a tax professional without a computer and some basic computer skills.

In tackling your tax return, do so with the interest of a professional. Read the instructions thoroughly. If you own rental property, sold stock, contributed to an individual retirement account, sold your residence, or did anything else that might complicate the return, get the free IRS publication that explains that particular transaction. The IRS will mail you the publications or you can download them from the IRS Web site at www.irs.gov. If you have hired a tax preparer in the past, have that person review your return after you complete it, if you like. The fee will be less than if you asked the preparer to prepare the return, and you will have begun your tax education.

You can get even more experience by preparing returns for family and friends. Do not be too aggressive in offering this free help, however,

To see if you will like the work, take charge of your own tax return with the interest of a professional.

because some family and friends might not be eager to share the intimacies of their financial affairs with you. They also might not have much faith in your tax expertise at this point.

After this brief exposure, sit back and contemplate how you would like doing about 500 returns during a three-month period. Consider the fact that with knowledge and experience, your efficiency would greatly improve.

## *Become a VITA Volunteer*

There is an even better way to get the feel of an actual tax practice prior to changing careers or investing much time in education. That is to become a Volunteer Income Tax Assistance (VITA) volunteer. VITA is an IRS program that trains volunteers to prepare basic tax returns for low-income individuals, individuals with disabilities, ESL (English-as-a-second-language) people, and elderly people. I have been involved with VITA for several years as a trainer and site coordinator.

People from all professions, not just tax professionals, serve as volunteers. You will find this gratifying work and will learn a great deal from the experience. It will provide you the opportunity to receive professional tax training with the investment of only time on your part. You will get a chance to deal with real clients, so to speak, rather than just friends and relatives. It will allow you to meet and work with others who are interested in or working in the tax profession as well as IRS personnel.

This is a great way to break in because clients tend always to be cooperative and grateful for your help. You might make mistakes from time to time, but VITA volunteers cannot be held personally responsible and cannot be charged preparer penalties by the IRS.

Many of my students whom I recruit as VITA volunteers become enthralled with the tax business and go on to make a career of it. They continue to return as VITA volunteers, even during the harried busy season of tax professionals, because of the gratification they receive from it.

Sign up with a friend and make it a social event as well as a learning opportunity.

At the VITA site on the University of Minnesota campus, we specialize in returns for nonresident aliens because of all the international students and scholars on campus. One student got a job in Geneva, Switzerland, preparing tax returns for expatriates, largely because of the international tax experience he gained as a VITA volunteer.

Tax counseling for the elderly (TCE) is another IRS program through which you can lend a helping hand while getting free tax training. TCE offers free tax help to people who are 60 years or older. The local IRS district taxpayer education coordinator (TPEC) is the person to contact to find out about volunteer opportunities through VITA or TCE. You can find the TPEC in your area through a list contained in the appendix.

## *Part-Time Employment*

If you really want a taste for the tax business, there are plenty of part-time opportunities with the large franchise tax services, large CPA firms, and independent practitioners. Your duties would be entry level at the beginning, but it would be a good way to get training in professional tax preparation.

Because tax work is largely seasonal, especially for the practitioners who prepare low-end tax returns, there is always a demand for temporary help during tax season. Getting a part-time job as a tax return preparer will not only provide valuable experience and allow you to determine if you would like to go further in the profession, but it will also introduce you to professional contacts who might prove valuable in your career.

In seeking part-time employment, the opportunity to gain experience rather than pay level is the key.

# EDUCATION AND CERTIFICATION OPTIONS

## *Becoming an Unenrolled Practitioner*

The tax profession accommodates people with various educational backgrounds. You can become an unenrolled practitioner in most states, or an enrolled agent, without even a high school diploma. Additionally, in most states there is no certification or licensing requirement for an unenrolled practitioner. Only in California and Oregon must unenrolled practitioners be registered with the state.

**California** In California, unenrolled practitioners are called tax preparers if they are self-employed and tax interviewers if they are employed by a tax service. Tax preparers and interviewers must be registered by the California Department of Consumer Affairs. Enrolled agents, CPAs, attorneys, and tax preparers employed by banks, savings and loans, or loan companies that operate tax preparation services are exempt from registration.

Applicants for registration in California must be at least 18 years old, with a high school diploma or the equivalent. They must have had either 60 in-class hours of approved instruction in basic personal income tax law, theory, and practice or two years of equivalent work experience preparing personal income tax returns. Both the instruction and work experience must cover California State tax law. Applicants must also post a $5,000 surety bond. Because many community and four-year colleges only cover federal taxation, students must take additional instruction in California State tax laws.

In order to be registered on the basis of work experience, applicants must have worked full time for two tax seasons or part time for four tax seasons, preparing both federal and state returns. Registration with the State of California must be renewed annually. Renewal requires the completion of 20 hours of continuing education.

**Oregon** In Oregon, anyone preparing personal income tax returns for a fee must be licensed by the Oregon State Board of Tax Service Examiners. The only people exempt from this law are CPAs, public accountants (PAs), and attorneys who are members of the Oregon State Bar and who prepare returns for their clients. ("Public accountant" is a designation under which individuals still practice but is not available to new applicants.)

There are two types of licenses. A tax preparer license enables a person to prepare personal income tax returns under the supervision of a "tax consultant," a CPA, a PA, or an attorney. A tax consultant license enables a person to prepare individual income tax returns in Oregon for a fee as a self-employed or an independent tax practitioner.

In order to become a tax preparer, an applicant must be at least 18, have a high school diploma, and complete a minimum of 80 hours of basic income tax education through a course of study that has been approved by the Board of Tax Service Examiners. The applicant must then pass the tax preparer examination administered by the board. This exam is no cakewalk—the success rate averages around 50 percent.

A tax preparer cannot take the exam to become a tax consultant until after working at least 780 hours in work directly related to tax preparation. The tax consultant examination is even tougher than the tax preparer exam. An enrolled agent need not take the federal tax portion of the exam but must pass the part on Oregon tax law, the Oregon Income Tax Service Law, and the Tax Board Code of Professional Conduct.

## Becoming an Enrolled Agent

Enrolled agents (EAs) have been around since 1884, when President Chester Arthur signed an act to provide rules to regulate persons who represent citizens in dealings with the Treasury Department. Enrolled agents specialize in taxation. They are not necessarily trained in financial accounting, auditing, personal finance, or anything else.

They have demonstrated technical competence in taxation by either passing an exam administered by the IRS or working for the IRS for at least five years. As explained in Chapter 1, they are authorized to practice before the IRS. Like CPAs and attorneys, they are generally unrestricted as to what taxpayers they can represent, what types of tax matters they can handle, and what IRS offices they can practice before. They are involved in preparing returns for and advising and representing all of the tax reporting entities: individuals, partnerships, corporations, estates, and trusts.

Enrolled agents have demonstrated competence in taxation. They are not necessarily trained in accounting, auditing, or personal finance.

There are two ways to become an enrolled agent. You can work for the IRS for a least five years at a level that involves regularly interpreting the provisions of the Internal Revenue Code and regulations relating to income, estate, gift, employment, or excise taxes. Or you can pass a rigorous two-day exam, called the Special Enrollment Examination (SEE), given in September of each year by the IRS. You also must pass a background check to insure that you have not engaged in any conduct that would justify the suspension or disbarment of an attorney, CPA, or enrolled agent from practice before the IRS. If you pass the exam, there is no minimum work requirement in order to receive the enrolled agent designation.

**SEE Exam** The areas tested on the SEE are as follows. Part 1 covers individual income taxes. Part 2 deals with sole proprietorships and partnerships. Part 3 tests on corporations (including S corporations), fiduciaries, estate and gift tax, and trusts. And Part 4 tests on ethics, record-keeping procedures, appeal procedures, exempt organizations, retirement plans, practitioner penalty provisions, research materials, and collection procedures.

Parts 1, 2, and 3 of the SEE are each three hours long. Each of these parts consists of 80 questions: 20 true/false, 25 multiple choice, and 35 multiple choice computational. Part 4 is two hours long. It consists of 80 questions, 40 true/false and 40 multiple choice.

**Applying and Studying for the SEE** You apply for the SEE on IRS Form 2587, *Application for the Special Enrollment Examination*, which can be downloaded from the IRS Web site at www.irs.gov, or ordered by calling 800-829-3676. The application deadline is generally the end of July each year, and no extension of time is allowed. You can get up to four years to pass all four parts. The current fee for taking the entire SEE in one year is $55, and $45 to take fewer than four parts. The examination is given at over 90 locations throughout the United States and at several international sites. A list of the test sites is included with Form 2587.

The IRS provides a free SEE study kit that contains the IRS forms, instructions, and publications that provide much of the basic information to assist you in preparing for the examination. You can also download from the IRS Web site (www.irs.gov) a copy of last year's exam and official answers to help you study for the current year's test. You can also get free exam information by contacting one of the following organizations:

National Association of Enrolled Agents
200 Orchard Ridge Drive, Suite 302
Gaithersburg, MD 20878
301-212-9608
301-990-1611 (fax)
www.naea.org

National Association of Tax Practitioners
720 Association Drive
Appleton, WI 54914-1483
800-558-3402 (U.S.)
800-242-3430 (WI)
800-747-0001 (fax)
www.natptax.com

National Society of Accountants
1010 North Fairfax Street
Alexandria, VA 22314
703-549-6400
703-549-2984 (fax)
www.nsacct.org

National Society of Tax Professionals
P.O. Box 2575
Vancouver, WA 98668-2575
360-695-8309
360-695-7115 (fax)
ATTN: EA Exam Department
www.nstp.org

**Applying to Practice before the IRS** You should receive word from the IRS about the results of the exam within four months. The IRS is currently implementing a system whereby you'll be able to look up your score on the IRS Web site. With the notice that you have passed all four parts of the SEE, you will be sent Form 23, *Application for Enrollment to Practice Before the Internal Revenue Service*. The fee for filing this application is currently $80. It takes the IRS four to six months to process your application because it first must do a background check.

Once you have been enrolled to practice before the IRS, you are required to complete 72 hours of continuing professional education (CPE) every three years, with at least 16 of those hours completed each year. Your Enrollment to Practice is renewable every three years. You will be sent Form 8554, *Application for Renewal of Enrollment to Practice Before the Internal Revenue Service*, when your enrollment expires. It is your responsibility to make sure that you have renewed in a timely manner and taken the appropriate number of hours of CPE.

## Becoming a Certified Public Accountant

CPAs have been around since the 1890s. The first CPA exam was given in New York in 1896, following passage of the first state CPA law. CPA legislation was enacted in all 48 states by the 1920s, most of it calling for a high school diploma or the equivalent.

A variety of career paths are open to you as a CPA. CPAs audit the financial records of businesses and attest to their fairness, and are the only professionals licensed for such purpose. They also serve as financial and tax advisors to businesses and individuals. As a CPA, you are bound by a strict code of professional ethics. You can become qualified, through education, training, and experience, to provide a wide range of tax services relating to personal and business decisions.

To become a CPA, you need to meet the requirements of the state or jurisdiction in which you wish to practice. These requirements vary from state to state, and are established by state law and administered by state boards of accountancy. To qualify for certification, you must:

- ✔ Complete a program of study in accounting at a college or university.
- ✔ Pass the uniform CPA Examination, which is developed and graded by the AICPA.
- ✔ Have a certain amount of professional work experience in public accounting. (Not all states require this. See Table 3.2, later in this chapter, detailing current state requirements.)

Once you become a CPA, most states require you to take continuing professional education courses annually to retain your license to practice.

The training you must receive to become a CPA provides a variety of career paths.

**150-Hour Requirement** Until very recently only a four-year degree in accounting, which is generally 120 semester hours, was required to sit for the CPA exam in most states. Now nearly all states have passed legislation requiring, or to require in the future, 150 semester hours of education to obtain the CPA certification. Colleges and universities in these states determine the curriculum for the required education of CPAs. Requirements are typically a good balance of accounting, business, and general education.

The American Institute of Certified Public Accountants is the premier organization for CPAs in the United States with over 340,000 members. According to the AICPA, a traditional four-year undergraduate program is no longer adequate for obtaining the requisite knowledge and skills to become a CPA for the following reasons:

✔ Significant increases in official accounting and auditing pronouncements and the proliferation of new tax laws have expanded the knowledge base that professional practice in accounting requires.

✔ Business methods have become increasingly complex. The proliferation of regulations from federal, state, and local governments requires well-educated individuals to ensure compliance. Also, improvements in technology have had a major effect on information systems design, internal control procedures, and auditing methods.

✔ With more sophisticated approaches to auditing and the increase in business demands for a variety of highly technical accounting services and greater audit efficiency, the requirements for effective professional practice have increased sharply. The demand for a large number of people to perform many routine auditing tasks is rapidly diminishing.

To obtain 150 semester hours of education, you do not necessarily have to get a master's degree. You can meet the requirement by taking additional courses at the undergraduate level, or get a bachelor's degree and take some courses at the graduate level. You also can meet the requirement by choosing one of the following:

You do not need a master's degree to satisfy the 150-hour requirement.

After the year 2000, if you become licensed as a CPA without satisfying the 150-hour requirement, you will not be eligible to join the AICPA.

✔ Combine an undergraduate accounting degree with a master's degree at the same school or at a different one.
✔ Combine an undergraduate degree in some other discipline with a master's in accounting or a master of business administration (MBA) degree with a concentration in accounting.
✔ Enroll in an integrated five-year professional accounting school or program leading to a master's degree in accounting.

If the 150-hour requirement has not yet kicked in in your state, you may still be allowed to sit for the CPA exam with only a four-year undergraduate accounting degree. However, with less than 150 hours of education, you will no longer be permitted to join the AICPA, which is the official body of CPAs. Also, if you become licensed in your state with less than 150 hours of education, you will not be granted reciprocity to practice in other states that have implemented the 150-hour requirement.

Therefore, even though your state does not require it, you should make plans to satisfy the 150-hour requirement. Shop around for a business school that has implemented a program to satisfy this requirement. Get a good reference book on business schools, such as *Business Week Guide to the Best Business Schools* (McGraw-Hill). You will have to take it upon yourself to satisfy the requirement if the school you wish to attend does not have a five-year program. Be sure to talk to your academic advisor about this.

Table 3.1 shows the status of the 150-hour requirement in the states as of the summer of 2000.

**CPA Exam** You must pass the uniform CPA examination to qualify for a CPA certificate and license (that is, permit to practice) to practice public accounting. The examination is given twice each year, in May and November, and its duration is $15\frac{1}{2}$ hours. You must apply to your state's Board of Accountancy to take the examination. Most boards require the

**TABLE 3.1  Jurisdictions That Have Passed the 150-Hour Education Requirement**

| State/Jurisdiction | Enacted Date | Effective Date |
|---|---|---|
| Alabama | 1989 | January 1, 1995 |
| Alaska | 1991 | January 1, 2001 |
| Arizona | 1999 | June 30, 2004 |
| Arkansas | 1990 (Reg.) | January 1, 1998 |
| Colorado | 1998 (Reg.) | January 1, 2002 |
| Connecticut | 1992 | January 1, 2000 |
| District of Columbia | 1995 | January 2, 2000 |
| Florida | 1979 | August 1, 1983 |
| Georgia | 1991 | January 1, 1998 |
| Guam | 1994 | June 1, 2000 |
| Hawaii | 1977 | December 31, 1978 |
| Idaho | 1993 | July 1, 2000 |
| Illinois | 1991 | January 1, 2001 |
| Indiana | 1992 | January 1, 2000 |
| Iowa | 1992 | January 1, 2001 |
| Kansas | 1990 | June 30, 1997 |
| Kentucky | 1990 | January 1, 2000 |
| Louisiana | 1990 | December 31, 1996 |
| Maine | 1997 | October 2, 2002 |
| Maryland | 1993 | July 1, 1999 |
| Massachusetts | 1998 | July 1, 2002 |
| Michigan | 1998 | July 1, 2003 |
| Minnesota | 2000 | July 1, 2006 |
| Mississippi | 1990 | February 1, 1995 |
| Missouri | 1993 | June 30, 1999 |
| Montana | 1989 | July 1, 1997 |
| Nebraska | 1991 | January 1, 1998 |
| Nevada | 1993 | January 1, 2001 |
| New Jersey | 1995 | July 2, 2000 |
| New Mexico | 1999 | July 1, 2004 |
| New York | 1998 | August 1, 2009 |

*(Continued)*

| TABLE 3.1 *(Continued)* | | |
| --- | --- | --- |
| *State/Jurisdiction* | *Enacted Date* | *Effective Date* |
| North Carolina | 1997 | January 1, 2001 |
| North Dakota | 1993 | January 1, 2000 |
| Ohio | 1992 | January 1, 2000 |
| Oklahoma | 1998 | July 1, 2003 |
| Oregon | 1997 | January 1, 2000 |
| Pennsylvania | 1996 | January 1, 2000 |
| Puerto Rico | 1994 | January 1, 2000 |
| Rhode Island | 1992 | July 1, 1999 |
| South Carolina | 1991 | July 1, 1997 |
| South Dakota | 1992 | January 1, 1998 |
| Tennessee | 1987 | April 14, 1993 |
| Texas | 1989 | August 31, 1997 |
| Utah | 1981 | July 1, 1994 |
| Virginia | 1999 | July 1, 2006 |
| Washington | 1995 (Reg.) | July 1, 2000 |
| West Virginia | 1989 | February 15, 2000 |
| Wisconsin | 1996 | January 1, 2001 |
| Wyoming | 1993 | January 1, 2000 |

application at least 60 days before the examination date. Requirements to take the examination may include work experience and a separate ethics examination as well as the appropriate education in your state. The CPA exam is a four-section test broken down as follows:

1. Business Law and Professional Responsibilities (LPR): Covers the CPA's professional responsibilities and the legal implications of business transactions, particularly as they relate to accounting and auditing. (Time: 3 hours)
2. Auditing (AUDIT): Covers generally accepted auditing standards and procedures and the skills needed to apply them in auditing and other attestation engagements. (Time: $4\frac{1}{2}$ hours)
3. Accounting and Reporting—Taxation, Managerial, and Governmental and Not-for-Profit Organizations (ARE): Covers federal

taxation, managerial accounting, and accounting for governmental and not-for-profit organizations and the skills needed to apply them in public accounting engagements. (Time: $3^{1}/_{2}$ hours)

4. Financial Accounting and Reporting (FARE): Covers generally accepted accounting principles (GAAP) for business enterprises and the skills needed to apply them in public accounting engagements. (Time: $4^{1}/_{2}$ hours)

This is a tough exam. Saddam Hussein would describe it as the mother of all exams. A number of professional CPA review courses are available to candidates, and many colleges and universities offer review courses. Some of the courses are self-study and others involve classroom training. You should take one of these review courses to give yourself the best opportunity to pass all four parts of the CPA exam. The appendix provides a partial list of professional providers.

**Experience Requirements** Most states/jurisdictions require at least two years of public accounting experience to become licensed as a CPA. Many states/jurisdictions also except non–public accounting experience (such as industry or government), but the number of years deemed acceptable is typically higher than for public accounting. In some jurisdictions both the CPA exam and the experience requirement must be fulfilled to obtain both the certificate and license. Others have a two-tier system in which you can obtain the certificate upon passing the exam, then must fulfill the experience requirement to obtain a license to practice in public accounting. Once you become licensed, you must complete a minimum number of continuing professional education hours each year, determined by the state, to retain your license. The AICPA requirement, of 120 hours every three years, with no fewer than 20 hours each year, is typical. Table 3.2 shows the current education and work experience requirements for each state and jurisdiction.

If you pass two parts of the CPA exam, usually you can sit for the remaining two parts without retaking the entire exam. However, in some states, you must make a substantial effort on all four parts to get credit for the parts that you pass.

| TABLE 3.2 Education and Experience Requirements for Each State and Jurisdiction | | |
|---|---|---|
| State | Education Requirement | Experience Requirement |
| Alabama | At least a bachelor's degree (150-hour requirement in effect) | None to get certificate; two years' public experience or five years' nonpublic experience to get license |
| Alaska | At least a bachelor's degree (150-hour requirement effective date January 1, 2001) | Two to three years' public and four to six years' nonpublic experience to get certificate and license |
| Arizona | At least a bachelor's degree (150-hour requirement will take effect June 30, 2004) | Two years' public or nonpublic experience to get certificate and license |
| Arkansas | At least a bachelor's degree (150-hour requirement in effect) | None to get certificate; two years' public or nonpublic experience to get license; less with an advanced degree |
| California | At least two years college study | With bachelor's degree, two to three years' public or two to four years' nonpublic experience to get certificate and license |
| Colorado | At least a bachelor's degree (150-hour requirement effective date January 1, 2002) | One year public or nonpublic experience to get certificate and license; none with an advanced degree |
| Connecticut | At least a bachelor's degree (150-hour requirement in effect) | Two to three years to get certificate; two to three years' public or three years' nonpublic experience to get license |
| Delaware | At least two years college study | With bachelor's degree, none to get certificate; two years' public or four years' nonpublic experience to get license; less with an advanced degree |

*(Continued)*

| | TABLE 3.2 *(Continued)* | |
|---|---|---|
| State | Education Requirement | Experience Requirement |
| District of Columbia | At least a bachelor's degree (150-hour requirement effective date January 1, 2000) | None to get certificate; two years' public or nonpublic experience to get license |
| Florida | At least a bachelor's degree (150-hour requirement in effect) | None to get a certificate and license |
| Georgia | At least a bachelor's degree (150-hour requirement in effect) | None to get certificate; two years' public or five years' nonpublic experience to get license |
| Guam | At least a bachelor's degree (150-hour requirement in effect) | None to get certificate; two years' public or nonpublic experience to get license; less with an advanced degree |
| Hawaii | At least a bachelor's degree (150-hour requirement effective date December 31, 2000) | Four and a half years' public experience to get certificate and license; less with an advanced degree; nonpublic experience is not accepted |
| Idaho | At least a bachelor's degree (150-hour requirement effective date July 1, 2000) | Two years' public or two years' plus nonpublic experience to get certificate and license |
| Illinois | At least a bachelor's degree (150-hour requirement effective date January 1, 2001) | None to get certificate; one year public or nonpublic experience to get license |
| Indiana | At least a bachelor's degree (150-hour requirement effective date January 1, 2000) | Three years' public or three to six years' nonpublic experience to get certificate and license; less with an advanced degree |

| | **TABLE 3.2** *(Continued)* | |
|---|---|---|
| State | *Education Requirement* | *Experience Requirement* |
| Iowa | At least a bachelor's degree (150-hour requirement effective date January 1, 2001) | None to get certificate; two years' public experience to get license; nonpublic experience is not accepted |
| Kansas | At least a bachelor's degree (150-hour requirement in effect) | None to get certificate; two years public experience to get license; less with an advanced degree; nonpublic experience is not accepted |
| Kentucky | At least a bachelor's degree (150-hour requirement in effect) | Two years' public or nonpublic experience to get a certificate and license; less with an advanced degree |
| Louisiana | At least a bachelor's degree (150-hour requirement in effect) | None to get certificate; two years' public or four years' and nonpublic experience to get license; less with an advanced degree |
| Maine | At least a bachelor's degree (150-hour requirement will take effect October 2, 2002) | Two years' public experience to get certificate and license; less with an advanced degree; nonpublic experience also allowed |
| Maryland | At least a bachelor's degree (150-hour requirement in effect) | None to get certificate and license |
| Massachusetts | At least a bachelor's degree | Three years' public or six to nine years' nonpublic experience to get certificate and license; less with an advanced degree |
| Michigan | At least a bachelor's degree (150-hour requirement will take effect July 1, 2003) | Two years' public or nonpublic experience to get certificate and license; less with an advanced degree |

*(Continued)*

## TABLE 3.2  *(Continued)*

| State | Education Requirement | Experience Requirement |
|---|---|---|
| Minnesota | Don't necessarily need college study (150-hour requirement will take effect July 1, 2006) | With bachelor's degree, up to one year to get certificate; two to three years' public or nonpublic experience to get license |
| Mississippi | At least a bachelor's degree (150-hour requirement in effect) | None to get certificate; one year public or nonpublic experience to get license |
| Missouri | At least a bachelor's degree (150-hour requirement in effect) | None to get certificate; two years' public or two to four years' nonpublic experience to get license |
| Montana | At least a bachelor's degree (150-hour requirement in effect) | None to get certificate; one year public or two years' nonpublic experience to get license |
| Nebraska | At least a bachelor's degree (150-hour requirement in effect) | None to get certificate; two years' public or three to three and a half years' nonpublic experience to get license |
| Nevada | At least a bachelor's degree (150-hour requirement effective date January 1, 2001) | Two years' public experience to get certificate and license; nonpublic experience also allowed |
| New Hampshire | At least a bachelor's degree | None to get certificate; two years' public or nonpublic experience to get license; less with an advanced degree |
| New Jersey | At least a bachelor's degree (150-hour requirement in effect) | One year to get certificate; one year public or three years' nonpublic experience to get license |
| New Mexico | At least a bachelor's degree (150-hour requirement will take effect July 1, 2004) | One year to get certificate; one year public or three years' nonpublic experience to get license |

| | TABLE 3.2 *(Continued)* | |
|---|---|---|
| *State* | *Education Requirement* | *Experience Requirement* |
| New York | Don't necessarily need college study (150-hour requirement will take effect August 1, 2009) | With a bachelor's degree, two years' public or nonpublic experience to get certificate and license; less with an advanced degree |
| North Carolina | At least a bachelor's degree (150-hour requirement effective date January 1, 2001) | Two years' public experience or five years' nonpublic experience to get certificate and license; less with an advanced degree |
| North Dakota | At least a bachelor's degree (150-hour requirement in effect) | No experience required to get certificate and license |
| Ohio | At least a bachelor's degree (150-hour requirement in effect) | Two years to get certificate; two years' public or six years' nonpublic experience to get license; less with an advanced degree |
| Oklahoma | At least a bachelor's degree (150-hour requirement will take effect July 1, 2003) | No experience required to get certificate and license |
| Pennsylvania | At least a bachelor's degree (150-hour requirement in effect) | Two years' public or nonpublic experience to get certificate and license; less with an advanced degree |
| Puerto Rico | At least a bachelor's degree (150-hour requirement in effect) | No experience required to get certificate and license |
| Rhode Island | At least a bachelor's degree (150-hour requirement in effect) | Two years' public experience to get certificate and license; less with an advanced degree; nonpublic experience is not accepted |
| South Carolina | At least a bachelor's degree (150-hour requirement in effect) | Two years' public or nonpublic experience to get certificate and license |

*(Continued)*

| TABLE 3.2 *(Continued)* | | |
| --- | --- | --- |
| State | Education Requirement | Experience Requirement |
| South Dakota | At least a bachelor's degree (150-hour requirement in effect) | None to get certificate; one year public experience to get license; nonpublic experience is not accepted |
| Tennessee | At least a bachelor's degree (150-hour requirement in effect) | Two years' public or two to three years' nonpublic experience to get certificate and license; less with an advanced degree |
| Texas | At least a bachelor's degree (150-hour requirement in effect) | Two years' public or nonpublic experience to get certificate and license; less with an advanced degree |
| Utah | At least a bachelor's degree (150-hour requirement in effect) | One year to get certificate; one year public or three years' nonpublic experience to get license |
| Vermont | At least 60 semester hours | Two years to get certificate; two years' public experience to get license; nonpublic experience is also accepted |
| Virgin Islands | Don't necessarily need college study | With bachelor's degree, three years' public or nonpublic experience to get certificate and license; less with an advanced degree |
| Virginia | At least a bachelor's degree (150-hour requirement to go into effect July 1, 2006) | No experience needed to get certificate; two years' public or three years' nonpublic experience to get license |
| Washington | At least a bachelor's degree (150-hour requirement in effect) | No experienced needed to get certificate; one year public or nonpublic experience to get license |
| West Virginia | At least a bachelor's degree (150-hour requirement in effect) | No experienced needed to get certificate; one year public or nonpublic experience to get license |

| State | Education Requirement | Experience Requirement |
|-------|----------------------|------------------------|
| | **TABLE 3.2** *(Continued)* | |
| Wisconsin | At least a bachelor's degree (150-hour requirement effective date January 1, 2001) | Three years' public or nonpublic experience to get certificate and license |
| Wyoming | At least a bachelor's degree (150-hour requirement in effect) | No experienced needed to get certificate; two years' public experience to get license; nonpublic experience not accepted |

**Master's of Taxation Degree** A master's degree in taxation offers accelerated, comprehensive tax training. There are between 100 and 150 graduate tax programs around the country, excluding the Masters of Law (LLM) programs that are exclusively for attorneys. An accounting degree is not generally required for a candidate to be admitted to a graduate taxation program, but core requirements might include some accounting courses.

There are several different categories of master of taxation programs. Some offer courses exclusively relating to technical areas of taxation, such as partnerships, corporations, estates and trusts, etc. At the other end are tax concentrations within Master of Business Administration programs, which offer a large number of business courses and a select number of tax courses. Some programs bridge the two extremes, offering a few required nontax courses, the remainder being technical tax courses. The other major choice of graduate tax programs is between the day program for full-time students and the evening program for part-time students.

My colleague Fred Jacobs is the director of the Master of Business Taxation (MBT) program at the University of Minnesota's Carlson School of Management. The University's program is primarily one for working professionals, offering classes exclusively at night for the benefit of practitioners working in the tax field. All of the Big Five firms, and many local firms, finance the program for their employees.

Fred described the benefit of the MBT program over simply having the experience of working in the field. "What our program can provide is a systematic look at a particular subject area. In practice, you tend to accentuate your client's needs, so if a client has a need you get yourself geared up in that particular area. But you don't have time to systematically go through a subject field such as partnership tax or corporate tax. That's what we provide here in the MBT program. Systematically looking at the various important subject areas for each course, tying them together so that when an issue arises, student/practitioners who are taking these courses have an awareness of the various problem areas and can relate to their clients' problems."

According to Fred, graduates of the MBT mostly value the immediate benefit in terms of helping their clients. "I often hear from students that they might be discussing a topic in class and a couple of days later they meet with a client who has an issue. The student realizes that what they were talking about in class was right on point and they have an answer for the client."

The only comprehensive listing of graduate tax programs that I am aware of is at the Web site of TaxSearch, Inc. (www.taxsearchinc.com), which is a specialty search firm dedicated exclusively to the recruitment of tax professionals. There you will find contact information for all full-time, part-time, and evening graduate tax programs. At this site you can even participate in a salary survey, which allows you to compare salaries for the same technical criteria with an undergraduate degree only versus an advanced degree.

A master's of taxation degree provides comprehensive knowledge of various technical areas that is not learned in practice.

### Becoming an Attorney

If you are thinking of going to law school, you are not alone. According to David Leonhardt of the *New York Times*, law schools are enjoying their first increases in applications since the 1980s.[2] Law school applications are up about 3 percent in 2000 from 1999, when they also had increased. This trend reverses a string of declines that accounted for a 30 percent overall drop from 1991 through 1998. Leonhardt says the law schools seem to be benefiting from corporate America's willingness to hire lawyers for a broader range of jobs than in the past and from a heightened interest in public interest work after a long economic expansion.

Law school applications are up after many years of decline.

Attorneys are recruited out of law school into the tax departments of the Big Five CPA firms. "We don't hire out of law school but I wish we did," said Jay Zack of RSM McGladrey, Inc. With communication skills at the top of every recruiter's list, it is understandable why law school gradu-ates are sought after. E. Burke Hinds, a tax attorney in Minneapolis, began his career with a Big Five firm. "I was better than the accountants at com-munication and research but was not as good when it came to working with the numbers," said Burke. Attorneys who do not have an undergrad-uate background in accounting must rely on continuing education and graduate tax programs to get up to speed in taxation, because law school generally does not provide sufficient training.

Law school graduates who wish to practice law must pass the bar exam. This exam is administered by each state, but most states use the stan-dardized Multistate Bar Examination. This is a six-hour, 200-question mul-tiple-choice examination covering contracts, torts, constitutional law, criminal law, evidence, and real property. Most states also require the Multi-state Professional Responsibility Examination, which is a two-hour 50-question, multiple-choice exam. Some states also require the Multistate Essay Examination and/or the Multistate Performance Test. The essay exam is a three-hour exam covering agency and partnerships, commercial paper, conflict of laws, corporations, decedents' estates, family law, federal civil procedure, sales, secured transactions, and trusts and future interests. The Multistate Performance Test is a four-and-a-half-hour skills test covering le-gal analysis, fact analysis, problem solving, resolution of ethical dilemmas, organization and management of a lawyering task, and communication.

Because law school provides a broad-based, general education in law, many graduate law programs, called LLM programs, offer focused instruc-tion on a particular legal specialty. The equivalent of a master's of taxation degree for a nonattorney is an LLM in taxation degree for an attorney.

Law school graduates are recruited into the tax departments of the Big Five firms more for their communication skills than their technical tax knowledge.

A lot of guides are available to investigate law school admission. One is *The Official Guide to U.S. Law Schools* (Times Books). Tons of information also are available on the Internet. Try www.lawschool.com and the American Bar Association's www.abanet.org for a start. At www.taxsearchinc.com you will find a survey of all law school programs with an emphasis on taxation.

# Your Business Plan

*Let us not make the income tax so high that the man whose money*
*we want to use in business prefers not to take the risk.*

—Wendell L. Willkie

## START WITH A SOLID BUSINESS STRATEGY

Mention the necessity of a business plan to many small business owners and they will tell you they have no time for such a thing—they are too busy doing what needs to be done. They envision detailed forecasts and financial projections in which they see little value. Probably most entrepreneurs underrate the use of a business plan as a planning tool, putting it off until it comes time to apply for a business loan or attract venture capital. But simply planning what needs to be done is really the first and most vital part of your business plan.

Save the numbers for later if you would like, but it is critical to develop a solid business strategy before you begin. You must consider specifically what it is you want to do and the type of clients you wish to serve. You must look at the market, the industry, and strengths and weaknesses of competitors, and plan how to use your skills to win over clients. Vying for business in the tax services industry is extremely competitive. It is necessary to focus on a competitive strategy. Developing a niche, which is discussed later in this chapter, is a great way to attract clients who will seek your specialized expertise.

> Save the numbers for later if you would like, but make sure you develop a solid business strategy before you begin.

## Focus on What You Want

In Chapter 3 you considered the question of whether you have the character and temperament required to become an entrepreneur. You carefully thought about the sacrifices and the risks involved. Now ask yourself what it is you want from a tax practice. Envision the idyllic tax practice— the one that you see yourself owning. Are you in a large plush office with many employees, associates, and perhaps partners, or are you working solo from your home office? Would you thrive on the responsibilities of a larger practice, or is being freewheeling and independent more important to you? Maybe you see yourself strictly as a part-time tax professional. Or perhaps you see yourself in the less traditional role of running a Web-based tax service. (For more on this see Chapter 8.)

> Envision your idyllic practice and develop a plan to work toward that goal.

## Academic and Professional Experience

Whatever your vision, consider your current level of education, training, and experience. Then devise a strategy to acquire the academic and professional qualifications that you need.

It is important to work for someone else for a period of time before striking out on your own. Adequate training and technical knowledge is essential. If you wish to become a CPA, most states require you to work for a CPA to be eligible for certification. Regardless of the certification requirement, knowledge of business practices and tax return processing is very important.

You must be prepared to be an office administrator and direct the promotional activities for the growth of your practice. You must have experience in supervising and training personnel; practice organization, administration, and development; billing and collection; planning and budgeting; and client relationships.

The length of time it will take as an employee to develop these skills depends on where you work and the quality and breadth of your experience. In *On Your Own! How to Start Your Own CPA Firm,* author Albert S. Williams recommends a minimum of five years of public accounting experience for a CPA who wishes to start a full-service practice.[1] Less time is needed to gain the experience necessary to run a specialized tax practice. But the amount of experience you have will bear a direct relationship on your probability of success.

Catherine Holtzclaw, CPA and owner of Holtzclaw & Associates in St. Paul, Minnesota, received a master's degree in taxation from the University of Minnesota's Carlson School of Management. Catherine worked for both a local CPA firm and an international CPA firm for about seven years before buying into her own practice. "I had a master's degree, but until I really got down in the trenches and was doing research and spotting the issues, I was not ready for my own practice. You cannot simply come out of graduate school and hang up a shingle."

Catherine also recommends using the time you are working for someone else to get out into the community and start networking. "You can't wait until you are about to start a practice to know people. You have to go and join a committee for a cause that you are interested in and start to meet people. It takes a while to break in. People have to know you and trust you before they will refer business to you. It's a lot of work. In your job you might not get any recognition or even support for networking, but if your ultimate goal is to start your own practice you must have your network."

Regardless of your academic background, the experience gained by working for someone else is critical before striking out on your own.

## GOING IT ALONE VERSUS PURCHASING A FRANCHISE

Franchising is a method of product and service distribution that is governed by a contract. Franchising is not a form of business ownership. It generally represents only the license to operate the franchisor's business for the term of the franchising agreement. Purchasing a franchise does not guarantee success, and it might not even increase your odds of success over starting an independent business that is not franchised.[2]

**Franchising:** A method of product or service distribution. It is not a form of business ownership.

But if you pick a good franchise, one that has an established value to the trademark, a solid business plan behind it, and fair protections for the franchisee, it could be a great way to break into the crowded tax services industry.

Buying into a franchise is very much like starting a business, except for the hefty fees you must pay for the business concept. There is generally an initial franchise fee, periodic royalty payments, and a national advertising fee. You can discover what these costs are by talking to existing franchisees in the system you are investigating. Fee information also can be obtained by contacting franchisors, either by mail or through their Web sites.

There is not necessarily a correlation between the fees charged and how profitable your investment eventually will be, so be sure to shop around. Because the ongoing fees are typically based on gross revenue, they can seriously cut into your profit. For example, if your pretax profit margin is 10 percent, but your franchise fee is 5 percent, your profit is cut in half. You must evaluate what you are getting when buying into a franchise and how valuable what you are buying will be to you in several years.

## *Structured Environment of a Franchise*

If you are considering a franchise, be aware that being a franchisee is not quite the same as being an entrepreneur. The franchise agreement of today generally dictates every aspect of the enterprise. The concept of "trade dress" characterizes the modern franchise agreement. This philosophy encompasses not just the look and feel of a business's decor but every detail of the way business is conducted.

Years ago franchising was different from what it is today. Franchise agreements were fairly short documents that gave the franchisee control

Franchising is not the same as being an entrepreneur, because the modern franchise agreement dictates every aspect of the enterprise.

over many aspects of the business. Early franchises were not generally royalty based but were dependent on purchase agreements between the franchisee and the franchisor.

Franchising was changed dramatically by Ray Kroc, founder of the McDonald's franchise. Kroc believed that by carefully controlling and repeating the business format of a very successful hamburger stand in San Bernardino, California, he could achieve predictable success time and time again. He was right, of course, and it is his model that is generally followed today. Ray Kroc brought the assembly line to the fast food industry and the concept of a trade dress to the franchising business.

In order to ensure uniformity and quality of service throughout a franchise system, franchisors of today must exercise substantially more control over their franchise owners. Because uniformity tends to ensure success when the franchise concept is sound, franchise buyers accept these nonnegotiable contracts.

The enormous popularity that franchising has enjoyed over the last few decades has put franchisors in the driver's seat by allowing franchise agreements to become more restrictive and one-sided. Many are not a good deal for the franchisee, so be cautious and do your research thoroughly. A good book to read on the current state of franchising is *Franchising 101: The Complete Guide to Evaluating, Buying and Growing Your Franchise Business.*[3]

Many franchise agreements today unfairly favor the franchisor, so do your research thoroughly.

## What's Available

The following are excerpts from the promotional literature of several franchisors of tax return preparation services. *The claims made have not been verified and I cannot vouch for them.* The list is not necessarily all-inclusive.

Econotax
365 West Northside Drive
Jackson, MS 39206
601-366-5631
800-748-9106
www.econotax.com

The literature says:

> Econotax established its first franchise in 1968 in Picayune, Mississippi. It is still operating under the same owner. The market for an Econotax franchisee is the working public—blue- and white-collar workers who generally make less than $50,000 a year, usually by working for wages. The customer does not have the time or inclination to study the current tax code and cannot afford the cost of hiring an accountant or a CPA. Econotax is a viable option for this individual. Here, the individual finds competent tax consultants who will calculate both his federal and state returns quickly and efficiently for a relatively small fee. By holding to our policy of calculating the largest number of returns efficiently and in a reliable manner that is satisfactory to each individual client, Econotax has seen a steady history of profit.

**H&R Block**
H&R Block World Headquarters
4400 Main Street
Kansas City, MO 64111
816-753-6900
www.hrblock.com

H&R Block is the oldest and most established tax service franchise. Beginning as a bookkeeping company in the early 1950s, Henry and Richard Bloch transformed their company into a tax service in 1955. In 1956 H&R Block began opening franchise offices.

> By 1978, H&R Block offices prepared more than one out of every nine tax returns filed in the United States.
>
> H&R Block is the number one tax firm in the world. As a franchise owner, you benefit from brand name recognition and trust built over 45 years of consistent tax preparation services. All franchisees are provided advanced WinTPS software. H&R Block just completed construction of a state-of-the-art service center. The service center takes all customer calls and tracks down complaints and client needs.

H&R Block claims to have fairly priced franchise fees.

**Jackson Hewitt Tax Service**
4575 Bonney Road
Virginia Beach, VA 23462-3831
800-277-3278
754-473-3300
www.jacksonhewitt.com

Jackson Hewitt, the fastest growing national tax service, is a pioneer in the industry. From its humble beginnings in 1982, the company quickly established itself as a fast, accurate and professional tax service, and now operates approximately 3,000 locations nationwide.

The literature asks:

> Why consider a Jackson Hewitt Franchise? You don't need to have tax experience to own and operate a Jackson Hewitt franchise, because we've created a proven method of doing business, which doesn't require our franchisees to have extensive tax experience. Whether you have an existing tax business, or are entering the industry for the first time, all you need is the willingness to follow a proven system, and the commitment to providing quality tax preparation and excellent customer service. If you do have tax experience or currently operate a tax business, Jackson Hewitt can offer you the strength of a nationally recognized brand name and the power of a leader in the Tax preparation industry.

Jackson Hewitt provides franchisees with state-of-the-art proprietary software that takes the preparer through the process step by step, national advertising and regional marketing support, professional tax and software support, a comprehensive management training program, and comprehensive franchise services support.

With respect to costs, the literature says, "like other franchises, there is an initial franchise fee, but with a relatively small start up fee, low overhead, and employees needed for only a portion of the year, investment costs can range from $45,000 to $75,000."

**Liberty Tax Service**
4575 Bonney Road
Virginia Beach, VA 23462
800-790-3863

757-493-8855
757-493-0169 (fax)
www.liberty.com

According to its literature:

> Liberty Tax Service is a retail income-tax preparation firm that is
> changing the way people think about income-taxes. Backed by
> leading authorities in tax preparation and franchising, Liberty Tax
> Service offers an opportunity to become part of the fastest grow-
> ing tax service in North America. In 2000, Entrepreneur Maga-
> zine ranked Liberty Tax Service #68 overall on their list of the top
> 500 franchises, up from #144 in 1999 and #405 the previous year.
>
> John Hewitt, founder and CEO of Liberty Tax Service,
> also founded Jackson Hewitt Tax Service. At Jackson Hewitt, he
> grew the chain from six offices in 1982 to over 1,300 offices
> when he left in 1996 to start Liberty Tax Service.

Here are some advantages that Liberty Tax Service offers, according
to its literature.

- ✔ Liberty Tax Service offers interested individuals the advantage of
  low startup costs. Most offices can open with under $20,000 in
  operating capital.
- ✔ We have the #1 corporate culture in the industry. We are setting
  standards and constantly improving and all the while we're having fun.
- ✔ "Try Before You Buy" offer. Come and work for us and see what
  it's all about.
- ✔ We're the fastest growing company in the industry.
- ✔ Our influence is present in both the United States and Canada.
- ✔ Our average office in the United States prepares approximately
  1000 returns.

Its literature shows an initial franchise fee of $12,500 and estimated start-
up costs of $24,300 to $35,150.

**Peoples Income Tax**
4915 Radford Avenue, Suite 100A
Richmond, VA 23230
800-984-1040

804-204-1040
804-213-4248 (fax)
www.peoplesinc.com

Peoples calls itself the upscale tax service. Its literature says:

> We will provide complete tax and business training, as well as support. No prior tax industry experience is necessary.
>
> Our proven operating and marketing systems are designed to build a client base with a higher average income and more complex tax returns. Target clients include upwardly mobile executives and small business, in addition to middle income taxpayers. These clients are more loyal than low-income taxpayers and represent higher average fees, resulting in greater profitability. Tax reform and technology may result in diminishing lower-income tax clients, but taxpayers with more complex returns should always need professional tax assistance. Don't compete in the crowded national mass-market tax service arena. Build a stable upscale tax business with a Peoples Income Tax Franchise!

Peoples offers its franchisees proven tax office operating systems, effective marketing methods, access to discounted computer systems and tax software, and ongoing training and support. Peoples currently offers its franchises in only a limited number of states.

**Professor Tax**
Professor Tax of FL, Inc.
3501 W. Highway 98
Panama City, FL 32401
850-914-0999
800-220-8775
850-914-0993 (fax)
www.professortax.com

According to its literature:

> Professor Tax was founded in 1981 by Henry C. Baurley, III, who had carefully developed a plan to provide small businesses with bookkeeping, tax preparation, and management counseling services. His plan worked well. In 1985, the business expanded to

include tax and bookkeeping training schools, and by 1994 Henry began opening additional Professor Tax locations. He chose to invite others to share in his success by offering Professor Tax franchises. Today, Professor Tax, Inc. is one of the most successful businesses of its kind, with an ever-growing list of company-owned stores and franchises throughout the United States.

Professor Tax franchise fee is $34,500 to $39,000 plus $10,000 to $12,000 in startup costs. If purchasing a super franchise, the fee starts at $100,000. A super franchise is a Professor Tax franchise that is sold as a fully established business, which means it already has a location, employees, and a solid client base. Super franchises are owned and supervised by the Executive Offices of Professor Tax until the time of their sale.

## START A PRACTICE OR PURCHASE ONE?

Probably your biggest challenge when you begin your practice is in acquiring a sufficient number of quality clients in the early years. One way to do so is to acquire the client list and files from another practitioner. Doing so will save you many hours of practice development time and provide you with an established base on which to build your practice. Depending on your situation and that of the other practitioner, you might wish to acquire only part or all of the client list, or the entire practice. The entire practice could include all tangible and intangible assets, including leaseholds and improvements, organizational structure and policy, franchise fees, and employment contracts. If you are inexperienced in the profession, bankers tend to look more favorably on a loan to acquire a well-established firm in the area.

### Determining a Value

If you decide to purchase the accounts or the entire practice of another practitioner, be very prudent in choosing the seller and settling on a price. The cost of purchasing an existing client base could range from 30 to 125 percent of the most current 12 months of gross fees, with 75 percent being typical. A revenue multiplier at the high end of the range would be justi-

You may wish to acquire part or all of a client list or the entire practice, including tangible assets.

fied only for a highly profitable firm with a high fee structure, a high client retention level, and a good reputation. The multiplier should be lower for lower-end clients and newer accounts.

The value indicated by the use of the multiplier is specifically for the client base and excludes the value of any other tangible or intangible assets. The value of tangible and other intangible assets, if included in the purchase, must be added to the value indicated by the multiplier. The amount added for these other assets should be their current fair market value minus liabilities.

Among the factors that should be considered in the valuation of a tax practice are ease of the transferability of the client base, the historical retention rate of the client base, client characteristics, management and personal characteristics of the seller, and willingness of the seller to assist in the transition. If an entire practice is being purchased, the previous owner or a key employee generally stays with the new firm for a period of time. Failure of the seller to assist in the transition will, more than likely, decrease future revenues.

Here are some attributes that tend to increase the likelihood of client retention.

- ✔ The buyer and the clients are located in the same city, especially when the city is small.
- ✔ The seller has served the clients for more than three years.
- ✔ The seller guarantees a letter of introduction for the buyer.
- ✔ The technical abilities of the seller and the buyer are similar.
- ✔ Practice management style does not change drastically.
- ✔ The personal characteristics of the seller and the buyer are fairly similar.
- ✔ The seller is actively and effectively engaged in the transition process.
- ✔ The seller intends to retire, leave the area, or leave the profession. (If the seller intends to stay in the area but leave the profession, he or she should sign a noncompete agreement.)

**Revenue multiplier:** Value of a list of accounts based on a percentage of gross receipts. The revenue multiplier is based on your assessment of the future value of the accounts.

The downside of purchasing a client list, or an entire practice, are the risks that you will not retain the clients on the list and that the clients retained are not a good match for you. Carefully study the characteristics of the clients included in the client base that you intend to purchase. Ensure that they are the type of clients with whom you wish to work and are compatible with your training and experience. Business clients, especially those who receive full-service accounting and financial planning from the seller as well as tax services, tend to be the most loyal. If you intend to provide only tax services for these clients, they might opt for another full-service practitioner. Individual clients, on the other hand, especially those with simpler returns, tend to be the least loyal. The revenue multiplier should be adjusted accordingly.

Because of the uncertainty of client retention, probably the best arrangement for purchasing a client list is to pay the seller a percentage of the fees collected from clients who continue with the practice for a specified period of time. For example, you could agree to pay a percentage of all fees charged to existing clients for up to five years. In this case, the true value of the transaction is not known until the end of the five-year period. At any rate, do not pay the price agreed to for a client list in cash. Typically payment is made over a term of three to five years.

Assess the type of clients on the list and determine if they are compatible with your training and experience and whether they are likely to be retained.

Catherine Holtzclaw of Holtzclaw & Associates in St. Paul, Minnesota, has purchased various parts of practices through the years. "Typically the way we have done it has been on a percentage of actual collections over a period of time. I would never buy a practice with money up front, because you never know how much you're going to keep. The percentage paid depends on the accounts, with business clients carrying a higher value than individuals. Our percentages have ranged from 15 percent to 25 percent over three years."

The payment for a client list is typically made over a term of three to five years.

## Example: Determining the Value of a Practice

You should start by analyzing the seller's financial information for the previous three to five years. Study and analyze the current client accounts in order to arrive at a revenue multiplier or a percentage to be paid to the seller. If you are purchasing other assets of the practice, adjust the balance sheet to reflect the fair market value of assets.

### Income and Expense Summary for 12 Months Ending June 30

| | |
|---|---|
| Total Fees (Based on previous 12 months) | $380,000 |
| Operating Expenses (Based on previous 12 months) | $300,000 |
| Net Operating Profit | $80,000 |

### Balance Sheet Summary at June 30

| | | *Restated at Market Value* |
|---|---|---|
| *Assets* | | |
| Current Assets: | | |
| Cash | $10,500 | $10,500 |
| Accounts receivable | $115,000 | $90,000 |
| Work in progress | $6,000 | $4,000 |
| Total Current Assets | $131,500 | $104,500 |
| Fixed Assets: | | |
| Furniture, leasehold | | |
| Improvements and equipment | | |
| (Net of depreciation) | $50,000 | $60,000 |
| Total Assets | $181,500 | $164,500 |
| *Liabilities* | $75,000 | $75,000 |
| *Tangible Equity* | $106,500 | $89,500 |
| *Formula Valuation Using Gross Revenue Multiplier* | | |
| Gross Fees | | $380,000 |
| Assumed multiplier | | × 75% |
| Indicated Value of Accounts | | $285,000 |

Plus Adjusted Market Value of Tangible Assets

| | |
|---|---:|
| Current | $104,500 |
| Fixed | $60,000 |
| Total Gross Value | $449,500 |
| Less Liabilities | $75,000 |
| Net Value of Equity | $374,500 |

## ESTIMATED START-UP COSTS

For franchisees, start-up costs will vary depending on the franchisor and your local area, but the following is a starting point for determining your required investment. If you are opening your own practice without a franchise, your costs will be roughly the same, minus the franchise fee. If you are starting your practice from your home office, you can reduce your costs by rent and utilities. If you are starting your practice on a part-time basis from home, your current wage can finance your working capital.

### *Example: Figuring Start-up Costs*

| | |
|---|---:|
| Initial Franchise Fee | $12,500–$50,000 |
| *Public Relations and Promotion:* | $1,000–$5,000 |
| Logo design (optional for non-franchisee only) | |
| Stationery and business cards | |
| Announcements & postage | |
| Advertising | |
| *Library Costs:* | $500–$2,500 |
| Tax services & professional publications | |
| *Initial Training (for franchisee):* | $0–$2,500 |
| Travel and lodging while training | |
| *Office Furniture:* | $1,000–$5,000 |
| Desks and chairs | |
| Lamps and tables | |
| Filing cabinets | |
| *Office Equipment:* | $500–$1,500 |

Computer hardware and software
Contract for annual tax software
Photocopier
Laser printer
Telephone system
Fax machine
Office supplies

*Other Start-up Costs:*                                   $2,000–$5,000

Two months' rent deposit
Legal advice and/or documents
Internet and e-mail access
Web site and design (optional)
Registration fees
Liability insurance
Other miscellaneous costs

*Other Working Capital:*                                  $10,000–$12,000

Funds to cover costs before sufficient
receipts from services

Total Estimated Start-up Costs:                           $27,500–$83,500

## SPECIALIZATION AND FINDING A NICHE

The tax services industry is not one market but a conglomeration of many markets, all serviced by individuals with divergent skills and expertise. Rita Benassi, with Deloitte & Touche in San Francisco, does high-level tax planning for large multinational corporations. E. Burke Hinds is an attorney in Minneapolis who does sophisticated estate planning for wealthy entrepreneurs. Craig Wilson is a CPA in Minneapolis who directs not only the tax planning but the general financial planning for his small business clients. He finds it is the tax consulting that opens the door to the broader field. Bob Lindgren and Ed Pyle are practitioners in Bloomington, Minnesota, who do primarily tax compliance for individual clients. Ben Ostfield is a tax practitioner in Edina, Minnesota, who specializes in negotiating property tax adjustments for owners of commercial buildings.

These practitioners are very good at what they do. At the same time, each would be less than competent in doing the job of any of the

The tax services industry is many markets. Successful practitioners have established their personal niche by developing special skills and expertise.

others. They have all developed a great deal of expertise in their particular specialty. They can service their clients more effectively and efficiently than a practitioner who deals with a broader range of issues. In competing with other practitioners for clients who fall into their niche, they can demonstrate greater knowledge and experience; they can identify issues that others might miss; they can perform their work effectively with less basic research and in less time and thereby demand a higher hourly rate.

Tax work performed by an individual or small firm is specialized by necessity because of the vastness of the field. It should also be specialized by design if the practitioner is to have a successful and rewarding practice. For example, James Tilsner is a CPA in Minneapolis who had a busy small practice, but who gave it up because of the stress of tax work. James is now looking for another profession. He started his own practice after only about a year with another practitioner. "One of my problems was that I really did not have enough time working for someone else—there was such a learning curve all on my own," said James. "Another problem was that I never really established a niche. I did about 100 personal and about 25 corporate and partnership returns. I was doing all different kinds of industries." Even the most skilled and talented of individuals, such as James, can easily become overwhelmed in a field that is too broad for one person to master.

Catherine Holtzclaw saw her niche in small businesses, especially those owned by women entrepreneurs. "A large percentage of my business owners are women, which kind of goes with the demographics of who is starting businesses these days—there are a lot of women starting businesses. There is a niche in the fact that you are still not going to find very many CPA firms that have women as partners, and a lot of women who are entrepreneurs like to do business with other women."

Catherine recognized a niche based on her gender and the fact that female business owners like to deal with female tax practitioners. You can imagine the same dynamics occurring based on your race, your religion, your hobbies, or the industry in which you currently or previously worked. Many types of businesses and professions are subject to special tax rules. Having worked in a particular industry that you would like to

A successful small practice must be specialized by design.

target for tax services gives you special knowledge and an edge over the competition. Similarly, any segment of the population with which you have something in common can be a niche.

For example, if you are currently in real estate sales but wish to enter the tax profession, you might strive to become a tax specialist for salespeople who are self-employed. Besides having a ready base of contacts, you can market your services as one who has special knowledge of the industry. Or if you are currently a member of the clergy or are actively involved in a religious organization, you might want to focus your practice on the special tax rules that are unique to clerics and religious organizations. A Web search will reveal several practitioners who practice exclusively in this area.

You can create a niche from your race, gender, religion, age, or former occupation.

You may be concerned that your chosen niche is too small and unable to generate a sufficient number of clients for you to make a living. First, if you are overly specialized, you can always have more than one niche. Second, niches tend to expand over time. For example, you might become very knowledgeable regarding the tax rules pertaining to real estate salespeople. These people tend to have real estate investments as well as friends and clients who are also real estate investors. Referrals for tax advice on real estate investing would prompt you to expand your specialty to this area, which is vast and complex. Last, in today's high-tech environment, it is possible to serve clients adequately regardless of where they live. In Chapter 8 I tell you about my Web-based tax service for nonresident aliens, through which I deal with clients who are located all over the world.

Areas in which you specialize tend to expand over time.

# FINANCIAL CONSIDERATIONS

The amount of capital that you will need to get started will vary considerably depending on whether you purchase a franchise, purchase a practice, or start from the ground up, and whether you start full time or part time. Consider the following questions.

- ✔ Is your current personal debt burden low?
- ✔ Do you have personal equity on which to borrow?
- ✔ Will it be necessary for a nonworking spouse to obtain employment to help support the venture?
- ✔ Will it be necessary to make adjustments in your standard of living?

As a beginning tax practitioner, you will likely make less in your first few years than you did in your prior employment, resulting in less disposable income. If this will cause undue financial pressure on the home front, make certain that your family is prepared for the adjustment.

## *Avoid Borrowing If Possible*

The less you must borrow initially will reduce the time it takes to turn a profit. However, without adequate financing at the outset, you might be tempted to accept marginal clients and lower fees. While this might pay the bills in the short term, it can hamper the long-term development of your practice. Should it be necessary to supplement your income, find activities that are compatible with your tax practice and that will enhance your professional image.

Frank Claymon, president of Frank E. Claymon, Ltd., in St. Louis Park, Minnesota, began his CPA practice nearly 30 years ago. "When I first went out on my own I got a job teaching at the Academy of Accountancy in downtown Minneapolis. I did that from about 7:30 to 9:00 in the morning. I enjoyed teaching and did that for several years. I also got an office with another CPA who gave me X amount of work to do

Plan to have less income in the first few years of your practice than you made in your previous job.

and didn't charge me rent or use of his secretary. I therefore had two sources of income until I built up my practice." Frank found what are considered the best supplemental sources of income for a beginning practitioner. Teaching not only enhances your professional image but also forces you to learn more about your work. Contracting with another practitioner provides experience and might result in long-term networking advantages.

> Supplemental sources of income that are compatible for a beginning practitioner are part-time teaching and contracting with another practitioner.

## If You Must Borrow

If borrowing is necessary, the most convenient, easiest, and least expensive source of funds is the equity in your home. If you have sufficient equity but are unwilling to risk it, perhaps you do not possess the confidence that is essential to launch a business successfully. If you do not possess sufficient equity in your home, and if other sources of unsecured financing are unavailable, then it will be necessary to acquire a business loan.

> Be prepared to risk the equity in your home for the easiest, most convenient, and least expensive source of funds.

The first step in acquiring a business loan is to develop a projection of your financing needs based on a detailed business plan. Go out and find a good book on writing business plans, such as Bob Adams's *Complete Business Plan*.[4] In addition to the plan, the lender will consider the following:

✔ *Character.* This includes your integrity, determination to prudently manage business assets, and assurance that the debt will be repaid.

✔ *Capital.* Usually a lender will require you to invest and accept a portion of the risk.

✔ *Capacity.* Your ability to manage the firm is probably the most important attribute a lender will consider. Capacity means that you have sound tax and business management experience. Entering the profession with little or no experience working for another practitioner can be a serious drawback to obtaining financing.

✔ *Collateral.* Often a lender will ask for collateralization of the debt. The most valuable asset for a service business, such as a tax practice, is its clients. This value will not be realized for the first few years of a new business. If something were to happen to you before your new firm realizes any profits, and if the loan were unsecured, the lender would not be in an adequate position. That is why lenders tend to seek collateral when possible.

✔ *Insurance Coverage.* Can you withstand major losses, and have you obtained adequate insurance coverage to protect your business assets? Sole practitioners are particularly vulnerable to this risk. The greatest potential loss is your death or disability. This should be covered by an insurance policy equal to the amount of the loan. Or, if you have partners, a well-drafted practice continuation agreement should be in effect.

Once a lender is satisfied that the above conditions have been met, and assuming you have presented a well-prepared and well-documented plan, you should be able to obtain the funds needed to start a practice.

To obtain a business loan that is not secured by your home equity, you must present a well-prepared and well-documented plan.

## LOCATION AND FACILITIES

When considering your office space, you probably will realize that what you can afford and what you would like to have are two different things. Here are some guidelines, from the *AICPA Management of an Accounting Practice Handbook*,[5] to consider if you plan to locate your office outside your home.

✔ The site should be accessible for you, your employees, and particularly clients.

✔ The site should be located near restaurants, banks, and a post office.

✔ Consider the convenience of the site to main arteries, public transportation, and ample parking.

✔ Be sure your building has adequate rest room facilities and proper heating, cooling, lighting, and maintenance service.

✔ If you are going to run a franchise or lower-end tax service, the site should be located where your sign is visible to a high volume of traffic. Walk-in traffic is common for a lower-end tax service. If you are a CPA serving business clients, you might not benefit greatly from the visibility of your sign.

Affordability and location are key factors when considering your office space.

## Home-Based versus Outside Office Space

Some of the preceding considerations do not pertain to a home office, but working from home saves money and commuting time. Many tax practitioners begin their careers from a home office. It is the least expensive and most convenient way to go. If you intend to start part time, it is essential to minimize office costs. Even full-time practitioners are burdened by unused office space during the slack season. An added advantage of a home office is the liberalized rule on home office deductions described in Chapter 6.

The major drawback to operating your business from home is not being able to project a professional image when meeting with clients. There is also the potential for interference with personal and family obligations. A home office might convey the appearance of impermanence and negatively influence clients' expectations of service and fees.

Catherine Holtzclaw has never worked out of a home office. "As a woman I feel a bit more of the pressure of having a professional presence so as to not be discounted. I think some people believe that if they go to a woman working out of her home that they're going to get a cheap price."

Conversely, Craig Wilson, a CPA in Burnsville, Minnesota, began his

When considering a home office, balance cost and convenience with the need to project a professional image and to divide work and home life.

practice from his home office after working several years with other firms. Craig now uses a combination of his home office and an office-sharing arrangement with another firm. Craig said, "I started my practice out of my home, in part from an economical standpoint and in part to get more time to be with my family."

Craig was working for a CPA firm in downtown Minneapolis before starting his practice. He said that during busy season, he virtually did not see his children five days out of the week. One morning during busy season he got up to go to work and his three-year-old daughter happened to have gotten up extra early. She said to Craig, "Oh, Daddy, you're going to work, aren't you?" Craig said, "Yes, I am." His daughter then asked, "That's where you live, isn't it?"

"That hit me pretty hard," Craig said, "and got me thinking about going out on my own and working from home." Craig said that this was probably the best thing that ever could have happened because of the way it changed the dynamics of the relationships he had with his business clients.

"I have met with some individual clients at home, but to meet with business clients, it forced me out of my office to their office. In going to their office, suddenly they didn't see me as the high-priced professional who held the keys to the relationship and who they didn't want to call unless they absolutely had to. It conveyed the perception that they were the most important party in the relationship rather than me, and I got to learn a lot more about what they did. So from this two things happened. One, I was able to give them a lot better advice, because I was more knowledgeable about their business; and two, I was able to become a much more critical member of their professional team and was able to become their key advisor. So out of that I have developed some very strong relationships with these business clients."

With the advent of the Internet and e-mail, home offices are becoming much more accepted today than ever before. Perhaps, in order to maintain professionalism while holding down costs, you could arrange for temporary office space outside the home to meet with clients but perform most of your work in a home office. Be sure to read Chapter 6 about the tax advantages of such an arrangement.

A home office might forge a closer connection with clients by shifting client meetings to their offices.

### Office Sharing

A compromise between an exclusive office outside the home and a home office is an office-sharing arrangement. Office-sharing arrangements have been popular among doctors and lawyers for many years and are gaining in popularity in the accounting and tax professions. In such an arrangement, usually a group of sole practitioners maintain separate executive offices but share a secretary, receptionist, reception room, library, conference room, photocopy machine, and lunchroom or coffee area. Sometimes sole practitioners, like Craig Wilson, make such an arrangement with a larger firm.

Office sharing offers economy and professionalism for the sole practitioner.

James Tilsner, a CPA in Minneapolis, said, "I would definitely suggest an office-sharing arrangement for someone who is going out on their own. It's the next best thing to a partnership. You have someone to help with questions and to bounce ideas off of."

Taken a step further, this can actually be a form of ownership known as a "shared-expense association." Advantages of such an arrangement are:

- ✔ *Coverage for illness and vacations.* Arrangements can be made for an associate practitioner to step in temporarily for emergencies.
- ✔ *Practice continuation in the event of death or disability.* A buy/sell agreement with an associate familiar with your clients and practice has a greater chance of success.
- ✔ *Public image.* If the image of your associates is good, your image may be enhanced.
- ✔ *Opportunities for professional discussion.* Associates provide an opportunity for the exchange of ideas.
- ✔ *Shared overhead.* You can have an office with all the amenities at a much lower cost.

There are a few disadvantages, such as:

- ✔ *Self-interest.* Your success depends on the growth of your practice. The growth and development of the association, therefore, is secondary.
- ✔ *Lack of staff development and incentives.* Because you and your associates tend to share staff, there may be lack of coordination

of supervision. This might cause employee confusion and discontent.

✔ *Public confusion.* Your clients and the general public might not understand the true nature of the organization.

## TIMING

Because you will obtain most of your new clients between January 1 and April 15, plan to open your practice so that you will be up and running a couple of months prior to that time. Give yourself enough time to organize your office and make personal contacts, taking into account the lack of cash flow during the setup phase. Do not let the opening of your practice be controlled by unrelated events, such as losing your current job or the sudden availability of good office space. Do all of your planning before you start, and be mindful of the services that must be fully in place when tax season begins. For example, check on how much lead time is necessary to obtain a listing in the phone book. Find out how long it will take to get customized letterhead stationery, envelopes, business cards, and client tax return folders. If you plan to do business on the Web, you must design and launch your Web site early enough to be listed in search engines.

Be prepared to open your office well ahead of the busy season.

## SETTING YOUR FEES

Fees are a topic for which there are no hard and fast rules. Setting fees is more of an art than a science, based on both objective and subjective considerations. One objective factor is what your competition is charging, which you should monitor regularly. But your fee structure should not be based solely on this. Your fees tell a client how much you think you are worth, and it is your job to convince the client that your knowledge, expertise, and experience are worth what you ask. If you charge too much, you won't have much to do. If you charge too little, prospective clients will think that you couldn't be very good, nor could your advice be worthwhile.

In economic terms, what you can charge involves the elasticity of demand for your services. If your elasticity of demand is low, you will attract clients regardless of your fee. If your elasticity of demand is high, the more you charge, the fewer clients you will attract. Generally, elasticity of

**Elasticity of demand:** The degree of change in demand for services associated with a change in the price charged.

demand is high for routine, low-end tax return preparation. In other words, there is a lot of price competition for this work. However, if you have an established reputation of excellence, clients will accept your fees even if they are above the norm.

Bob Lindgren, an unenrolled practitioner in Bloomington, Minnesota, uses the fees he charges to screen his clients. His current clients know that he is knowledgeable and accurate, and are willing to pay his fees. Also, clients who come to him by referral, which is his best source of new business, are familiar with his reputation and accept his fees. Clients who contact him through promotions or his listing in the Yellow Pages are generally more reluctant to accept his high fees. "I can often convince those who are more concerned about getting the job done right," said Bob, "but those who are simply shopping for the lowest price go somewhere else."

Fees can be set in several ways. Some practitioners charge strictly by the hour, others charge by the job, others charge a stated fee for each form that must be included in a return, and some use a combination of the foregoing. For low-end compliance work, it is generally more acceptable to charge by the job or the forms required to prepare the return and to give the client a certain price at the initial meeting. Higher-end return preparation and consulting work tends to demand a higher fee and is typically charged by the hour.

When charging by the job or the forms required to prepare a return, practitioners attempt to aim at an average hourly rate. For example, if you charge $50 for each Form 1040-EZ that you prepare, it might be based on your assumption that, on average, you can prepare and completely process such a form in half an hour. You know that some Form 1040-EZs will be completed in 15 minutes, while a few will take 45 minutes, but on average you will earn $100 an hour for your work. Clients tend to enjoy the certainty of this arrangement.

Of the sole-practitioner CPAs with whom I spoke, the highest fee (as of the summer of 2000) was $130 per hour. The lowest was around $100

Practitioners tend to charge by the hour for consulting or higher-end compliance work and by the job for more routine compliance work.

Regularly monitor the fees your competitors charge.

per hour. This contrasted with high-level attorneys and CPA partners with large firms, whose firms charged up to $265 per hour for their work. Self-employed unenrolled practitioners and enrolled agents averaged about $90 per hour. This was strictly a small sample survey in the Twin Cities area and might differ from the average in your area. It is advisable to keep track, on a regular basis, of what your peers in your area charge so that your fees are not too out of line.

## MARKETING YOUR SERVICES

Marketing your services as a tax professional should involve much more than placing an ad in a newspaper and the Yellow Pages. Your basic marketing strategy should be to maximize awareness of your tax practice to taxpayers you would like to attract as clients and interact, on a professional level, with as many people as possible, making them aware of your competency.

Advertising alone provides awareness, which is important, but does not set you apart from competitors with similar qualifications. Focused awareness is necessary to achieve maximum results at the least cost. It is generally advantageous to make taxpayers in the immediate vicinity of your practice aware of your services, if they are the type of clientele you wish to attract. Prospective clients often start their search for a tax advisor closest to where they live or work. Bob Lindgren attracted many of his original clients by sending notices announcing the opening of his practice to people who lived in the surrounding area. You should also make business, social, and personal acquaintances aware of your new practice by sending them announcements.

Another very effective form of focused awareness is through other professionals. Becoming active in civic organizations, the chamber of commerce, and the Parent Teachers Association (PTA) will put you in contact with professionals in the community, such as attorneys, insurance agents, bankers, and brokers. As these individuals become aware of your value to the organi-

Prospective clients often start their search for a tax advisor closest to where they live or work.

Networking with attorneys, insurance agents, bankers, and brokers is an effective form of marketing.

zation and your diligence in performing assigned tasks, they will develop confidence in you as a tax practitioner. From that confidence, referrals will develop. Catherine Holtzclaw, like most of the other CPAs I interviewed, markets her services mostly through networking with lawyers, bankers, and brokers who are willing to trade referrals. Once they know your practice, they will tend to send you clients of the type with whom you wish to work. This networking must begin while you are still gaining experience by working for someone else. While there is a risk that some of the contacts developed during this period will become your current employer's clients, it is still necessary to have your network in place when you go out on your own.

Awareness is enhanced when you make prospective clients aware of your professional competence through personal interaction. A favorite method of doing this is to volunteer to teach free community seminars on tax topics. Contacting private and civic organizations that sponsor such seminars will generally evoke a grateful acceptance.

You also can contact the local office of the IRS and say you would like to volunteer for the Community Outreach Tax Education program. In this program individuals conduct lectures or seminars on some aspect of tax law. The presentations are targeted at groups of taxpayers that have a common occupation or tax concern, such as farmers, retirees, and small business owners. This is a great way to make personal professional contact with a targeted audience. Ed Pyle, an enrolled agent in Bloomington, Minnesota, has volunteered to teach a small business seminar for the IRS for several years. Besides gaining exposure and demonstrating his technical competence to prospective clients, Ed also gets a chance to improve his communication skills.

Another way to make prospective clients aware of your technical competence is through interaction that is not face to face. For example, many practitioners mail newsletters to clients and prospects. It is now popular, and much cheaper, to e-mail these newsletters.

Another form of promotion that tax professionals are beginning to use is a Web site that offers plain-language explanations of tax rules for a

Volunteer through the Community Outreach Tax Education program sponsored by the IRS.

Launch a Web site that offers plain-language explanations of the tax rules for a particular audience.

particular audience. I have such a site at www.thetaxguy.com. My site provides tax information for international students and scholars who are visiting the United States to study, teach, or do research. It was not originally intended as a promotional site. As a VITA site coordinator at the University of Minnesota, I found that the number of these people requiring help was much larger than what we could serve. I therefore put enough information on my Web site to allow many of them to prepare their own returns. As traffic on the site grew, along with e-mail inquiries, I developed the idea of starting a part-time Web-based tax service for these taxpayers. The free and useful information still attracts the taxpayers to my site. After being convinced of my competency, some of them opt to become clients rather than tackle the chore on their own. (See Chapter 8 for complete details on my Web-based tax service.)

## PROJECTED INCOME STATEMENT

Here is a sample income statement that you can use as a starting point for your projections. It is based on fees charged at an hourly rate of $100 and 800 chargeable hours, totaling gross fees of $80,000. If you consider working an average of 48 hours per week over 50 weeks during the year, the total number of hours worked is 2,400. If you charge one-third of the total time spent on the job as a sole practitioner, you are doing very well. You may wish to reduce your projection significantly for the first year and increase it gradually over the first five years.

The projection includes wage expenses for a bookkeeper/secretary, whom you may or may not employ. The fee estimate does not include hours charged for this employee. The hourly rate for an employee will vary greatly, depending on that person's ability and experience. Gross fees for an employee also will vary greatly by the person's involvement with return preparation and processing. Most of the following numbers are from the *AICPA Management of an Accounting Practice Handbook*.

**Chargeable hours:** The time spent performing client services that you can charge in full to the client.

## Example: Projected Income Statement for Sole Proprietor Tax Service

| | |
|---|---|
| Gross fees | $80,000 |
| Billing adjustments | ($8,000) |
| Net fees | $72,000* |
| Bookkeeper/secretary salary (part time) | $12,000 |
| Payroll taxes | $800 |
| Medical, disability, and term life insurance | $3,000 |
| Professional development (CPE) | $1,000 |
| Professional dues | $400 |
| Office rent | $7,000 |
| Equipment repairs | $500 |
| Depreciation expense | $2,000 |
| Promotional expenses | $1,000 |
| Client entertainment | $500 |
| Insurance | $1,000 |
| Library publications | $500 |
| Stationery, printing, and supplies | $2,000 |
| Postage and Express Mail | $1,200 |
| Other taxes | $400 |
| Telephone | $2,000 |
| Total Operating Expenses | $35,300 |
| Nonoperating expenses | |
| Interest | $2,000 |
| Provision for doubtful accounts | $2,000 |
| All other expenses | $400 |
| Total nonoperating expenses | $4,400 |
| Total operating and nonoperating expenses | $39,700 |
| Net income before state and federal income taxes and self-employment tax | $32,300 |

*Note: Franchisees also must account for the royalty fee and national advertising fee, both of which come out of your gross receipts.

# Chapter

# Choices for
# Business Organization

*It's a game. We [tax lawyers] teach the rich how to play it so they can stay rich—and the IRS keeps changing the rules so we can keep getting rich teaching them.*

—John Grisham

One of the first questions you will get from a client who wishes to start a business is "What type of entity should I form?" This, coincidentally, is one of the first issues you should consider in setting up your practice. In this chapter and the next, you will learn a few things about setting up a business that you can use not only for yourself but also in advising your new business clients.

Carefully think about what form of business organization is best for you. If you are by yourself, you could operate as a sole proprietor or a limited liability company (LLC), or you could incorporate and operate as a C corporation or an S corporation. If you have partners or associates, you could operate as a corporation, a partnership, or as an LLC or limited liability partnership (LLP). Both LLCs and LLPs are treated as partnerships for tax purposes when there is more than one owner. This

One of the first things to consider is what type of entity to form.

chapter discusses the characteristics of the various forms of business and compares their benefits and drawbacks.

# SOLE PROPRIETORSHIPS

A sole proprietorship is any unincorporated business owned entirely by one individual. It is the simplest form of business and has the advantage of low cost in its formation, operation, and termination. If you are just going into business, you might want to choose a name for your business that is different from your own. Contact your state's secretary of state and ask how to do this. Also contact the state and city or county department of revenue to find out about sales tax and other filing requirements.

## *General Tax Treatment*

Sole proprietors file Schedule C ("Profit or Loss from Business") with their Form 1040. Proprietors who are farmers file Schedule F ("Profit and Loss from Farming") with their Form 1040. Owners of rental real estate, who are not otherwise in the real estate business, report rental income and expenses on Schedule E ("Supplemental Income and Loss") to be filed with Form 1040. Royalties from nonworking interests in oil, gas, or mineral properties or from copyrights and patents are also reported on Schedule E. The income or loss from the business is combined with the taxpayer's other income and deductions and taxed at the individual rates.

## *Self-Employment Tax*

Sole proprietors must also pay self-employment tax on the entire net income from Schedule C or Schedule F (but not Schedule E), one-half of which they can deduct on page 1 of Form 1040. You could be an employee for your regular job in addition to having a part-time business, the net income from which is subject to self-employment tax. But any wages

**Sole proprietorship:** A type of business organization owned entirely by a single individual that is not a separate entity from the owner.

you earn reduce the self-employment tax base for retirement and disability benefits. For example, if you earned over $76,200 in wages in 2000 and also had Schedule C income, the Schedule C income is only subject to self-employment tax at the rate of 2.9 percent. See the expanded discussion of self-employment tax in Chapter 6.

> You must pay self-employment tax on the entire net income of your sole proprietorship.

## Who Can Be a Sole Proprietor?

The word "proprietor" might bring to mind a shop owner, but you can operate any business under this form as long as you are the only owner. You could operate a large company with hundreds of employees as a sole proprietorship, or you could be a one-person consulting firm. You could operate a sole proprietorship on a full-time or part-time basis, and you can have more than one proprietorship if you want. A sole proprietorship must be a business—not an investment activity or a hobby.

If you work primarily or exclusively for one company but are not classified as an employee for income tax purposes, you are a type of sole proprietor referred to as an "independent contractor." Sometimes there is a very fuzzy line between being an independent contractor and being an employee, but the distinction has important tax implications. As an independent contractor, your business expenses are deductible "above the line" on Schedule C (Form 1040). This means they are deductible even if you claim the standard deduction. As an employee, on the other hand, all of your unreimbursed employment-related expenses must be deducted on Schedule A (Form 1040) as "Miscellaneous Itemized Deductions." You don't get the full benefit of these deductions because they are reduced by 2 percent of adjusted gross income. (See Schedule A.)

An advantage of being an employee is that you only pay one-half of your social security tax; your employer pays the other half. You also qualify for employee benefits offered by your employer that you do not get as an independent contractor.

> If you do work as an independent contractor, report your income and deductions as a sole proprietor.

## Tax Accounting Methods and Periods

**Accounting Methods** A sole proprietorship is not an entity separate from the individual proprietor, so any income or loss from the proprietorship is combined with income and deductions from other sources on Form 1040. However, you can choose a method of accounting for your business that is different from the method you use for your other income and deductions. In fact, you can run several businesses as sole proprietorships and use a different accounting method for each one. For example, you are a cash-method taxpayer when you report wage income and non-business deductions, but you can adopt an accrual method for your sole proprietorship. If you have two separate businesses, you can use the cash method for one and an accrual method for the other. You should report each business on a separate Schedule C. The general rules for the cash and accrual methods can be found in IRS Publication 538, *Accounting Periods and Methods*, which can be downloaded from the IRS Web site at www.irs.gov.

You can choose a method of accounting for your business that is different from the method used for your other income and deductions.

**Taxable Year** You report the income from your business for the 12 months ending on the last day of the business. Wouldn't it be neat if you could adopt January 31 as the year end for your Schedule C, so 11 months of your income from this year would not be reported until you file next year's return? Forget it—you cannot do that. Unlike the rule for accounting methods, as an individual you can use only one accounting period for all your income and deductions. Individuals are required to use a calendar year unless, when they file their first return, they have a bookkeeping system in place and adopt a fiscal year. As a practical matter, individuals rarely meet this requirement. As a result, they are required to use the calendar year. Once adopted, a taxable year cannot be changed without the approval of the IRS.

**Calendar year:** A taxable year ending on December 31.

**Fiscal year:** A taxable year ending on the last day of any month other than December.

Individuals must use a calendar year, with limited exceptions, and must use the same taxable year for their sole proprietorships.

## Retirement Plans

As a sole proprietor, you can set up a simplified employee pension (SEP) or a Keogh plan, or both, and make deductible retirement contributions for yourself and your employees. Alternatively, you may be able to set up a "Savings Incentive Match Plan," known as the SIMPLE retirement plan, for yourself and your employees (if you have any). Enacted as part of the Small Business Job Protection Act of 1996, this type of plan does not have to meet many of the requirements of qualified plans. Deductible contributions to the above plans and the earnings on them remain tax-free until you or your employees receive distributions from the plans in later years. These plans are available for your own retirement even if you do not have employees. Contributions for employees are claimed on Schedule C (Form 1040) or Schedule F (Form 1040), but your own contributions are deductible on page one of Form 1040. That means contributions for your account do not reduce self-employment income in computing self-employment tax. IRS Publication 590, *Retirement Plans for the Self-Employed*, is a good source for information on this stuff.

You can set up a variety of retirement plans as a sole proprietor.

## Health Insurance

You can also deduct, "above the line" (that is, in arriving at adjusted gross income), a percentage of the amount you pay during the year for health insurance for yourself, your spouse, and your dependents. The above-the-line deduction cannot exceed your earned income from the business for which

You can deduct 60 percent of your health insurance premiums as a business expense until 2001, 70 percent in 2002, and 100 percent thereafter.

the plan was established. Also, you cannot deduct health insurance premiums above the line if you are eligible to participate in a health insurance program sponsored by your own or your spouse's employer. The portion of health insurance costs that are not deductible above the line are deductible on Schedule A as medical expenses, subject to the $7\frac{1}{2}$ percent of adjusted gross income (AGI) reduction. The above-the-line portion is deductible on page 1 of Form 1040 rather than on Schedule C, so it does not reduce your self-employment income in computing self-employment tax.

Under the Tax and Trade Relief Extension Act of 1998, the above-the-line percentage for 1999 through 2001 is 60 percent. The percentage deductible above the line increases to 70 percent in 2002 and is 100 percent in 2003 and later.

### Liability for Sole Proprietorship Debts and Claims

Because a sole proprietorship is not a separate legal entity, the owner has unlimited liability for debts and other claims against the business, so it would be wise to review your insurance policies. If you are doing business from your home, you might want a business liability policy separate from your home owner's policy. If you are dealing with customers, at least be sure to have the "office, school, or studio" option in effect with your home owner's policy.

The quest for limited liability is the most common reason some small business owners believe it is prudent to incorporate or to form a limited liability company. C corporations, S corporations, and LLCs are entities independent from their owners and are legally responsible for their own debts and liability claims. However, creditors of home-based and small businesses typically require the owners to cosign for any significant debt. Also, if a civil action is brought against a small start-up business, the claimant typically will seek action against the individual owner

You have unlimited liability for debts and claims against your sole proprietorship.

or owners as well. That means the promise of limited liability by these more complex forms of business is often illusory.

## PARTNERSHIPS

A partnership is an association of two or more persons to carry on a business, with each contributing money, property, labor, or skill and expecting to share in the profits and losses. Four types of entities are treated as partnerships for tax purposes: general partnerships, limited partnerships, LLPs, and LLCs.

A general partnership consists of one or more general partners, each of whom is personally liable for the debts of the partnership. A general partner can be held personally liable for a malpractice judgment brought against the partnership, even though the partner is not the one who committed the malpractice. Limited partners and members of LLPs and LLCs are protected against personal liability.

Like a sole proprietorship, a partnership is not considered a separate entity for computing income tax, but acts as a conduit through which income and deductions are passed to the partners. For certain other purposes, however, a partnership is considered an entity separate from its partners. Although the theory of partnerships seems simple enough, it can be an extremely complex way to conduct business from a tax standpoint. This section highlights only the general rules and concepts for partnerships. Get IRS Publication 541, *Partnerships*, for additional information.

A partnership is a conduit through which income and deductions are passed, to be reported on the partners' individual tax returns.

### Family Partnerships

You are not a candidate for a partnership if you are going it alone. However, if you and your spouse, or another member of your immediate family, carry on a business together and share in the profits and losses, you might be partners whether you have a formal partnership agreement or not. Forming a partnership could reduce your family's tax burden. For example, if you could make your three children partners in your business and shift income to them so that business profits are being split four ways, your family's combined tax liability might be lower than if all the income was taxed to you. Doing this will work as long as it is a legitimate partnership and not a facade to reduce taxes. However, if the children are still being visited by the Tooth Fairy and have no equity in the partnership, do not count on the IRS allowing you a tax break. The government makes it difficult to establish family partnerships for tax purposes precisely because of this tax avoidance potential. Family members are considered to be legitimate partners only in the following cases:

✔ Capital is a material income-producing factor in the partnership, and the family member has bona fide ownership and control of a capital interest (even if the interest was acquired by gift from another family member).

✔ Capital is not a material income-producing factor, but the family member contributes services that are substantial and vital to the partnership.

Capital is a material income-producing factor when the business depends on machinery and equipment or inventories to generate a substantial portion of gross income rather than services of the partners.

A family partnership could reduce your tax burden, but family members must have a legitimate partnership interest.

### General Tax Treatment

A partnership does not pay any income tax at the partnership level. Its income or loss is reported on Form 1065 (U.S. Partnership Return of Income), which informs the IRS of partnership profit or loss and each partner's share on Schedule K-1 (Partner's Share of Income, Credits, Deductions, etc.). Each partner reports his or her share of partnership net profit or loss as shown on Schedule K-1, regardless of whether distributions are made by the partnership or not. Income that is not distributed or withdrawn increases the basis of a partner's partnership interest. The character of any item included in each partner's share is the same as if the partner recognized it directly. So things like tax-exempt income, interest, dividends, royalties, long-term and short-term capital gains and losses, and charitable contributions are stated separately on Schedule K-1.

A knowledgeable tax attorney should be involved in drafting the partnership agreement if special allocations are desired.

**Partnership Agreement** The partnership agreement can be as simple or as convoluted as the partners wish to make it. A partnership affords great flexibility in how gains, losses, assets, and liabilities are shared by the partners. Each partner has a capital-sharing ratio, which is the partner's percentage ownership in the assets and liabilities of the partnership, and a profit-and-loss-sharing ratio. The partnership agreement can provide for "special allocations" of certain items to specific partners, or it can allocate items in a different proportion from the general profit-and-loss-sharing ratios. For a special allocation to be recognized for tax purposes, it must have "substantial economic effect," meaning it must not simply be a tax reduction scheme.

**Reporting Income and Deductions** Partners report their share of partnership income and deductions on their Form 1040, even if a distribution has not been made. The partners' share can include several types of income that may have to be reported in separate places on their tax returns. For example, ordinary business income or loss from the partnership is reported on Schedule E (Supplemental Income and Loss) whereas capital gains and losses are reported on Schedule D and charitable contributions are reported on Schedule A.

**Self-Employment Tax** Partners must pay self-employment tax on their net earnings from self-employment allocated to them from the partnership. Net earnings from self-employment include an individual's share, whether distributed or not, of income or loss from any trade or business carried on by a partnership. An exception excludes a limited partner's distributive share of partnership income or loss, but guaranteed payments as compensation for services are classified as earnings from self-employment, whether made to a general or a limited partner.

## *Partnership Contributions and Basis in the Partnership*

**Contributions** When partners contribute property or money to a partnership in exchange for an interest in the partnership, they generally do not recognize gain or loss. The partnership simply takes the property with the same

> **Basis:** The face value of money and generally the cost of property, minus depreciation deductions and losses claimed relating to the property.

basis as it had when owned by the contributing partner. There are exceptions to this rule, however. For example, if the partner contributes property and receives property or money in addition to an interest in the partnership, the transaction is treated as a sale in which gain or loss is recognized. Also, if a partner contributes property that is subject to a liability greater than the basis of the contributed property, the partner might recognize gain. Further, any partner who contributes services (rather than money or property) to the partnership in exchange for a partnership interest must generally recognize income equal to the value of the partnership interest received.

**Basis in the Partnership Interest** Partners must each keep track of their basis in their partnership interest because they cannot deduct losses from the partnership in excess of their basis. A partner's basis in the partnership is increased by the sum of money contributed, the adjusted basis of property contributed, and the amount of any income recognized from the contribution of services to the partnership.

Liabilities also affect the partners' basis—and this gets a little tricky. Because a partnership is an aggregation of the partners' assets and liabilities, any increase in a partner's share of partnership liabilities is considered a contribution of money to the partnership and increases that partner's basis in the partnership. Conversely, any decrease in partnership liabilities, or an assumption by the partnership of a partner's liabilities, decreases the partner's basis. See Example 5.1.

Once a partner's initial basis in the partnership is determined, it is subject to continual change. It is increased by the partner's share of partnership income and additional contributions by the partner, and it is decreased by the partner's share of partnership losses and distributions of money and property to the partner. If money is distributed to a partner in excess of the partner's partnership basis, the partner must recognize gain on the distribution. (Remember that a decrease in part-

> Losses from the partnership cannot be deducted in excess of your basis.

Raoul and Ramona contribute property to become equal general partners in the RR Partnership. Raoul contributes cash of $30,000. Ramona contributes land with a fair market value of $45,000 and an adjusted basis of $12,000. The land is subject to a liability of $15,000, which the partnership assumes. The partnership borrows $100,000 to finance the construction of a building on the contributed land. Raoul and Ramona's bases in their partnership interests are determined as follows:

| Raoul's Basis | | Ramona's Basis | |
|---|---|---|---|
| Contributed cash | $30,000 | Basis in contributed land | $12,000 |
| Share of construction loan | 50,000 | Share of construction loan | 50,000 |
| Share of debt on land | 7,500 | Share of debt on land | 7,500 |
| | | Less: debt assumed by partnership | (15,000) |
| Total | $87,500 | Total | $54,500 |

**EXAMPLE 5.1**

nership liabilities is considered a distribution of money to the partners.) See Example 5.2.

**Allocation of Debt** A partnership could owe two types of debt. *Recourse debt* is debt for which the partnership or at least one of the partners is personally liable. *Nonrecourse debt* is secured only by a particular partnership asset, so creditors can have no claim on other assets of the partnership or of the partners. The two types of debt are allocated differently for purposes of determining each partner's partnership basis.

Allocation of debt used to be fairly straightforward; recourse debt was shared among the partners according to their loss-sharing ratios and nonrecourse debt was shared according to the way the partners shared profits. The rules are much more difficult than that now, though, since a complex set of regulations were issued a few years ago regarding nonrecourse debt. IRS Publication 541, *Tax Information on Partnerships*, gives you limited information on this, then refers you to the regulations. If your or a client's partnership owes nonrecourse debt,

Assume the same facts as in Example 5.1, except the partnership incurred an ordinary loss of $100,000 in the first year of operation. Raoul and Ramona each deduct a $50,000 loss, and their respective bases are $37,500 and $4,500. In the second year, the partnership generated no income or loss but repaid $40,000 of the construction loan. The $20,000 reduction of each partner's share of liabilities is treated as a money distribution to the partners. As a result, Raoul's basis is reduced to $17,500 and Ramona's basis is reduced to zero. (It can never be less than zero.) In addition, Ramona must report $15,500 of gain, because she is deemed to have received a money distribution of $15,500 in excess of her partnership basis.

**EXAMPLE 5.2**

you should become familiar with the regulations under Section 752. See Chapter 7 for information on how to find the regulations.

Allocation of debt affects your partnership basis, and can be tricky if you have any nonrecourse debt. You must become familiar with the regulations under IRC §752.

## *Tax Accounting Methods and Periods*

**Accounting Methods**  A partnership is treated as an entity for purposes of adopting accounting methods in computing its taxable income. As with a sole proprietor, the partnership can adopt a separate accounting method for each separate business of the partnership.

Most small business partnerships can use the cash method of accounting if they wish, but Section 448 of the tax code bars use of the cash

Most small business partnerships can use the cash method, but some partnerships with losses are required to use an accrual method.

method for certain partnerships with losses. These partnerships must use an accrual method, which makes the tax accounting process a little more complicated. See IRS Publication 541, *Tax Information on Partnerships*, for more information.

**Taxable Year** A partnership is considered a separate entity for the purpose of adopting a taxable year, but its taxable year generally must be the same as its partners. So if you are a partner on a calendar year, and all of your partners are on a calendar year, the partnership is generally required to be on a calendar year. If you and your partners are on different taxable years, the Code provides specific rules for what taxable year the partnership generally must adopt. See IRS Publication 541. Under certain limited exceptions, partnerships can adopt fiscal years different from their partners. For details see IRS Publication 538, *Accounting Periods and Methods*.

## Retirement Plans and Health Insurance

Partnerships can set up a Keogh plan, a simplified employee pension (SEP) plan, or a SIMPLE plan in the same manner as a sole proprietor. Contribution limits for the partners are based on their net earnings from self-employment from the partnership.

If the partnership pays health insurance premiums and other fringe benefits for its partners, the partners must include the amount of such payments in their gross income. The deduction for a percentage of health insurance premiums above the line is available to partners in the same manner as sole proprietors. The above-the-line deduction cannot exceed a partner's net earnings from self-employment derived from the partnership.

## Liability for Partnership Debts and Claims

**General Partnerships** There is a difference among the entities that are taxed as partnerships with respect to who is ultimately responsible to pay the bills. All *general partners* are subject to the same personal liability for partnership debts and malfeasance claims as sole proprietors, even if the claims are due to the actions of one of the other partners. That is why it is wise to check out anyone with whom you plan to enter into a general partnership.

As a general partner, you are liable for all of the debts and legal claims against the partnership.

**Limited Partnerships** In contrast, *limited partners* are liable only to the extent of their investment in the business and their obligation to make further investments. Limited partners cannot take an active part in the management of the partnership. A limited partnership must have at least one general partner (which could be a corporation) but can have as many limited partners as it wants. Limited partnerships are popular for financing things like movies and real estate developments.

**Limited Liability Partnerships** A type of entity that has only recently been authorized by state statutes is the limited liability partnership. It is just like a general partnership except for one important difference: In most states, partners in a registered LLP are jointly and severally liable for commercial partnership debt but are not personally liable for the malpractice and torts of their partners. In some states, LLP partners are granted complete limited liability. In 1994 all of the then–Big Six accounting firms (now Big Five) changed from general partnerships to LLPs.

**Limited Liability Companies** Limited liability companies are also new. They combine partnership tax treatment with limited personal liability for all the owners of the entity. All states have passed legislation permitting the establishment of LLCs in some form. More details are provided later in the chapter (page 149).

## C CORPORATIONS

When you form a corporation, you create a separate tax-paying entity. Unlike sole proprietorships and partnerships, income earned by a regular corporation is taxed at corporate rates, unless corporate shareholders elect to be an S corporation. Regular corporations are called C corporations because Subchapter C of Chapter One of the Internal Revenue Code is where you find all the general tax rules affecting corporations and their shareholders. The rules for S corporations are found in—you guessed it—Subchapter S!

### Forming a Corporation

Forming a corporation is a fairly straightforward process. It involves submitting articles of incorporation to the secretary of state of the state in which you want to incorporate. The articles contain the name and purpose of the corporation, the name of a registered agent in the state where mail can be sent, the name of the incorporator, number of shares authorized, and the classes of stock authorized. The state of incorporation does

> A corporation is a legal entity separate and distinct from its shareholders.

not have to be the state in which you will be conducting business. For example, a lot of businesses incorporate in the State of Delaware because of that state's flexible, well-developed, and corporate-friendly laws. Before you jump into this, however, read the rest of this chapter. Also, *be sure to check the franchise tax and filing requirements for the state in which you choose to incorporate.* You might find that your small business will pay a lot of extra money to the state just for being a corporation.

If you hire a lawyer to file the articles of incorporation, he or she probably will do what lawyers do best—charge you a lot of money. Since incorporating is a straightforward process, you might want to save on the lawyer's fees and just do the incorporation yourself. The secretary of state's office in most states will send you a "form" Articles of Incorporation that allows you to simply fill in a few blanks, pay a fee, and voilà!—you are a corporation.

On the other hand, you might want to hire an attorney if you have questions about which state of incorporation is best, the liability protection granted, and how to make an "S election" (discussed later). Also, if other shareholders are involved, considerations like buy-sell agreements come into play where legal advice might be crucial. It is also nice to have a handy person to holler at if it gets screwed up.

> An attorney can answer important questions in the forming of a corporation.

### Reporting Taxable Income

A C corporation reports taxable income on Form 1120 (U.S. Corporation Income Tax Return) or Form 1120-A (the corporate short form) and pays tax on its taxable income using the rate schedule for corporations. Most small business corporations can use the graduated rate schedule shown in Table 5.1. However, if you are a CPA or an attorney, your corporation will be a "qualified personal service corporation" (QPSC). A QPSC is a C corporation that earns substantially all of its income from services in the fields of health, law, engineering, architecture, accounting, actuarial science, performing arts, or consulting. The taxable income of these entities is taxed at a flat rate of 35

| TABLE 5.1　Corporation Income Tax Rates | | |
|---|---|---|
| Taxable Income Over | Not Over | Tax Rate |
| $0 | $50,000 | 15% |
| 50,000 | 75,000 | 25 |
| 75,000 | 100,000 | 34 |
| 100,000 | 335,000 | 39 |
| 335,000 | 10,000,000 | 34 |
| 10,000,000 | 15,000,000 | 35 |
| 15,000,000 | 18,333,333 | 38 |
| 18,333,333 | . . . . . . | 35 |

percent. If you are an unenrolled practitioner or an enrolled agent doing primarily tax return preparation, you will not be classified as a QPSC.

For C corporations that are not QPSCs, the top rate imposed on taxable income under $100,000 is 34 percent, which is about 5 percent less than the top individual tax rate of 39.6 percent. It may not be advantageous to be taxed as a corporation, however, because corporations have a two-tier tax structure. This means that if earnings are paid to an owner (shareholder) as a dividend, the money is taxed once at the corporate level and again at the shareholder level. Therefore, carefully consider how the corporate tax regime will affect you before deciding to incorporate as a C corporation. Table 5.1 shows the rates for C corporations that are not QPSCs.

If Ed, in Example 5.3, had the corporation pay him an additional $50,000 of wages, the corporation would have zero taxable income after wages, which would eliminate the double taxation. Wages are deductible by the corporation under Section 162 of the Code only if they are "reasonable." If the IRS thinks Ed has received more in pay than his services are worth, the IRS will reclassify the money as a dividend and the reclassified amount will still be subject to the two-tier tax system.

**Employment Taxes** Employment taxes are another consideration in deciding how corporate earnings should be distributed. A corporate shareholder pays social security and Medicare taxes (FICA) only on compensation for services, not on dividends. If the shareholder is an employee, the corporation and the employee each pay one-half of these taxes, and the corporation can deduct its half. Example 5.4 provides another look at Ed's situation.

Ed's Corporation, which is not a QPSC, files Form 1120 and reports taxable income of $50,000 after paying its shareholder-employee, Ed, his wages. The corporation pays corporate income tax of $7,500. The balance of its taxable income, $42,500, is distributed as a dividend to Ed. Ed is in the 39.6 percent tax bracket and pays tax of $16,830 on the dividend. The total income tax paid on the $50,000 of corporate earnings is $24,330 ($7,500 + $16,830). If Ed operated instead as a sole proprietorship, income tax on the $50,000 of income would be only $19,800 ($50,000 × 39.6%).

**EXAMPLE 5.3**

If Ed's Corporation in Example 5.3 used its $50,000 of taxable income as wage expense, the corporation would have no taxable income, so it would not pay corporate income tax. However, the combined corporate/employee liability for social security taxes on the additional wages to Ed would be as much as 15.3 percent or as little as 2.9 percent. The rate depends on whether Ed had already been paid the base amount of wages ($76,200 in 2000) for retirement and disability benefits. If the entire $50,000 was subject to tax at 15.3 percent, the additional tax would be $7,106 ($3,553 FICA paid by the corporation and $3,553 FICA paid by Ed on $46,447 of wages). Note that Ed would not get the full $50,000, because the corporation would need $3,553 for its share of the social security tax, which it also could deduct ($46,447 + $3,553 = $50,000). In addition, Ed would pay income tax on the additional $46,447, unreduced by the social security tax. So total social security and income tax on the additional $46,447 of wages would be $25,499 ($46,447 × 15.3% + $46,447 × 39.6%). This is more in total tax than if the corporation had simply paid Ed the $50,000 as a dividend. If Ed operated, instead, as a sole proprietorship, his combined tax on the additional $50,000 would be about the same, considering self-employment tax of 15.3 percent and Ed's allowable deduction of one-half of it.

**EXAMPLE 5.4**

## Accumulating Earnings for Future Expansion

Another option available for excess corporate earnings is to retain them in the corporation for future expansion. For corporations that are not QPSCs, the corporate tax rate on taxable income up to $50,000 is only 15 percent, which is generally lower than what a shareholder would pay if the money was paid out in wages. If your goal is to build equity in the company and eventually to use the money for expansion, this is the cheapest way to do so. Also, any investment earnings on the excess capital will be taxed at the lower corporate rates. There is a special "dividends received deduction" available to C corporations that receive dividends from other domestic corporations. The deduction is generally 70 percent of the dividends received. That puts the tax rate on dividends, for a corporation with taxable income of $50,000 or less, at 4.5 percent (15% × 30%). If you were to build up the value of the corporation in this way, you could eventually sell the stock at a price reflecting the increased value and be taxed at the favorable capital gains rates. Alternatively, you could just keep the stock and pass it on to your heirs when you die. That way, no one would pay tax at the individual level on the built-up income in the corporation because the heirs would get fair market value bases in their stock. You would have to figure a potential estate tax liability into this plan, however.

**Here Is the Catch** Congress realized that it is more attractive from a tax perspective for shareholders of a corporation to accumulate earnings in the corporation rather than to distribute them as dividends. That is why there is an "accumulated earnings tax" on every corporation "formed or availed of for the purpose of avoiding the income tax with respect to its shareholders . . . by permitting earnings and profits to accumulate instead of being . . . distributed." This penalty tax is imposed at the rate of 39.6 percent on undistributed current-year earnings that are not necessary for the reasonable needs of the business. A corporation is not subject to this tax until it accumulates over $250,000 of earnings in the business. Even if a corporation has more than $250,000

A tax of 39.6 percent is imposed on the accumulated earnings of a corporation in excess of $250,000 if they are not for reasonable business needs.

of earnings, it will not be subject to the tax if it can prove that the accumulation is for reasonable business needs.

Another penalty tax is imposed at the rate of 39.6 percent on undistributed income of a "closely held corporation"—that is, a "personal holding company." A corporation is closely held if over 50 percent of its stock is owned, directly or indirectly, by five or fewer individuals. It is a personal holding company only if at least 60 percent of its income (with a few adjustments) is from dividends, interest, royalties, and other types of investment income.

This tax is aimed at preventing high-income individuals from building up their investment portfolio in a corporation and avoiding the tax at the individual level, then selling the stock and recognizing long-term capital gain. In any one year, however, the IRS cannot impose both the accumulated earnings tax and the personal holding company tax. Also, both of these taxes can easily be avoided by making appropriate distributions to the shareholders.

## *Contributions to the Corporation*

A newly formed corporation is no more endowed than a newborn baby—with financial assets, that is. To start the new entity out in life, operating assets and money are contributed by its organizers in exchange for stock in the corporation. If a business is already being run as a sole proprietorship or partnership when it is incorporated, assets of the business must be transferred to the corporation in order for the corporation to claim any related deductions.

The general rule, when two parties exchange assets, is that gain or loss is recognized by both of them, just as in a sale. Each transferor reports as gain or loss the difference between the basis of the asset given up and the value of the asset received. However, in several special situations the recognition of gain or loss is not justified. The contribution of property to a corporation is one of them.

When a corporation receives money or property in exchange for its own stock, the corporation never recognizes any gain or loss. Also, Section 351 of the Code says the shareholders do not recognize gain or loss on property transferred in exchange for stock if they are "in control" (explained a lit-

The contribution of property or money to a corporation in exchange for stock is tax-free to shareholders who are in "control" of the corporation.

tle later) of the corporation after the exchange. Property received by the corporation takes the same basis as it had in the hands of the shareholder who transferred it, increased by any gain recognized to the shareholder. A separate rule says that losses are never recognized by an individual on property contributed to a corporation if the individual owns, directly or indirectly, over 50 percent of the outstanding stock of the corporation.

For purposes of Section 351, the term "property" is pretty comprehensive, including both tangible and intangible assets. Yet one item that the Code specifically excludes from the definition of property is services rendered to the corporation. So any shareholder who contributes services (rather than money or property) to the corporation in exchange for stock must recognize income equal to the value of the stock received.

**80 Percent Test**  Section 351 of the Code says that no gain or loss is recognized to the contributing shareholders if they are "in control" of the corporation "immediately after the exchange." That means that the person or persons transferring the property must own 80 percent of the stock of the corporation immediately after the transfer. This test applies either to a single transferor or to several people transferring property for stock at about the same time. Transfers by several people in an integrated transaction do not have to be simultaneous to satisfy the "immediately after the exchange" requirement, but they have to be fairly close together. If the control test is not met, the transferors must recognize any gain on the property transferred, just as if cash was received instead of stock. See Examples 5.5 and 5.6.

**When "Boot" Is Received in Addition to Stock**  When a shareholder receives anything other than corporate stock from the corporation as compensation for the property transferred, it is referred to as *boot*. Whenever boot is received, the shareholder must recognize any gain on the transfer up to the amount of boot received. A loss is never recognized. See Example 5.7.

---

Betty exchanges property with a basis of $50,000 and fair market value of $80,000 for 70 percent of the stock of B&D Corporation. The other 30 percent of the stock is owned by Don, who acquired it several years ago. Betty receives stock with a fair market value of $80,000 and recognizes taxable gain of $30,000 on the transfer. The 80 percent control test is not satisfied.

---

**EXAMPLE 5.5**

Larry, Moe, and Curly incorporate their respective businesses together and form the Stooge Corporation. Larry exchanges his property for 334 shares of Stooge stock on July 1, 2000. Moe contributes his property for 333 shares of Stooge stock on July 10, 2000, and Curly transfers his property for 333 shares of Stooge stock on August 15, 2000. The three exchanges are part of a prearranged plan, so none of the shareholders recognizes gain or loss on the exchange; the control requirement is met.

**EXAMPLE 5.6**

**Basis in Corporate Stock** Shareholders receive basis in their stock equal to the basis of the property they contribute to the corporation, reduced by any boot received from the corporation and increased by any gain recognized on the exchange. If the corporation makes a distribution of money or property that is not out of corporate earnings, it is nontaxable to the shareholders only to the extent of the basis of their stock. Any distribution in excess of basis is taxable as capital gain. Also, the shareholders must keep track of their stock basis in order to determine gain or loss on the sale of their stock.

**Treatment of Gain or Loss on Disposition of Stock** The general rule when corporate stock is sold or exchanged is that the gain or loss is capital gain or loss. The maximum rate on *long-term* capital gains (the asset is owned for over a year for sales after 1997) is 20 percent. The top rate on ordinary income, on the other hand, is currently 39.6 percent. Capital losses are fully deductible against capital gains, but if losses exceed gains

Julie owns all the stock of Julie's Corporation. She transfers a computer to the corporation that has a basis of $1,000 and is valued at $3,000. In exchange, the corporation gives Julie $500 in cash, a note for $1,000, and issues her stock worth $1,500. Because the cash and note are boot, Julie must recognize gain of $1,500, which is the smaller of her realized gain ($2,000) and the amount of boot received ($1,500).

**EXAMPLE 5.7**

> Corporate stock sold at a gain gets capital gain treatment, while an ordinary loss can be claimed if the stock becomes worthless.

you can only deduct up to $3,000 of the excess loss against ordinary income. Capital losses that cannot be deducted in the current year are carried over to future years. The $3,000 limit is reduced to $1,500 for married persons filing separately.

A special rule in Section 1244 of the Code allows shareholders of certain small business corporations to deduct a loss from the sale or worthlessness of their stock as an ordinary loss rather than a capital loss. That means the loss can be deducted in full rather than being subject to the limitations on capital losses.

Another special break in Section 1202 of the Code says you can exclude from income 50 percent of the gain on "qualified small business stock" held for more than five years at the time of sale. In general, qualified small business stock must be issued after August 10, 1993, in a C corporation that is conducting an active business and does not have gross assets in excess of $50 million.

## Tax Accounting Methods and Periods

**Accounting Methods** As a separate taxable entity, a corporation can adopt any acceptable accounting method. One limitation on accounting methods for C corporations does not apply to other entities. The cash method is generally not allowed for corporations with gross receipts greater than $5 million. As with sole proprietorships and partnerships, a corporation can adopt a separate accounting method for each separate business of the corporation.

**Taxable Year** Most new C corporations can adopt either a calendar year or any fiscal year, regardless of the taxable years of their shareholders. They are even permitted to change their fiscal or calendar year after 10 years without permission from the IRS, if they meet some conditions contained in the regulations.

A "personal service corporation" (PSC) is the one type of C corporation that is required to adopt a calendar year. The definition of a PSC for this purpose is a little complex. Generally it is a C corporation that has employee owners who perform services in the fields of health, law, engineering, architecture, accounting, actuarial science, performing arts, or

A "personal service corporation" must adopt a calendar year unless it can establish a business purpose for a fiscal year.

consulting. Under certain limited exceptions, PSCs can adopt fiscal years different from those of their shareholders. For details see IRS Publication 538, *Accounting Periods and Methods.*

## Retirement Plans and Health Insurance

A variety of qualified retirement plans are available for corporate employees. Qualified plans must meet stringent requirements under the Code with respect to participation, contributions, and distributions. They have the advantage of providing tax-deferred retirement benefits to employees while allowing the corporation a current deduction for contributions. It used to be that corporate plans allowed greater contributions than retirement plans for unincorporated businesses, but that is no longer the case. Keogh plans for self-employed people are now subject to the same general rules as qualified corporate plans. One difference is that owners in corporate plans can borrow from the plan, with certain restrictions, but loans from Keogh accounts are prohibited. A corporation that does not want to be bothered with the complexities of a qualified plan can set up a simplified employee pension (SEP) plan or a savings incentive match (SIMPLE) plan. For more details see IRS Publication 560, *Retirement Plans for the Self-Employed.*

An advantage of being a corporate employee is that you can have the corporation pay and deduct all of your family's health insurance premiums. Self-employed individuals can currently deduct only 60 percent of their health insurance premiums as a business expense, but that amount rises to 100 percent in 2003.

## Liability for Corporate Debts and Claims

A corporation is a legal entity, chartered under state law, that is separate and distinct from its shareholders and officers. It is a vehicle designed to foster investment by protecting the investors from liabilities of the business. Limited liability is probably the chief reason most businesses incor-

A corporation can pay and deduct all of your family's health insurance premiums.

Incorporating as a small closely held corporation probably will not protect you from the claims of creditors or from civil actions.

porate (although I am convinced that a lot of people incorporate just to be able to call themselves Mr. or Ms. President).

Shareholders and officers of a corporation usually are not personally responsible for creditor claims unless they provide a personal guarantee. Unfortunately, for start-up and home-based businesses with few assets, a personal guarantee is exactly what many creditors demand. Bankers will tend to treat your fledgling corporation more like a minor child than a separate business entity. As the corporation acquires more assets and a good credit rating, there will be fewer creditor demands for personal guarantees.

Even if there are no personal guarantees from shareholders, under common law creditors are sometimes allowed to "pierce the corporate veil." That means they can pursue corporate owners directly for corporate claims. In some states, shareholders can be sued directly for unpaid wages and employee benefits. Shareholders also can be held liable for corporate debts when the corporation has not been operated in a manner that indicates it is truly separate from the personal finances of its stockholders.

Additionally, if you perform services for the corporation that result in some kind of civil action, you will be sued along with your corporation. State laws used to prohibit professional individuals (such as accountants, attorneys, architects, and doctors) from incorporating. Now they are allowed to incorporate, but they are not provided limited liability for the performance of professional services.

In summary, if your primary purpose for incorporating your business is to gain limited liability, you might be better advised to save the time and expense and purchase additional business liability insurance instead. If you are a service professional, you probably will not be able to create liabilities for which the corporation alone will be responsible. Of course, if your *real* purpose for incorporating is to be called Mr. or Ms. President, none of this advice really matters.

## S CORPORATIONS

Operating as an S corporation combines the advantages of a single level of taxation at the shareholder level with limited liability for corporate shareholders. An S corporation has the same corporate characteristics as a C corporation. It is a legal entity, chartered under state law, which is separate

An S corporation provides a degree of limited liability and a single level of taxation.

and distinct from its shareholders and officers. The only difference is that, after incorporating, it has filed an election with the IRS to be treated differently for federal tax purposes. The election generally permits the income of the S corporation to be taxed to the shareholders of the corporation rather than to the corporation itself. The election can be made for a new entity, or it can be made for an existing corporation that has been taxed as a C corporation. When S status is no longer an advantage to the corporate shareholders, the election can be revoked.

S status has been available ever since the late 1950s, and its use enjoyed a steady increase over the years. It was in the late 1980s, though, that it became really popular. That is because for a few years after the Tax Reform Act of 1986, the top individual tax rate was less than the top corporate rate. Now the top rate for individuals (39.6 percent) is five points above the top rate paid by most small corporations (34 percent), and LLCs, which are authorized in all states, offer more advantages than S corporations for many taxpayers. Nevertheless, the popularity of S corporations has not diminished. The IRS estimates that S corporation filings will first exceed C corporation filings in 2000 and projects that S corporations will be the fastest-growing type of business tax entity through 2005,[1] although the accuracy of this prediction has been questioned.[2]

Doing business as an S corporation is complex from a tax standpoint. Tax accountants drool over clients with S corporations. This is an area in which you can become an expert and establish a niche, with some determined effort. This section highlights only the general rules and concepts. For information on the tax requirements for S corporations, the best free source is the IRS instructions for Form 1120S. Also see the instructions for Form 2553 (S election).

## Making the Election

A corporation will not be treated as an S corporation unless a proper election is made in a timely manner. The election is made on Form 2553 (Election by

Although the continued popularity of S corporations has been predicted, limited liability companies, which are authorized in all states, offer more advantages than S corporations for many taxpayers.

A corporation must make a proper election in a timely manner in order to be treated as an S corporation.

a Small Business Corporation), which must be filed with the IRS before the sixteenth day of the third month of the corporation's tax year for which the election will be effective. An election made after the fifteenth day of the third month but before the end of the taxable year is generally effective for the next year. However, as part of the changes made by the Small Business Job Protection Act of 1996, the IRS is granted authority to cut taxpayers some slack if they make a late election or inadvertently fail to make an election. The IRS may treat a late election or a nonexistent election as timely made if the IRS determines that there was reasonable cause for the failure to file the election on time. See the instructions to Form 2553. Each shareholder must consent to and sign the election.

An S election made with the IRS might not be effective for state tax purposes. While most states simply follow the federal law on this, some do not. A state that allows S status might require a separate election to be filed with the state. Be sure to check the laws of your state before making an S election.

## Who Can Make the Election?

A corporation can be an S corporation only if it meets the following six tests:

1. It is a domestic corporation.
2. It has no more than 75 shareholders (increased from 35 in 1996). A husband and wife are treated as one shareholder for this purpose, but everyone else is a separate shareholder.
3. It has only individuals, estates, or certain trusts, financial institutions, and tax-exempt entities as shareholders. The types of eligible S corporation shareholders were significantly expanded for 1997 and later years by the Small Business Job Protection Act of 1996.
4. It has no nonresident alien shareholders.
5. It has only one class of stock.
6. It has a "permitted tax year." That means, with certain exceptions, its tax year is the calendar year. The rules for taxable years are the same as discussed for partnerships.

If the corporation violates any of these rules while it is an S corporation, the S election will automatically terminate and the corporation will be taxed as a C corporation, unless the shareholders take steps to correct the problem. If there is no violation of the rule, the election stays in effect until the shareholders choose to terminate it.

## General Tax Treatment

An S corporation is treated much the same as a partnership, in that it generally does not pay tax at the corporate level. Its income or loss is reported on Form 1120S (U.S. Income Tax Return for an S Corporation), and flows through to be reported on the shareholders' individual returns. Schedule K-1 (Shareholder's Share of Income, Credits, Deductions, etc.) is completed with Form 1120S for each shareholder. These schedules tell the shareholders their allocable share of corporate income and deductions. Shareholders, therefore, must pay tax on their share of corporate income, regardless of whether it is actually distributed.

A potential disadvantage, for an S corporation with more than one shareholder, is that income and deductions from an S corporation must be allocated according to the shareholder's ownership interest. They cannot be specially allocated to shareholders as they can from a partnership.

One exception to this rule prevents tax avoidance by family members, similar to the family partnership rules. Any individual who is a member of a family of S corporation shareholders must receive adequate compensation for services or capital provided to the corporation. For example, if you are allocating corporate profits among your six minor children, the IRS is authorized to allocate more profits to you to adequately reflect the services and capital you provide to the corporation.

**Basis in Stock and Debt** A shareholder's basis in an S corporation's stock is adjusted in much the same way a partner's partnership interest is adjusted. Losses from the S corporation attributable to a shareholder are limited to the shareholder's stock basis. There is a major difference, though, in the way corporate debt is treated. Remember that a partner's basis in the partnership interest includes the partner's direct investment plus a ratable share of any partnership liabilities. For S corporation share-

Tax treatment of an S corporation is generally similar to that of a partnership.

Unlike partnership taxation, your basis in S corporation stock is not increased by debt owed by the S corporation to third parties, even if you guarantee the debt.

holders, however, corporate borrowing has no effect on their stock basis. S corporation shareholders get a separate tax basis in any debt the corporation owes *directly to them*, but not in any other corporate debt. Here is a tip: If you form an S corporation that you expect to incur losses, and the corporation needs to borrow money, *do not have it borrow money directly from someone else* if you are going to have to guarantee the loan anyway. A loan from a third party does not increase your basis for deducting losses. Borrow the money yourself and lend it to the corporation.

Losses allocated to shareholders in excess of their stock basis are suspended until their basis is increased. Shareholders who have outstanding loans to the corporation can deduct additional losses to the extent of the loans. This feature of S corporations gives individual shareholders a lot of flexibility in choosing when to recognize losses from the corporation.

**Corporate-Level Taxes** Unlike partnerships, there are some special situations in which tax is paid directly by an S corporation. One involves built-in gains of a C corporation that converts to an S corporation. Built-in gains are gains related to appreciation on assets held by a C corporation that converts to S corporation status. Another applies when passive investment income of an S corporation having C corporation earnings and profits exceeds 25 percent of gross receipts. The last corporate-level tax applies when a C corporation using LIFO (last-in, first-out) inventory converts to an S corporation. All of these special taxes affect S corporations that were formerly C corporations. If you form a corporation and immediately elect S status, the S corporation will never be taxed at the corporate level.

### Reporting Income and Deductions

Shareholders report the income and deductions from an S corporation in much the same way as they report partnership income and deduc-

There are no corporate-level taxes to S corporations that were never C corporations.

> Shareholders report S corporation income and deductions much the same as partners report partnership income and deductions.

tions. The character of any item included in each shareholder's pro rata share is the same as if the shareholder recognized it directly. So things like tax-exempt income, interest, dividends, royalties, long-term and short-term capital gains and losses, and charitable contributions are stated separately on each shareholder's Schedule K-1. Individual shareholders report their share of ordinary business income or loss from the corporation on Schedule E (Supplemental Income and Loss). The separately stated items are reported on the appropriate schedules of Form 1040.

**Employment Taxes** S corporation employee/shareholders are treated the same as if they were employees of a C corporation. Income or loss of the corporation is allocated to the shareholders after the deduction for wages. The shareholders are not subject to self-employment tax on any income they receive from the corporation.

This is a potentially lucrative advantage of doing business as an S corporation. For a sole proprietor, the entire net income on Schedule C is subject to self-employment tax. General partners and active limited liability shareholders must also pay self-employment tax on their share of partnership income. But S corporation employee/shareholders who are paid a reasonable wage will escape employment taxes on the remaining income of the corporation. This benefit might be as high as 15.3 percent or as low as 2.9 percent, depending on the amount of wages the shareholder has received from the corporation and other sources. Caution is in order here, though. If you are the sole shareholder of an S corporation earning income from your services, the IRS could argue that all of the corporate service income should reasonably be recognized by you as wages. Example 5.8 demonstrates potential savings.

Although Laura, in Example 5.8, saves over $3,700 in taxes by treating only $50,000 of her corporate income as wages, the IRS may treat all of the corporate income attributable to her services as wages.

> An S corporation can potentially save self-employment tax over a partnership or sole proprietorship.

Laura owns all the stock of Laura's S Corporation. The corporation earned net income of $100,000 from Laura's services as a consultant in 2000 and paid Laura $50,000 in wages for her services. The remaining corporate income is taxed to Laura as a dividend. Assuming Laura is in the 36 percent tax bracket, and ignoring personal deductions, Laura's after-tax corporate income is about $3,700 greater than if all of the service income was treated as wages to Laura.

| | |
|---|---:|
| Total earned | $100,000 |
| Less: | |
| $50,000 × 15.3% (corporate and employee FICA) | ($7,650) |
| $50,000 × 36% (income tax on wages) | ($18,000) |
| $46,175 × 36% (income tax on corporate income after wages and employer FICA) | ($16,623) |
| After tax corporate income | $57,727 |

If Laura's S corporation paid Laura all of its income in wages, her after tax corporate income would be:

| | |
|---|---:|
| Total earned | $100,000 |
| Less: | |
| $76,200 × 15.3% (corporate and employee FICA) | ($11,659) |
| $17,709 × 2.9% (corporate and employee Medicare tax after corporate FICA) | ($514) |
| $93,913 × 36% (income tax on wages after employer FICA) | ($33,809) |
| After tax corporate income | $54,018 |

**EXAMPLE 5.8**

## Tax Accounting Methods and Periods

**Accounting Methods**   An S corporation adopts its own accounting methods in computing its taxable income. Like partnerships, most S corporations are permitted to use the cash method of accounting if they wish, with the exception of accounting for the purchase and sale of inventory for which an accrual method must be used. However, Section 448 of the tax code denies the use of the cash method to certain S corporations that have incurred losses. These corporations are required to use an overall accrual method. See Chapter 4.

S corporations generally must adopt a calendar taxable year.

**Taxable Year** S corporations have a required taxable year, like partnerships and personal service corporations. Under limited circumstances they can adopt a fiscal year. See IRS Publication 538, *Accounting Periods and Methods*, for more information.

### Retirement Plans and Health Insurance

The variety of qualified retirement plans available to employees of C corporations is also available to employees of S corporations. A simplified employee pension plan is also an option for S corporations.

Remember that an advantage of being an employee of a C corporation is that you can have the corporation pay and deduct all of your family's health insurance premiums, and some other benefits, without the amounts being included in your gross income. That does not apply for S corporation shareholders who own more than 2 percent of the corporation's outstanding stock. They are treated like partners for this purpose. If the corporation pays health insurance premiums for these shareholders, the amount is deducted by the corporation as wages and included in the shareholders' gross income. The deduction for a percentage of health insurance premiums above the line is available to the shareholders in the same manner as partners and sole proprietors.

### Liability for Corporate Debts and Claims

An S corporation offers shareholders the same limited liability protection that a C corporation does. See the discussion under "C Corporations."

## LIMITED LIABILITY COMPANIES

### Background

Limited liability companies are a fairly recent phenomenon in the United States, though European countries have been using the concept for quite a while. Wyoming passed the first LLC legislation in the United States in 1977. Now all the states and the District of Columbia have LLC statutes.

Limited liability companies are organizations that are formed under state law to provide limited liability for their owners, who are called "members," in the same way corporate shareholders are protected. They are not corporations under state law, however, and the IRS has ruled that they may be treated as partnerships rather than corporations for federal income tax purposes. This ruling was necessary under regulations in effect prior to 1997 when the IRS could tax any unincorporated entity as a corporation if it had more corporate characteristics than noncorporate characteristics. The four characteristics that were used to distinguish an association taxable as a corporation from an association taxable as a partnership were:

1. Centralized management.
2. Continuity of life.
3. Free transferability of interests.
4. Limited liability.

These factors were given equal weight so that an organization was classified as a partnership if it lacked at least two of them.

Beginning in 1997, the IRS has decided to use a much simpler approach. The regulations have been changed to allow most unincorporated businesses the choice of whether they will be taxed as a corporation or not, even if all the owners have limited liability. Except for a business entity that is automatically classified as a corporation under the revised regulations, an entity with at least two members can choose to be classified as either an association taxable as a corporation or a partnership. A business entity with a single individual owner can choose to be taxed as a corporation or treated as a sole proprietorship. These business entities are automatically taxed as either a partnership (if the entity has more than one member) or a sole proprietorship (if the entity only has one member) unless the entity's owner(s) file Form 8832, electing to have the entity taxed as a corporation.

## Advantages

An ideal financial structure for a business entity would provide limited liability for its owners, a single level of taxation, maximum flexibility in dividing profits and losses, and uncomplicated rules for tax compliance. The LLC provides most of these attributes.

An LLC has characteristics of both a partnership for tax purposes and a corporation for liability purposes. An LLC functions like a partnership in that it provides single-level taxation for an entity with more than one

An LLC provides the same liability protection for its members that a corporation provides its shareholders and a single level of taxation without the complexity of an S corporation.

owner; it provides flexibility in dividing profits and losses; and it allows partners to increase the basis of their partnership interest with third-party debt of the partnership. An LLC functions like a corporation in that it provides limited liability to its members. The same benefits apply to a single-member LLC. The owner can achieve limited liability, maintain a single level of taxation, and avoid the complexities of S corporation status.

## Drawbacks

**State Tax Issues** State statutes differ in their treatment of LLCs, and state law is still evolving to determine treatment of LLCs formed in one state but doing business in another state. Some states, such as Texas and Florida, tax LLCs as corporations. Other states, such as Michigan, Illinois, New Hampshire, and the District of Columbia, impose entity-level taxes on LLCs.

Under the revised federal regulations discussed earlier, an LLC owned by a single individual is treated as a sole proprietorship for federal tax purposes by default. That means you file Schedule C and treat your LLC just like an unincorporated sole proprietorship for federal tax purposes. For a time, several states refused to allow single-member LLCs. However, most states have now indicated, through regulations or public rulings, that they will conform to the simplified federal classification for single-member LLCs. As noted, though, some impose a tax at the entity level. Alabama is a holdout on the classification of single-member LLCs, requiring partnership rather than sole proprietorship treatment. That means in Alabama you will file a Schedule C for federal tax purposes and an Alabama partnership return for state tax purposes.

If you wish to be an LLC and are performing professional services that require licensing under state law, you are typically required to form a professional limited liability company (PLLC or PLC) under separate statutes. A PLLC is granted the same limited liability as a corporation for creditor claims, but there is no limited liability with respect to claims arising out of your professional services. In other words, being an LLC will not prevent your clients from suing you personally for malpractice. Professional services generally include accountancy, architecture, engineering, law, medicine and surgery, chiropractic, registered nursing, psychology, dentistry and dental hygiene, pharmacy, veterinary medicine, surveying, landscape architecture, and certified interior design.

There is no limited liability from claims arising out of your professional services.

If you are considering LLC status, be sure to check the LLC provisions of your state and any state in which you plan to do business.

**Self-Employment Tax**   Self-employment income, on which self-employment tax must be paid, includes the gross income derived by an individual or partner from any trade or business. However, a *limited* parner's share of partnership income, except for guaranteed payments, is not subject to self-employment tax. There is no definition of the term "limited partner" in the Code or regulations. That brings up the question of whether, as an LLC member, you are considered a general or limited partner for this purpose.

A regulation proposed by the IRS in January of 1997 addressed this question. The proposed regulation said that generally, an individual will be treated as a limited partner for self-employment tax purposes unless the individual: (1) has personal liability for the debts of or claims against the partnership by reason of being a partner; (2) has authority to contract on behalf of the partnership under the statute or law pursuant to which the partnership is organized; or (3) participates in the partnership's trade or business for more than 500 hours during the taxable year. The regulation added that if substantially all of the activities of a partnership involve the performance of services in the fields of health, law, engineering, architecture, accounting, actuarial science, or consulting, any individual who provides services as part of that trade or business will not be considered a limited partner.

This proposed regulation caused quite an uproar. Some believed that the regulation exceeded the regulatory authority of the IRS and that it would effectively change the law administratively without congressional action. Therefore, as part of the Taxpayer Relief Act of 1997, Congress provided that no regulation could be issued or made effective by the IRS on the definition of limited partner for self-employment tax purposes before July 1, 1998. That means the IRS must now go back to the drawing board and come up with some rules that are not so expansive in imposing self-employment tax on LLC members and limited partners in general. New regulations have yet to be proposed.

**Loss Limitations**  The rules restricting passive activity losses have not been discussed previously because they usually affect taxpayers who are not active participants in their business, which generally include limited

There are currently uncertainties about how self-employment tax applies to LLC members.

partners. In general, a passive activity is a business in which the taxpayer is a passive investor and does not "materially participate" in management activities. A taxpayer's passive activity loss (PAL) is not allowed to offset income that is not from a passive activity in computing taxable income. A PAL that is disallowed can be carried forward to reduce passive income in the following year.

The passive loss rules are particularly restrictive for LLC members, because LLC members are classified as limited partners for this purpose, even when they are active in the business. A stricter test is required for limited partners to determine if they materially participate in the business. Basically, a business is considered a passive activity for any member of an LLC who devotes less than 500 hours per year to the business. Consequently, any LLC member who participates on a part-time basis (under 500 hours per year) and incurs losses might not be allowed to deduct them under the passive loss rules.

## WHICH BUSINESS FORM IS BEST?

The answer to that question is completely dependent on your particular circumstances and objectives. If you are the sole owner of a business and your primary goal is to keep things as simple as possible, there are surprisingly few tax advantages to organizing as anything other than a sole proprietorship. You can achieve limited liability and still file as a sole proprietor by forming a single-member LLC, but beware of the state tax pitfalls mentioned earlier. If you form an S corporation to achieve limited liability, you can say so long to simplicity. Yet a potential advantage of an S corporation is the ability of S shareholders to avoid employment taxes on their share of corporate income above a reasonable wage.

If you have partners or associates, a general partnership provides the maximum flexibility in dividing profits and losses while allowing a single level of taxation. If you are going to have a general partnership, there are very few reasons not to organize as an LLC or LLP if your state permits it. Organizing as an LLC or LLP provides limited liability and partnership tax treatment.

If you have clients who are producing or manufacturing a product

The best business form depends on your individual circumstances and objectives.

and they wish to build capital in the business for eventual worldwide domination of the market (why not be optimistic?), the corporate form is probably best for them. It might be prudent, however, to delay incorporating for a year or two, or initially to elect S status, or form an LLC and then convert it to a corporation, so they can take advantage of start-up losses on their personal returns.

## ADDITIONAL RESOURCES

For additional information on doing business as a sole proprietor, a good IRS publication for general guidance is Publication 334, *Tax Guide for Small Business*. As mentioned in the text, IRS Publication 541, *Partnerships*, provides guidance in filing Form 1065 and the related Schedules K and K-1. For information on the tax requirements of S corporations, the best free source is the IRS *Instructions for Form 1120S*. Also see the instructions for Form 2553 (S election). Tax information on doing business as a C corporation is in Publication 542, *Corporations*.

You can get these publications free by calling the IRS at 1-800-TAX-FORM (1-800-829-3676). If you have access to TTY/TDD equipment, you can call 1-800-829-4059. To download them from the Internet, go to www.irs.gov (World Wide Web) or ftp.irs.gov (FTP). If you would like to get forms and instructions (not publications) by fax, dial 1-703-368-9694 to reach IRS Tax Fax.

# A Little about Taxes, Permits, and Record-Keeping

*Though tax records are generally looked upon as a nuisance, the day may come when historians will realize that tax records tell the real story behind civilized life.*

—Charles Adams

I n this chapter you will find information that will not only help you get your own business up and running but that you can preach to your new business clients as well. Because you are now or soon will become a tax professional, the information presented is intended only to focus your awareness on certain tax and record-keeping issues related to the start-up of a business. It is up to you to fill in the details through the additional resources mentioned.

We will start with state and local taxes, fees, and permits. You will then learn about the home office deduction, self-employment taxes, estimated tax payments, and employment taxes for employees. Finally, you will get a few tips on keeping the books and record keeping.

## STATE AND LOCAL TAXES, FEES, AND PERMITS

One of the first things you should do as a new business owner is to call your state's Department of Revenue and ask to be sent information on all

> Check with your state and city government about taxes, fees and information.

the tax requirements for a small business operating in your state. Your business might be subject to state and local income taxes, franchise taxes, sales taxes, and occupational taxes. If you organize as a C corporation, S corporation, limited liability company, or limited liability partnership, you might be subject to entity-level taxes by your state government that do not apply at the federal level.

While you are on the phone with the Department of Revenue, you also might ask about other state agencies that offer information to small businesses. If the person you are speaking with does not know, hang up and start calling around. Often your state government has extremely useful free information. You might try the Commerce Department, the secretary of state, or any other department that looks promising. In Minnesota, for example, the Department of Trade and Economic Development offers a free "Guide to Starting a Business in Minnesota." This is a book of over 300 pages of extremely useful information for a new business owner.

If you hire one or more employees, contact your state unemployment insurance office to get details about your state unemployment tax obligations. (See "Employment Taxes," later in this chapter.) Also check with city hall, especially if you start out in a home office. As more people establish home businesses, cities are increasingly seeing revenue opportunities. Some cities charge business licensing fees and/or a gross receipts tax.

While you're on the line with city hall, find out about zoning requirements. Whether you start out from a home office or lease space, there might be restrictions. Some municipalities either prohibit businesses from operating in residential areas or require a special license or permit.

## HOME OFFICE DEDUCTION

Whether you begin your business full time or part time, you might want to start out in a home office. Probably most businesses begin at home—in the basement, the garage, or a home office. And what a great time for running a home-based business! The continuing advances in telecommunications and Internet technology have made working from home easier than ever before. As a further bonus, the rules on home office deductions are less restrictive now than at any time in the last quarter century. Even if you only do your book and computer work at home, and lease or barter

**Home office expenses:** Those expenses incurred in maintaining your home that are either directly related or allocable to your home office area.

for space outside the home for meeting with clients, you are still eligible to deduct home office expenses.

Following is a rundown of the basic rules on home office deductions. For additional information on this and other topics in this chapter, see my book *J.K. Lasser's Taxes Made Easy for Your Home-Based Business*, 4th edition.[1]

The rules on home office deductions are less restrictive now than at any time since 1976.

### Quick Summary of the Restrictions

Section 280A of the Internal Revenue Code says that you cannot deduct expenses for the business use of your home unless you use a portion of your home on a *regular* and *exclusive* basis:

- ✔ As the *principal* place of any business in which you are engaged; or
- ✔ As a place of business where patients, clients, or customers meet and deal with you; or
- ✔ In the case of a separate structure (like a garage) that is not attached to your house, in a use that is *connected* with any business in which you engage.

These rules apply to employees as well as self-employed individuals. But if you are an employee, using a home office must be for the convenience of your employer and not simply for your own convenience.

According to the IRS, in order for an employee to qualify for home office deductions, his or her employer must require work to be performed at home.

You also qualify to claim deductions for two additional uses that require *regular* use only (not *exclusive* use). They are:

✔ The use of space in your home for the storage of inventory or (for 1996 and later) product samples, if your business is selling products at retail or wholesale, but only if your home is the sole fixed location of such business; and

✔ The use of a portion of your home in your business of providing day care for children, for individuals 65 or over, or for physically or mentally handicapped people.

If you satisfy one or more of these use tests, you must then allocate a portion of the various expenses of maintaining your home to business use. This is generally done based on the square footage of your home office compared to the total square footage of your home.

**Net Income Limitation** Even if the use tests are met, deductions for the business portion of expenses may not exceed net income derived from business use. Expenses disallowed because of the income limitation may be carried forward and treated as home-based business expenses for next year. The carryover and the expenses incurred next year are subject to the income limitation for that year.

**What Expenses Are Limited?** The only expenses that are limited by Section 280A are those related directly or indirectly to the use of your home office that are not otherwise deductible. Expenses that are deductible regardless of their business connection are not subject to the limitation. That means gas, sewer, water, heat, electricity, garbage pickup, home owner's insurance, and depreciation allocable to your home office are limited. Cleaning and any direct repairs to your home office are also limited. The portions of your property taxes, mortgage interest, and any casualty loss allocated to your home office are specifically excluded from the limitation, because they are deductible regardless of their business connection.

Additionally, all of the other expenses you incur in your home-based business that are unrelated to the use of your home office are deductible without the limitations of Section 280A. However, they must qualify as ordinary and necessary business expenses, so any amount allocated to personal use must be excluded. For example, if you purchase a computer for use in your home office and use it 25 percent of the time for personal things and 75 percent of the time for business, you can only deduct 75 percent of the cost of the computer.

All business expenses incurred in your home-based business that are not directly related to use of your home office are deductible without limitation.

## Regular Use

Any qualified business use of your personal residence requires "regular" use. Regular use means "on a continuing basis." This means that using a portion of your home only occasionally for business does not count. The intent of this requirement is to disallow costs related to areas of your house that are primarily personal. If you have a seasonal business, you still can satisfy the regular use test even though the use is limited to the part of the year the business is active.

The determination of regular use is based on individual judgment rather than exact criteria. As a practical matter, if you have a business that requires both regular and exclusive use, it is the exclusive use test that you generally have to worry about. If you can show that an area of your home is used exclusively for business, an IRS agent probably will concede that you use it on a regular basis.

## Exclusive Use

"Exclusive use" means that the portion of your home used for business cannot be used for any other purpose. According to the Tax Court and the legislative history of Section 280A, this requirement is to be taken quite literally, meaning "the taxpayer must use a specific part of a dwelling unit solely for the purpose of carrying on his trade or business." That means you don't qualify if your home office is a space you have cleared off on the dining room table. Congress wants you to have an area set up just for doing business. You flunk the test if you do investment-related work, balance your personal checkbook, or let the kids play games on the computer.

This is a higher standard than you would have to maintain for an office outside the home. Admittedly it is harsh, ruthless, and downright unkind. It is there because Congress, in enacting Section 280A, wanted to prevent deductions for personal expenses and to allow deductions only for the business use of a residence. It would seem, however, that negligible nonbusiness use of your office would not violate the spirit of Section 280A. In fact, in at least one case the Tax Court ruled that a space satisfied the exclusive use test even though there was evidence of minimal personal use.

> Exclusive means exclusive! But negligible nonbusiness use probably will not disqualify your deductions.

For purposes of the regular and exclusive use tests, the "portion of your home" in which your home office is occupied does not have to constitute an entire room. You must have a separately identifiable space, but it is not necessary that it be marked off by a permanent partition. A separately identifiable space means you should not have personal use items mixed with business use items. To convince the IRS that the use is exclusive, you should take special care to show that your only activities in the business space are business activities.

### What Is Your Principal Place of Business?

**Supreme Court Restrictions**  This is the test most people rely on to qualify (so don't doze off—this is the important part!). The question is "What is a principal place of business?" Unfortunately, Congress did not bother to define the term when it enacted Section 280A. Consequently, the IRS and the courts have struggled with a definition over the years. The Supreme Court finally took up the issue in the 1993 case of *Commissioner of Internal Revenue v. Soliman.* The Court's definition in *Soliman* was so restrictive that it put home office deductions out of reach for most home-based business owners.

**Congress Rides to the Rescue, But on a Slow Horse**  Congress finally eased up on the restrictions as part of the Taxpayer Relief Act of 1997, but the new rules did not take effect until 1999. Amended Section 280A now provides that the term "principal place of business" includes a place of business that is used by the taxpayer for the administrative or management activities of any trade or business. To apply, however, there must be no other fixed location where the taxpayer conducts substantial administrative or management activities of that trade or business. The new

> The *Soliman* test basically said that your principal place of business was where you performed your primary moneymaking activity, which for many people is not their home office.

Under the new rule, you need only perform administrative or management activities in your home office to qualify for the deductions.

law does not change the regular and exclusive use requirements, or the condition that employee use must be for the convenience of the employer.

Under the new rule, a home office used for administrative or management activities will qualify as a principal place of business, regardless of whether such activities connected with the same trade or business are performed by others at other locations (such as billing activities). The fact that you also carry out administrative or management activities at sites that are not fixed locations of the business, such as a car or hotel room, will not affect your ability to claim home office deductions. In addition, if you conduct some administrative or management activities at a fixed location outside the home, you will still be able to claim home office deductions, as long as the administrative or management activities conducted at the other location are not substantial. Your ability to claim home office deductions under the new rule will not be affected by the fact that you conduct substantial nonadministrative or nonmanagement business activities at a fixed location of the business outside the home.

Therefore, under the new rule, you could have an outside office in which you meet with or provide services to clients but choose not to use for administrative or management activities. If you use your home office regularly and exclusively for administrative and management activities, such as doing the books and preparing tax returns, it will qualify as your principal place of business. If you are conducting business as an employee, however, the convenience-of-the-employer test still must be satisfied.

Congress revised the definition of principal place of business because it believes the *Soliman* decision unfairly denied home office deductions to a growing number of entrepreneurs who manage their business from their homes. It also believes that the new rule will enable more taxpayers to work efficiently at home, save commuting time and expenses, and spend additional time with their families. The new rule permits virtually all home-based business owners to structure their affairs so that they qualify for the deduction.See Examples 6.1 and 6.2.

## A Place to Meet Patients, Clients, or Customers

If your home office does not meet the principal place of business test just discussed, your home-business expenses still might be deductible (subject

Julie is a self-employed sales representative for several different product lines. Her only office is a room in her house used regularly and exclusively to set up appointments, store product samples, and write up orders and other reports for the companies whose products she sells. She occasionally writes up orders and sets up appointments from her hotel room when she is away on business overnight.

Julie's business is selling products to customers at various locations within the metropolitan area where she lives. To make these sales, she regularly visits the customers to explain the available products and to take orders. Julie makes only a few sales from her home office.

In 1998 Julie's home office would not have qualified as her principal place of business. Under the new rules, however, Julie's home office does qualify as her principal place of business. She conducts administrative or management activities there, and she has no other fixed location where she conducts administrative or management activities. The fact that she conducts some administrative or management activities in her hotel room (not a fixed location) does not disqualify her home office as her principal place of business. She can deduct her expenses, to the extent of the deduction limit, for the business use of her home for the years 1999 and beyond.

**EXAMPLE 6.1**

to the net income limitation). If you use your home office to meet or deal with clients or customers, the office does not need to be your principal place of business. To qualify, you must meet or deal with your clients or customers in the home office, not just talk with them on the phone or through fax or e-mail communications. In today's cyberspace environment this strict focus on face-to-face communication seems archaic, but that's the way the law is written.

If you regularly meet clients or customers there, your home office need not be your principal place of business to be deductible.

Albert is a self-employed consultant who meets with clients in their homes and offices. Albert spends about 40 hours of his work time per week at these client locations. He has a small office in his home that he uses regularly and exclusively, for about 10 hours per week, talking with clients on the telephone, reading professional journals, and reviewing the books of his business.

Albert does not do his own billing. He uses a local bookkeeping service to bill his customers.

In 1998 Albert's home office would not have qualified as his principal place of business. Under the new rules, however, Albert's home office does qualify as his principal place of business. He uses the home office for the administrative or managerial activities of his consulting business, and he has no other fixed location where he conducts these activities. His choice to have his billing done by another company does not disqualify his home office as his principal place of business. He can deduct his expenses, to the extent of the deduction limit, for the business use of his home for the years 1999 and beyond.

**EXAMPLE 6.2**

The office still must be used exclusively and regularly for your business. If you meet with clients or customers only occasionally in your home office, it will not qualify. Such meetings must be "substantial and integral" to the conduct of your business. Also, if you are an employee, the use of your home office must be for the convenience of your employer (discussed later in this chapter).

**This Can Be Your Second Office** As noted earlier, your home office does not have to be your main office to qualify for this rule. Therefore, doctors, attorneys, tax consultants, and other self-employed professionals can have an office downtown that they work at two or three days a week and also maintain a home office for meeting with patients or clients the rest of the time. In this case, it's a good idea to have an appointment calendar showing your home appointments. To further support your home business deductions, your advertising literature and business cards should show your home address and phone number.

## SELF-EMPLOYMENT TAX

Self-employment (SE) tax is what you pay as a self-employed individual to finance your coverage under the social security system. SE tax is computed on Schedule SE, *Self-Employment Tax* (Form 1040). The tax is based on your net earnings from self-employment, and the combined rate is 15.3 percent. The combined rate is the sum of 12.4 percent for social security (old-age, survivors, and disability insurance) and 2.9 percent for Medicare (hospital insurance). The maximum amount of earnings from self-employment subject to the social security part (12.4 percent) for 2000 is $76,200. All of your net earnings from self-employment are subject to the Medicare part (2.9 percent). If your net earnings from self-employment are less than $400 (less than $108.28 as a church employee), you do not have to pay SE tax.

As demonstrated in Example 6.3, this tax might be a real eye-popper for some people the first year they have income from their small business. As an employee, your employer generally pays half of your social security tax and withholds the other half from your paycheck. As a self-employed person, you are on your own for the whole bill. Because net earnings from self-employment are determined differently from your taxable income, you could have a substantial SE tax liability when you owe little or no income tax. Your combined obligation for SE tax and income tax on self-employment income should be paid in quarterly estimated payments, explained later in this chapter.

### Who Must Pay Self-Employment Tax?

Income received from carrying on a business as a sole proprietor (or independent contractor) or a member of a partnership is generally self-

---

Ed Nord had net earnings from self-employment in 2000 of $30,000. Ed and his wife file a joint return, and neither one received wages subject to social security and Medicare taxes. The Nords have five dependent children and claimed itemized deductions of $10,400 on their 2000 return. The Nords' taxable income is zero, so no income tax is due ($30,000 − $10,400 [itemized deductions] − $19,600 [7 exemptions × $2,800] = $0). However, they owe self-employment tax of $4,590 ($30,000 × 15.3%).

**EXAMPLE 6.3**

employment income. Your business need not be full time; you could have a small part-time business in addition to your regular job. Any wages you earn reduce the self-employment tax base for retirement and disability benefits, so that you do not pay this amount on more than $76,200 in SE and wage income.

You are subject to the tax only on active business income—not on investment income. To determine whether you have business income, the same rules generally apply as for income tax purposes. (See Chapter 2.) Even if you are retired from your regular job and receiving social security benefits, you will still owe SE tax on your self-employment income.

**Not Employees, Usually** Employees share their social security tax obligation (FICA) with their employers, so they do not pay SE tax. Sometimes employers try to classify employees as independent contractors to avoid their share of the social security tax. On the other side, IRS agents have been known to be overly zealous in trying to reclassify workers as employees. Nevertheless, whether someone is an independent contractor or an employee depends on the facts in each case, not on how the employer classifies him or her. If an employer misclassifies an employee as an independent contractor, the employer can be held liable for unpaid employment taxes for that worker plus a penalty.

Generally, you are an independent contractor if you are receiving payments from someone who has the right to control or direct only the result of your work, not specifically what you will do or how you will do it. You are generally not an independent contractor if the person paying you controls what you will do and how and when you will do it. This applies even if you are performing the work in your home office. What matters is that the employer has the legal right to control the details of how your services are performed.

The determination of whether you are an employee or are self-employed generally follows the same tests for both income tax and social security tax purposes, but there are some differences. Some people are classified as employees for social security tax purposes but are self-employed for income tax purposes. Others are treated just the opposite.

One of the biggest areas of dispute between the IRS and small business owners is over the classification of their workers for social security tax purposes.

**Statutory Employees** For example, if you earned wages as a "statutory employee," you are considered an employee for FICA purposes and do not pay SE tax. A statutory employee is anyone who performs services as an agent-driver or commission-driver, as a full-time life insurance sales representative, as a home worker, or as a traveling or city salesperson, under the conditions stated in the tax code. If you are a statutory employee, the box titled "Statutory employee" in box 15 of your Form W-2 (Wage and Tax Statement) that you get from your employer at the end of the year will be checked.

Although your employer withholds social security tax from your paycheck, you are not an employee for income tax purposes. You can report your wages on Schedule C (or Schedule C-EZ) and deduct any allowable related expenses. Doing so avoids having to claim these deductions on Schedule A as employee expenses where they are reduced by 2 percent of your adjusted gross income (AGI).

**Ordained Ministers** Conversely, if you are a duly ordained, commissioned, or licensed minister of a church, you are treated as self-employed for SE tax purposes but are probably an employee for income tax purposes. That means you must pay SE tax on your net earnings but cannot use Schedule C or C-EZ to claim related deductions. Your employee expenses must be claimed on Schedule A as itemized deductions, subject to the 2 percent of AGI reduction. As was mentioned in Chapter 4, the taxation of clergy has a few other little twists that make it a very good niche market in which to specialize.

**Form SS-8** If you are now confused and wondering whether you are an employee or self-employed, or are treating workers you hire correctly, get IRS Publication 15-A, *Employer's Supplemental Tax Guide.* This publication has information that helps to determine whether an individual is an employee or an independent contractor. If you believe you might be wrongly classified or might be wrongly classifying your workers, you can get a written determination from the IRS by completing and filing Form SS-8, "Determination of Employee Work Status for Purposes of Federal Employment Taxes and Income Tax Withholding." Either the employer or the worker, or both, can complete this form. See "Additional Resources" at the end of this chapter.

 The taxation of members of the clergy is a good niche area.

**Partners** If you are a general partner in a partnership that carries on a trade or business, your distributive share of income or loss from the trade or business is included in your income from self-employment. If you are a limited partner, only guaranteed payments for services performed during the year are included in your self-employment income.

If your partnership is not engaged in a business, then your distributive share of income or loss is not included in your income from self-employment. For example, if you are a member of an investment club partnership that limits its activities to investing in securities and collecting interest and dividends for its members' accounts, the income is not self-employment income.

## What Is Not Self-Employment Income

Even if you are self-employed, all the income or loss from your business might not be included in self-employment income. Here are a few things that are not included.

**Gains and Losses** Gains and losses from property that you are not in the business of selling are not included in self-employment income. Examples are gains and losses from investment property and depreciable property or other fixed assets used for business.

**Real Estate Rent** Rent from real estate and from personal property leased with the real estate is not self-employment income, unless you receive the income as part of your business as a real estate dealer. If you are a dealer, include the rental income and deductions with your other real estate income on Schedule C or C-EZ (Form 1040). If you are not a real estate dealer, include the income and deductions from rental property on Schedule E (Form 1040).

**Corporate Shareholders** The only self-employment income you might receive from a corporation is director fees. This is generally income you receive for going to directors' meetings or serving on committees, not compensation for your active involvement in the operation of the corporation.

Even if you own all the stock of a C corporation, your work performed for the corporation is in the capacity of an employee, and compensation you receive is not self-employment income. It is subject to withholding by the corporation for social security and Medicare taxes. If you are a shareholder in an S corporation, your share of the corporation's income is not self-employment income, even though you must report it

> As an S corporation shareholder, you do not pay self-employment tax.

for income tax purposes. Payments from your S corporation for services are employee wages, subject to withholding by the corporation.

## Computing the Self-Employment Tax

If you owe SE tax, you must file Form 1040 to report the tax, even if you owe no income tax. SE tax is shown on line 50 of Form 1040 and is computed on Schedule SE (Form 1040). If you file a joint return, you must compute the self-employment income of you and your spouse separately; if you both have self-employment income, you have to file two schedules.

**What Is Deductible?** The tax is computed on net earnings from self-employment, which is generally self-employment income reduced by the business deductions that are allowable for income tax. If you have more than one business, combine the net income or loss from each to determine your net earnings from self-employment. Some of the deductions that reduce taxable income for income tax purposes but do not count in determining net income from self-employment are the following:

✔ Deductions for personal and dependency exemptions.

✔ Standard deduction or itemized deductions.

✔ Net operating loss deduction (meaning business losses from other years that are carried to the current year).

✔ Contributions on your behalf to a retirement plan, including an Individual Retirement Account (IRA).

✔ Self-employed health insurance deduction.

For income tax purposes, you can deduct half of your SE tax computed on Schedule SE. This deduction goes on page 1 of Form 1040 rather than on Schedule SE. Instead of allowing this deduction for SE tax purposes (which would create a simultaneous equation), the Code allows you to compute the tax on only 92.35 percent of net earnings from self-employment (100% – 7.65%).

**How Much Is Taxable?** The maximum amount that is subject to the 12.4 percent rate is $76,200 in 2000, reduced by any wages you earned that were subject to social security tax. All of your net earnings from self-employment are subject to the additional 2.9 percent rate (Medicare). So if your combined wages and net earnings from self-employment were less than $76,200, all of your net self-employment earnings are taxed at 15.3 percent. If net earnings from self-employment are greater than the excess of $76,200 over wages, only the amount equal to the excess is taxed at 15.3 percent; the rest is taxed at 2.9 percent. Example 6.4 shows how the ceiling for the SE tax is affected by wages.

The instructions to Schedule SE tell you how to use either the non-farm or farm optional method to figure the tax if you have a loss or a small amount of income from self-employment and you want to receive credit for social security benefit coverage.

## FEDERAL ESTIMATED TAX PAYMENTS

Even though your final tax liability cannot be determined until you file your income tax return at the end of the year, the government wants you to pay your taxes in installments throughout the year. This requires you to estimate the amount of tax (including alternative minimum tax and self-employment tax) you expect to owe for the year, after subtracting tax credits and tax withheld by employers. If you are required to make estimated tax payments and do not send in enough each quarter by the due date, you might be charged a penalty, even though you are due a refund when you file your tax return. Corporations as well as individuals are required to make estimated tax payments.

Jeff Ferd had net income from self-employment of $70,000 in 2000 and received $20,000 in wages subject to social security and Medicare taxes. Jeff's net earnings from self-employment are $64,645 ($70,000 × 0.9235). The maximum income subject to the 15.3 percent SE tax rate is $56,200 ($76,200 − $20,000). The tax at 15.3 percent is $8,598.60. The balance of Jeff's net self-employment earnings is taxed at 2.9 percent. That amount is $244.91 ($8,445 × 2.9%). That makes Jeff's total SE tax $8,843.51 ($8,598.60 + $244.91). One-half of this amount, or $4,421.76, is deductible on page 1 of Form 1040.

**EXAMPLE 6.4**

You are required to make quarterly estimated tax payments for your self-employment tax liability, even if you have no income tax due.

## General Rules for Individuals

You might owe an underpayment penalty for 2001 (or any year) if you did not pay, in the form of withholding and/or equal quarterly estimated payments, at least the smaller of

- ✔ 90 percent of the tax shown on your tax return for 2000 (current year); or
- ✔ 100 percent of the tax shown on your tax return for 1999 (preceding year).

The tax shown on your return means all taxes you were required to pay, reduced only by the earned income credit and the credit for federal tax paid on fuels, not your withholding and estimated tax payments.

Higher-income individuals are required to pay a higher percentage based on the preceding year to avoid an estimated tax underpayment penalty. If your adjusted gross income on your 1999 return exceeded $150,000 ($75,000 for married taxpayers filing separately), your required annual payment in figuring 2000 estimated taxes is the lesser of 90 percent of the tax for 2000, or 108.6 percent of the tax for 1999. If the AGI shown on your 2000 return exceeds $150,000 ($75,000 for married taxpayers filing separately), your required annual payment in figuring 2001 estimated tax payments is the lesser of 90 percent of the tax for 2001, or 110 percent of the tax for 2000. The preceding year tax percentage goes up to 112 percent for 2001, then levels off at 110 percent for years after that.

You will not owe a penalty if you had no tax liability for the preceding year, and you were a U.S. citizen or resident for the entire year. Also, you will not be penalized for any year in which the tax liability shown on your return, minus withholding, is less than $1,000 for years after 1997 ($500 for prior years).

## General Rule for Corporations

A corporation is generally subject to an underpayment penalty if it has a tax liability of $500 or more for the current year and did not timely pay, in quarterly installments, at least the smaller of

You do not have to make your fourth estimated tax payment if you file your return and pay the tax by January 31.

✔ 100 percent of the tax liability on its current year return; or

✔ 100 percent of the tax liability on its preceding year return.

The preceding year is taken into account only if the corporation filed a return for the preceding year showing at least some tax liability.

## Making the Payments

For estimated tax purposes, the year is divided into four payment periods, and each period has a due date. If you do not pay enough tax by each of these due dates, you might owe a penalty. The due dates for a calendar year individual are: April 15 (for the first quarter), June 15 (for the second quarter), September 15 (for the third quarter), and January 15 of the following year (for the fourth quarter). You can skip the fourth-quarter payment if you file your return and pay the tax due by January 31.

The first three dates are the same for a calendar-year corporation, but the last payment is due on December 15 of the same year. A fiscal-year taxpayer uses corresponding dates for its taxable year. Due dates are always postponed to the next working day if they fall on a weekend or holiday.

You can use the Estimated Tax Worksheet in the instructions to Form 1040-ES (the payment vouchers) to compute your estimated tax payments for your individual return. To compute corporate estimated tax payments, use Form 1120-W, "Estimated Tax for Corporations."

The simplest and safest way to figure the payments for your individual return is to take the tax liability from your previous year return, subtract the tax you expect to be withheld during the current year on wages for you and/or your spouse (if filing jointly), and use the difference for your total estimated tax payments. You should send in one-fourth of the total by the due date for each quarter. See Example 6.5.

If you discover late in the year that your estimated payments and withholding will not equal at least 90 percent of your tax liability, and you or your spouse is earning wages subject to withholding, the best way to make up the deficit is to request that your (or your spouse's) employer increase the withholding. The penalty for each quarter is computed by assuming your employer withholds income tax proportionately throughout the year, even if it is all taken out of your last paycheck. Your estimated payments, however, are not applied until they are actually paid.

Jim and Julie showed a combined tax liability on their 2000 jointly filed Form 1040 of $13,000 (line 56) before any credit for withholding or estimated taxes. The tax was attributable to income tax on Julie's wages and to income and self-employment tax on Jim's home-based business income. In 2001 Julie expects to pay $9,500 in federal income tax withholding through her employer.

Jim and Julie will avoid underpayment penalties for 2001 if they pay, in equal quarterly installments, enough additional tax to equal 90 percent of their 2001 combined tax liability or 100 percent of their 2000 tax liability. To be safe, they make four quarterly payments of $875 beginning April 15, 2001, that is, $3,500 ($13,000 − $9,500) divided by four.

**EXAMPLE 6.5**

## Penalty

The underpayment penalty charged to individuals and corporations is redetermined by the Treasury each quarter and is tied to the current yield on U.S. government short-term bonds. As of this writing (September 2000), the rate is 9 percent for all taxpayers except for large corporations, which are charged 11 percent.

If you failed to make adequate estimated payments, you can compute the underpayment penalty for Form 1040 on Form 2210, "Underpayment of Estimated Tax by Individuals, Estates, and Trusts." The underpayment for corporations is computed on Form 2220, "Underpayment of Estimated Tax by Corporations." You do not have to compute the underpayment penalty if you do not want to. (It is complicated.) In fact, the IRS encourages you to send your return in and let it calculate the penalty. The IRS will send you a bill, and it will not cost you any more for the IRS to do it as long as your return is filed by the due date, and you pay the penalty by the date specified on the bill. If you want to do this, just leave the penalty line on your return blank (line 69 on Form 1040) and do not file Form 2210.

The IRS will gladly compute the underpayment penalty for you free of charge.

If you or a client operates a seasonal business where the income varies quite a bit during the year, you might be able to lower or eliminate some or all of the quarterly penalties by using the annualized income installment method to compute the penalties. See the instructions to Form 2210 or Form 2220. You must complete and file the form to do this.

All or part of an underpayment will be waived if the IRS determines that the underpayment was due to a casualty, disaster, or other unusual circumstance, and it would be inequitable to impose the penalty. If you wish to request a waiver, you must complete and file Form 2210 (or Form 2220) and follow the instructions for requesting a waiver. Do not count on much sympathy from the IRS unless your excuse is a pretty good one.

# EMPLOYMENT TAXES

You might work solo starting out but eventually have the need and desire for an employee. You should first learn about your employment tax obligations. You also might go out and buy an extra filing cabinet to handle all the paperwork.

## Employer Identification Number

Your employer identification number (EIN) is like a social security number for your business. You generally do not need an EIN if you are a sole proprietor without employees or a deferred compensation plan. But if you are considering hiring an employee, you should get one. There are four situations in which you must have an EIN. You are required to have an EIN if you:

1. Have employees.
2. Have a Keogh plan.
3. Operate your business as a corporation or partnership.
4. File any of these tax returns:
   a. Employment.
   b. Excise.
   c. Alcohol, tobacco, and firearms.

You can get an EIN by filling out Form SS-4, "Application for Employer Identification Number," and sending it in. It will take at least four or five weeks to get the number. A quicker way is to apply over the phone. To find the local phone number to call, either look in the instructions to Form SS-4 or call the IRS at 1-800-829-1040, and ask for the entity control phone number for your area. If you apply by phone you will get your number immediately.

### Tax Withholding

Your employees should fill out Form W-4, "Employee's Withholding Allowance Certificate," when starting work. You will use the filing status and withholding allowances shown on this form to figure the amount of income tax to withhold. Then you need to get IRS Publication 15, *Circular E, Employer's Tax Guide*, to calculate the proper withholding.

Social security and Medicare taxes are generally levied on both you and your employees. You must withhold and deposit the employee's part and pay a matching amount. The deposits for withheld income and social security tax are reported on Form 941 and are generally made quarterly. See Publication 15 for the details on when and where to send the deposits.

If you operate your home-based business as a sole proprietor, and you employ your child who is under 18, the child's wages will not be subject to social security and Medicare taxes. Also, wages of your child who is under the age of 21 are not subject to federal unemployment taxes (FUTA). These exemptions apply only to your child—just any kid will not do. In addition, the employment must be directly by you, the parent. If the child is employed by a partnership or corporation, even if controlled by you, the exemptions will not apply.

### Federal Unemployment Tax

The federal unemployment (FUTA) tax pays unemployment compensation to workers who lose their jobs. The FUTA tax rate is 6.2 percent through 2007, and the federal wage base is $7,000. Most employers pay both a federal and a state unemployment tax. Your state wage base may be different.

Here's a tax tip: By employing your child under 18 in your business, you will get a tax break. You can deduct your child's wages as a business expense. Also, you do not have to withhold social security tax if your child is under 18, and wages of up to $4,400 (in 2000) received by a dependent child will be offset by the child's standard deduction, so they will not be taxed to the child.

Contact your state unemployment insurance offices to receive your state reporting number, state experience rate, and details about your state unemployment tax obligations. The federal government allows a credit for FUTA paid, or allowed under a merit rating system, to your state. The credit cannot exceed 5.4 percent of the covered wages, so the amount you pay to the IRS could be as low as 0.8 percent (6.2 percent – 5.4 percent). You report and pay FUTA tax separately from withheld taxes, and it is all paid out of your funds. You use Form 940 or 940-EZ, "Employer's Annual Federal Unemployment (FUTA) Tax Return," to report this tax.

## GENERAL RECORD-KEEPING REQUIREMENTS

Adequate and accurate record keeping is fundamental to running any business. Records tell you what you own and what you owe, whether you are making a profit or are incurring a loss, and whether you are building equity in your enterprise. In addition, maintaining accurate records is the only way to ensure that you are paying the proper tax liability. It might also affect whether a loss will be allowed to you or a client, because it is one factor the IRS uses to determine whether an activity is a legitimate business or simply a hobby. Keep in mind that the IRS is not obliged to prove that an item is *not* deductible; it is up to you to show that it *is*.

You do not have to be a certified public accountant to keep adequate records (although it would not hurt). Even if you have no accounting background, you can maintain a very simple record-keeping system sufficient to show your profit or loss. Following are a few suggestions for general record keeping if you are operating a business.

### Your Business Checking Account and Credit Card

One of the first things you should do when you start a business is to open a separate checking account for it. Banks like to charge a lot of money for business checking accounts, so shop around. If you are a sole proprietor just starting out, and you do not have an assumed name for your business, you might try to operate your business through a personal checking account. The IRS will have no problem with this, but the bank might.

The burden of proof is on the taxpayer to substantiate claimed deductions.

All bank accounts should be reconciled at the end of each month.

Use this separate account only for business items, and do not run business items through your personal account. If you run out of money in your business account, transfer funds to it rather than writing checks from your personal account. Pay for all of your business expenditures with checks (or your business credit card) rather than cash, and avoid writing checks payable to cash; write checks to yourself only when you want to withdraw money from the business. Be sure to reconcile your checkbook with your bank statements on a regular basis and at the end of the year.

You also should get a credit card that is designated for business purchases. It does not have to be a "business" credit card. When you pay the credit card bill, use your business checking account. Your credit card charges are considered paid when you charge them, making them deductible at that time rather than when you pay the bill. So be sure that all unpaid credit card charges are recorded in your business books at the end of the year.

Simply keeping your business income and expenditures separate from your personal items will greatly simplify your record keeping. It also will demonstrate to the IRS that you are serious about your business. Your checking account and credit card receipts are your primary sources of information for recording transactions in your business books.

### Keeping the Books

The purpose of keeping books is to record and identify each transaction and to summarize all transactions at the end of the year to establish an accurate income statement and balance sheet. How you accomplish this is up to you, as long as you record sufficient information to accurately present your income or loss.

**Computer Programs** Since you will need a computer for your tax software, the easiest way to keep your business books may be to buy a computer bookkeeping program. Before you buy, though, get some advice on which one is best for you. The easiest ones are based on a simple single-entry system, allowing you to record receipts and expenditures just like in your checkbook. These programs also can replace your checkbook. They print out checks and even make electronic funds transfers. They reconcile your bank account and produce instant profit-and-loss statements, balance sheets, and other reports. If you get the program that is right for you, it will be a painless way to satisfy your record-keeping requirements.

**Manual Systems** If you are not a computer person, you can find complete single-entry bookkeeping ledger systems at you favorite office supply store for less than $30. One brand even gives you a lesson in bookkeeping with filled-in ledger sheets. You can get systems for either cash or accrual accounting. These systems make bookkeeping pretty easy, even for the completely uninitiated. It might be easier to start this way than to convert to a computer system.

**Bailing Out** You might be thinking you want to concentrate on the tax end of the business and leave the bookkeeping to someone else. Okay, if you can afford the luxury, hire someone. A good place to start might be a local college or university that has an accounting program. Talk to one of the professors about a recent graduate or senior who might be willing to set up a bookkeeping system for you. Alternatively, there are probably plenty of bookkeeping services in your area that employ qualified people at reasonable rates.

**Do Not Trust the Bookkeeper!** Whatever you do, do not turn over the entire financial affairs of your business to any one person. If you hire a bookkeeper, continue to write the checks and deposit the funds yourself; let the bookkeeper record the transactions. This is called internal control, and it is essential to safeguard the monetary assets of your business. If you grow to the point where you can no longer pay the bills and do the banking yourself, you had better hire an accountant to keep an eye on the bookkeeper. If the bookkeeper and the accountant get really friendly, fire one of them and hire someone else. The world abounds with those who tread the straight and narrow path simply for want of opportunity. Do not allow your business to become their fortuitous circumstance.

## Substantiating Your Expenses

For each business purchase, you should have evidence of the date, the amount, the payee, and the business purpose of the expenditure. Your canceled checks and credit card statements will provide evidence of the

If you need a bookkeeper, check with a local college or university for a recent top graduate.

> To substantiate a business purpose, you need an invoice or receipt from the vendor in addition to your canceled check or credit card statement.

first three, but you also need the invoice or receipt from the vendor to indicate business purpose.

For example, let's say you bought some office furniture for your home office in 2000 from Bob's Furniture, and it cost $1,000. You claim a deduction for the furniture on your tax return, and your friendly neighborhood IRS agent pays you a visit. The agent simply wants proof that you bought the furniture in 2000 and that you paid $1,000 for it. You can show the agent your record of the transaction in your books, and the agent can visibly inspect the furniture in your home office. But from viewing the books and inspecting the furniture, the agent still does not know for sure that you spent all or any of the $1,000 paid to Bob's Furniture on that particular furniture. You could have bought a dining room table from Bob's and received the office furniture as a gift from Aunt Harriett. What the agent needs to see is the invoice or receipt from Bob's Furniture showing that you did in fact pay $1,000 for office furniture.

## WHEN IS IT SAFE TO THROW STUFF AWAY?

If you are preparing tax returns for clients, Section 6107 of the Internal Revenue Code says you are to retain either a copy of the returns you prepare, or a list with the identifying information for each client, for three years after the close of the taxable year.

With respect to your own records and those of your clients, you should keep them as long as the transaction involved could be questioned by the IRS or has an effect on an item that could be questioned by the IRS. That generally means you should keep all records that support an item of income or deduction on a return until the period of limitations for that return expires. The period of limitations is the length of time after you file your return in which the return can be amended to claim a credit or refund or in which the IRS can assess additional tax.

> Never be too quick to throw anything away that is related to your tax return or the return of a client.

## Income and Expense Records

The normal period of limitations for your return generally expires three years after the return is filed. That means you should never throw anything away for at least three years. If you have a net operating loss in a later year, and you carry the loss back to the current year, the period of limitations for the current year can be as long as six years. In that situation you should keep all your records for at least six years. If the transaction relates to a bad debt deduction or a loss from worthless securities, the period of limitations is extended to seven years, so keep that stuff for seven years. If you have employees, you must keep all employment tax records for at least four years after the tax is due or is paid, whichever comes later.

## Asset Records

The IRS can question the cost of an asset and of any capital improvements for up to three years after you dispose of the asset in a taxable transaction. Keep all of your records until that time.

The gain or loss on certain asset dispositions is not recognized if the property is replaced, and this affects the basis of the replacement property. For example, if you trade in a business automobile, the basis of the new car is determined, in part, by the basis of the car you traded in. That means you have to keep the records for the old car as well as the new car. All records should be kept until the period of limitations expires for the year the new property is disposed of in a taxable sale.

Although most taxpayers no longer need to report the sale and purchase of a personal residence on their tax return, you still must establish a basis in your personal residence to claim a home office deduction, and it is still necessary to report gain on a sale attributable to claimed depreciation. It is a good idea, therefore, to keep a permanent file for each personal residence. The closing papers from the purchase of your home should go into this file as well as receipts for all capital improvements. Keep this file for at least three years after you have sold your house and moved to a retirement home.

## ADDITIONAL RESOURCES

The IRS publication that addresses home office rules is Publication 587, *Business Use of Your Home*. The IRS publication that addresses self-employment tax is Publication 533, *Self-Employment Tax*. For further guidance in determining whether you are an employee or self-employed, get IRS Publication 15A, *Employer's Supplemental Tax Guide*. IRS Publication 505, *Tax Withholding and Estimated Tax*, shows detailed examples of how to compute estimated tax payments and figure the underpayment penalty. IRS Publication 15, *Circular E, Employer's Tax Guide*, gives information on the computation and reporting of employment taxes. IRS Publication 1066, *Small Business Tax Workshop Workbook*, gives detailed lessons on how to comply with all the requirements related to having employees. Publication 583, *Starting a Business and Keeping Records*, contains an example of a simple manual bookkeeping system. Finally, *J.K. Lasser's Taxes Made Easy for Your Home-Based Business* (John Wiley & Sons, 2000) contains information on all of these topics and more.

You can get IRS publications free by calling the IRS at 1-800-TAX-FORM (1-800-829-3676). If you have access to TTY/TDD equipment, you can call 1-800-829-4059. To download them from the Internet, go to www.irs.gov (World Wide Web) or ftp.irs.gov (FTP). If you would like to get forms and instructions (not publications) by fax, dial 1-703-368-9694 to reach IRS Tax Fax.

As an alternative to downloading files from the Internet, you can order *IRS Federal Tax Products* on CD-ROM. This CD includes over 2,000 tax products, including all of the above publications and forms. It can be ordered by calling 1-800-233-6767. Also, Publication 3207, *Small Business Resource Guide*, is an interactive CD-ROM that contains information important to small businesses. It is available in mid-February. You can get one free copy by calling 1-800-829-3676.

# Tax Research and
# the Tools of the Trade

*When a tax controversy erupts, it is common for clients to blame their tax advisors as well as the IRS for the aggravation they are undergoing. . . .*

—William L. Raby

his chapter provides a basic introduction to tax research, which is an essential skill of a tax professional. It also introduces you to tax resources available primarily through the new technology of the tax profession—the Internet. Tax planning and compliance software is a fundamental tool for every tax practitioner, and there are many to choose from. This chapter gives you a brief overview of what these programs have to offer.

## YOUR LIFELINE TO EFFECTIVE CLIENT SERVICES

Regardless of the nature of the tax services you envision providing or the type of clients you wish to serve, you will find it necessary to engage in tax research. Your ability to find tax saving opportunities for your clients is limited only by the resources you have at hand and your skill at using them.

Tax rules, you see, are not designed to be committed to memory. Even if you specialize in a limited area, the rules are too vast for mortal

Tax research for a tax professional is unavoidable. Your efficiency in doing research will add to your bottom line.

memory banks. The exceptions, limitations, and special rules make memorizing even a short tax code section very risky. A misquote to a client who is relying on your tax advice to structure a future transaction might be very costly in terms of client relations.

Additionally, even if you did possess the ability to memorize the rules, they change quite frequently. Major tax legislation has been enacted almost annually for the past two decades. Even ignoring the frequent changes by Congress, our federal tax authority is extremely dynamic, with new court decisions and IRS rulings being written on a daily basis.

For these reasons, a large part of tax work consists of research. This research might simply involve looking up a tax rate or an exemption amount, or it could encompass a large planning project. It is generally done for the benefit of a specific client so it is, or should be, done on chargeable time. However, the inefficiency of many practitioners in conducting tax research renders much of their research time unproductive and nonchargeable.

### Example

Eliza has opened a tax practice for individuals, and Jeff and Joan Johnson, a husband and wife, have come to her to have their tax return prepared. Jeff and Joan have a fairly simple tax situation. Both earn wages and they have a few deductions, but they have incurred no business or investment expenses and no capital gains or losses or real estate transactions, so their return should be very straightforward. "Oh, by the way," says Jeff, "I have a cousin, Joe, whom we supported during the year, but he does not live with us. Someone told us he could be claimed as a dependent, and someone else said he couldn't be. We were wondering if there was a new ruling or a court case or something that says a cousin can be a deductible dependent." Eliza realizes that this is an issue with which some of her competitors are probably familiar but one that she will need to research. She assures Jeff and Joan that she will find the correct answer. She then boosts her quoted fee for half an hour of research, with the knowledge that charging more to resolve this question might send Jeff and Joan to another practitioner. Satisfied with the quoted fee, Jeff and Joan leave the office to return later for their tax return.

Now Eliza's work begins. Given the facts presented, how is she to determine if Jeff's cousin Joe is deductible? Her speed in finding the correct answer will determine her profitability for the job. We will assume Eliza is not well trained in the research process, like many other tax professionals, and goes about her search in a haphazard manner.

She starts with the instructions to Form 1040. On page 19 of the instructions she finds that to be claimed as a dependent, a person must be either the taxpayer's relative or have lived with the taxpayer for the entire year. Since Joe did not live with Jeff and Joan, he must qualify as a "relative" to be deductible. Now the question is, does a cousin qualify as a relative?

Eliza remembers seeing a list of individuals who qualify as relatives, for dependency purposes, in an IRS publication. She digs around for a couple of minutes and comes up with IRS Publication 501, which deals with exemptions, filing status, and the standard deduction. The list of relatives in the publication does not include cousins. Eliza therefore concludes that, according to Publication 501, a cousin who does not live with the taxpayer is not a deductible dependent. However, Jeff mentioned that a new case or ruling might have changed this result.

Eliza has access to one of the online tax services that are described later in this chapter. Such services contain all the latest developments. She logs on to the service on the Internet and keys in the words "cousin" and "dependent" as search terms. She also selects the databases she wishes to search to include IRS rulings and regulations and all federal court decisions that pertain to taxation. This search should reveal all current rulings, regulations, and court decisions that mention both "cousin" and "dependent." She presses the Search button and hopes that the number of documents matching her search criteria is manageable.

Eliza is disappointed to see that 78 documents meet her search criteria. Lacking the knowledge to refine her search further, she is compelled to examine all 78 documents for evidence of a change in the rule. Two hours later, after incurring a sizable bill for the database search, she is finally satisfied that Publication 501 is up to date and correct and that Joe is not deductible.

## Your Key to Profitability

This example demonstrates a simple question for which Eliza could not have charged more but that completely destroyed her profitability on Jeff

Eliza's lack of basic knowledge about the tax system cost her valuable chargeable time.

> The learning process in the tax profession is continuous;
> your key to profitability is to understand how to learn in an
> effective and efficient manner.

and Joan's return. A better understanding of the basic structure of the tax system and the relationship among the Internal Revenue Code, the courts, and the IRS would have reduced her research time to no more than 10 minutes.

Similar questions arise daily in a typical tax practice. Memorizing the answers to specific questions is not the solution, because the questions are unending. Consequently, learning is continuous—it cannot be avoided if you are to be successful. Your key to profitability is to understand how to learn in an effective and efficient manner. The more proficient and expeditious your research, the wealthier you will become.

Research competence is gained only through familiarity with the system in which the rules exist. As with any research, you must identify the proper sources of information and determine their level of validity. The next section, therefore, introduces you to the three primary sources of tax authority: (1) the law itself, (2) IRS regulations and rulings, and (3) judicial decisions. You will learn which rules take precedence over the others and how to evaluate the strength of conflicting authority.

## LEGISLATIVE, ADMINISTRATIVE, AND JUDICIAL AUTHORITY

Our government was established under the Constitution with a system of checks and balances. The Legislative Branch (Congress) enacts the laws, the Administrative Branch (the President and cabinet) administers and enforces the laws, and the Judicial Branch (the courts) makes sure the other two branches are operating legally and within their constitutional authority.

From the three branches of government come the three sources of primary tax authority. The law itself, and supporting documents, is called *legislative authority*. In the case of tax law, this is the Internal Revenue Code. The President delegates the administration of tax laws to the U.S. Treasury Department, which includes the IRS. From Treasury and the IRS comes *administrative authority* in the form of regulations and rulings. The courts give us *judicial authority*, also known as case law, in

> The three branches of our federal government produce the three types of primary tax authority—legislative, administrative, and judicial. Nothing else is relevant.

the form of court decisions that settle disputes between the IRS and taxpayers. These decisions can be used as precedent in future dealings with the IRS, although in many cases they are not binding on either party, as discussed later.

## Legislative Authority

When Congress enacts tax legislation and the President signs it into law, it adds to or amends the Internal Revenue Code of 1986 (which is Title 26 of the U.S. Code). The Internal Revenue Code contains all of our country's tax laws, which the IRS is required to administer and enforce.

**Begin Research with the Code** Keep in mind that the Internal Revenue Code is the highest form of tax authority, with the exception of the Constitution (as interpreted by the Supreme Court). Judicial and administrative authority generally only interpret the meaning of the Code when it is less than clear. The judicial branch can override the plain language of the Code only when the law is unconstitutional. (Remember the Supreme Court case of *Pollock v. Farmer's Loan & Trust Co.* in Chapter 2.) Administrative authority, in the form of regulations and rulings, can never overrule the Internal Revenue Code. It is important, therefore, for a tax professional to be familiar with the Code, because that is where your research should begin. The section entitled "Where to Find This Stuff" explains where to find the Code to read, in hard copy, CD form, and over the Internet.

Learning the structure and the ins and outs of reading the Code is well beyond the scope of this book. However, here is a brief look at part of one section:

> The Internal Revenue Code (legislative authority) is the law. Administrative and judicial authority interpret the meaning of the Code.

§ 152 Dependent defined.

(a) General definition. For purposes of this subtitle, the term "dependent" means any of the following individuals over half of whose support, for the calendar year in which the taxable year of the taxpayer begins, was received from the taxpayer . . . :

(1) A son or daughter of the taxpayer, or a descendant of either,

(2) A stepson or stepdaughter of the taxpayer,

(3) A brother, sister, stepbrother, or stepsister of the taxpayer,

(4) The father or mother of the taxpayer, or an ancestor of either,

(5) A stepfather or stepmother of the taxpayer,

(6) A son or daughter of a brother or sister of the taxpayer,

(7) A brother or sister of the father or mother of the taxpayer,

(8) A son-in-law, daughter-in-law, father-in-law, mother-in-law, brother-in-law, or sister-in-law of the taxpayer, or

(9) An individual (other than an individual who at any time during the taxable year was the spouse, determined without regard to section 7703, of the taxpayer) who, for the taxable year of the taxpayer, has as his principal place of abode the home of the taxpayer and is a member of the taxpayer's household.

As you can see, this Code section defines the individuals who can be claimed as dependents of another taxpayer. Only those individuals who meet the relationship tests of paragraphs (1) through (8) of Section 152 qualify, unless they live with the taxpayer for the entire year as provided in paragraph (9). Note that a cousin, who in Code talk would be labeled "a son or daughter of a brother or sister of the father or mother of the taxpayer," is not listed.

You know that a ruling from the IRS or a court decision cannot over-

Note that "a son or daughter of a brother or sister of the father or mother of the taxpayer," which in Code talk means "cousin," is not listed in Section 152.

Beginning your research with the highest form of authority can save valuable time.

rule the plain language of the Code. The Code is the law, which can only be *interpreted* by the IRS and the courts. Eliza, in the previous example, could have saved a great deal of time had she been Code literate and started her search with the Code.

If Eliza was unfamiliar with Code Section 152, she could have easily found it by looking in the Code's key word index under "dependent" or "exemptions." Having confirmed the rule in the Code section, her only task would have been to assure herself that she was referring to the current version of Section 152. This would have been a straightforward procedure, taking only a few minutes, and would have given her compete confidence in her conclusion.

**Committee Reports Add Clarification** Other Code sections are not always as explicit as Section 152 and sometimes need explanation. Documents produced during the legislative process help to determine the intent behind a Code provision and are also considered legislative authority. These documents are called committee reports and are written by the tax-writing committees of Congress to explain the provisions of proposed legislation to other members of Congress for the purpose of voting on it.

The House Ways and Means Committee is traditionally the first congressional committee to consider new tax legislation. *Ways and Means Committee reports* are written by the Ways and Means Committee when it writes tax legislation to be voted on by the full House. A tax bill passed by the House of Representatives is sent to the Senate, where it is referred to the Senate Finance Committee. The Finance Committee issues *Finance Committee reports* for its version of the bill to be voted on by the full Senate. When the House and Senate form a joint conference committee to hash out a compromise bill, the joint committee issues *Joint Conference Committee reports* for the benefit of both houses of Congress.

Once legislation is enacted, the courts, the IRS, and tax practitioners use all three sets of the committee reports to interpret the new law. Committee reports are most helpful to tax practitioners during the period following enactment, prior to the issuance of other guidance. It might be years after tax legislation is enacted before regulations are issued or litigation produces court decisions to follow.

Committee reports are most helpful in explaining the intent of new legislation before regulations and rulings are issued.

If Treasury writes regulations interpreting the new law, it will generally rely on information from the committee reports. Treasury regulations, along with all forms of rulings and announcements from the administrative branch of government, are forms of administrative authority, which is discussed next.

### Administrative Authority

As just mentioned, sometimes the tax laws written by Congress are unclear, or are not specific enough to apply to particular circumstances. In order to enforce these laws, it is necessary for the Treasury Department and the IRS to provide interpretations. That is why the Internal Revenue Code provides Treasury general authority to write regulations and rulings to interpret any Code section.[1] These interpretations generally come in the form of *regulations* from Treasury and *revenue rulings* and *letter rulings* from the IRS. The IRS also publishes *revenue procedures*, which are used to tell taxpayers about IRS administrative practices.

**"Cumulative Bulletin" and "Internal Revenue Bulletin"** Regulations, revenue rulings and revenue procedures are published by the IRS on a weekly basis in a pamphlet called "The Internal Revenue Bulletin." Each weekly volume contains everything issued by the IRS during that week. Every six months these bulletins are reorganized by Code section and published in a bound volume. The bound volume is the "Cumulative Bulletin." That means there are at least two "Cumulative Bulletins" per year. The first volume contains IRS pronouncements from the first half of the year, and the second volume has the stuff from the second half.

Besides rulings issued by the IRS, the "Cumulative Bulletin" also contains the entire text of any tax legislation enacted during the year and the committee reports that accompany it. Remember that committee reports are written by the tax legislative committees of Congress and provide explanation and insight into the congressional intent of the legislation. For any year in which major legislation is enacted, there will probably be more than two volumes of the "Cumulative Bulletin" to handle the legislation and committee reports. Locating the "Internal Revenue

Bulletins" and the "Cumulative Bulletin," as well as other sources of rulings and regulations, is discussed later under "Where to Find This Stuff."

**Regulations**  Regulations are the highest form of administrative authority. The purpose of regulations is to explain, in relatively normal language, the meaning of all or part of a Code section. They generally expand on the language of the Code section and provide examples to help taxpayers comply with the Code section.

Some regulations merely interpret what the Code section itself says. These are called *interpretive* regulations. In selected Code sections, however, Congress provides specific authority for Treasury to come up with certain rules on its own, as long as they comply with the overall intent of the Code section. These are called *legislative* regulations. For example, Congress might provide a general intent for a particular Code section but in the Code section ask the secretary of the Treasury to issue regulations that provide specific rules to carry out the intent. The regulations issued in response would be legislative regulations.

Legislative regulations carry the force and effect of the law itself, as long as they comply with the intent of the Code section under which they are issued. Legislative regulations are not actually the law, however, because the Treasury Department writes them. Although they are the highest form of administrative authority and carry more weight than interpretive regulations, they are, on occasion, successfully challenged by taxpayers in the courts when they go beyond the intent of Congress.

You can identify the reference to a regulation, as opposed to a Code section, by its citation (name). It will begin with the number 1 (if issued under an income tax Code section) followed by a decimal, then the number of the Code section. For example, Regulation Section 1.61-1 is the citation for the first regulation issued under Section 61 of the Code. You will also see it cited as Reg. §1.61-1.

**Revenue Rulings**  The National Office of the IRS issues revenue rulings. These are generally official replies by the IRS to specific questions raised by taxpayers. They also interpret tax law, but are not as authoritative as regulations (meaning the courts are more likely to disagree with

Regulations are the highest form of administrative authority, with "legislative regulations" carrying the most weight.

Revenue rulings are short legal memoranda addressing narrow issues.

them). They tend to deal with much more focused issues than regulations, often addressing a specific legal question. They are published to provide guidance in cases having similar facts to those presented in the rulings and are generally only one or two pages long.

Here is an example of the citation for a revenue ruling: Rev. Rul. 80-52, 1980-1 C.B. 100. The "80-52" means it was the fifty-second revenue ruling issued in the year 1980. The "1980-1 C.B." means this ruling can be found in the first volume of the 1980 "Cumulative Bulletin." The "100" at the end means it can be found on page 100 of that bulletin. You sometimes see "I.R.B." instead of "C.B." behind a revenue ruling. That means it can be found in the "Internal Revenue Bulletin" rather than the "Cumulative Bulletin."

**Letter Rulings** A letter ruling is issued to a particular taxpayer at the taxpayer's request and describes how the IRS will treat a proposed transaction. If the taxpayer carries through with the transaction exactly as described in the ruling request, the IRS is bound to abide by the ruling. If the taxpayer changes any of the facts of the transaction, the IRS is no longer obligated to follow the ruling. This is a way for your client to get an advance commitment from the IRS regarding its treatment of the tax effects of a particular transaction. Writing ruling requests is one aspect of your role as a tax consultant.

The IRS limits its letter rulings to only certain types of transactions and refuses to rule on some issues.[2] If a client wants the assurance of a letter ruling, the issue had better be pretty important. The IRS charges $5,000 for most ruling requests, but only $500 if your client's gross income is less than $150,000. And if your ruling request involves a business-related tax issue, such as home office expenses or residential rental property issues, you can get one for $500 for clients whose gross income is less than $1 million.[3]

Letter rulings used to be called private letter rulings, because they were not available to the public. Since 1976, however, they have been available to read, after all the information that could identify the taxpayer has been deleted. They are still private in another sense though. A letter ruling is a two-party contract between the IRS and the taxpayer who requested the ruling. The IRS is not obligated to treat a similar

> A letter ruling constitutes a contract between the IRS and a taxpayer regarding the treatment of a proposed transaction that is binding on the IRS if the facts are presented fairly and do not change.

transaction by another taxpayer in the same way. That means your clients cannot rely on someone else's letter ruling with certainty; they have got to get their own. With this in mind, letter rulings still provide evidence to the public of how the IRS will handle a transaction. Tax practitioners tend to use them to support their treatment of similar transactions. If enough taxpayers request rulings on the same question, the IRS will issue a revenue ruling stating its position, which can be relied on by all taxpayers.

Here is an example of the citation for a letter ruling: LTR 9824010. It is always a seven-digit number. The first two numbers indicate the year the ruling was issued, the second two indicate the week of the year the ruling was issued, and the last three numbers indicate the number among the rulings issued that week. So the letter ruling cited was issued in 1998 during the twenty-fourth week, and it was the tenth ruling issued that week.

Although the IRS makes letter rulings available to the public, it does not publish them. They can be found in private tax services, which are discussed more fully later in the chapter.

**Revenue Procedures**   Revenue procedures are issued in the same manner as revenue rulings, but they deal with different issues. They tell you about IRS practices and procedures instead of answering specific legal questions. Notice in the notes to this chapter that a revenue procedure is used to disclose the types of issues on which the IRS refuses to rule (Rev. Proc. 2000-3), and another is used to provide the rules on filing fees (Rev. Proc. 2000-1). A revenue procedure is also used to provide the annual inflation adjustments for everything in the Code that is supposed to be adjusted for inflation. These include individual tax rates, exemptions, the standard deduction, and several other things. This is useful information for doing tax planning for the current year.[4]

Revenue procedures are cited just like revenue rulings, except they begin with "Rev. Proc." rather than "Rev. Rul." They are also found in the "Internal Revenue Bulletin" (I.R.B.) and the "Cumulative Bulletin" (C.B.), for the period in which they are released.

**Example: Basic Research Using Administrative Authority** Here is an example of a Code section that has fairly simple wording. Section 61 of the Code provides a definition of *Gross Income* (the term Congress uses to define income subject to tax, before being reduced by allowable deductions). This is part of what it says:

Sec. 61. Gross Income Defined

(a) General Definition—Except as otherwise provided in this subtitle, gross income means all income from whatever source derived, including (but not limited to) the following items:

1. Compensation for services, including fees, commissions, fringe benefits, and similar items
2. Gross income derived from business
3. Gains derived from dealings in property . . .

This Code definition of Gross Income might seem understandable enough, but now let us try to apply it to an actual situation. Let's say you have a client, Ed, who is in the business of selling newspapers. Ed sold $500 worth of newspapers for cash during the year, and Ed's cost of the papers was $250. In addition, some guy came by one day on his way to work, carrying his lunch in a paper bag. He had forgotten his wallet but really wanted to buy a paper. Ed, being an astute businessman, traded the guy a newspaper for his lunch. We will assume the lunch had a value of two dollars.

What is Ed's gross income? Does it include the value of the guy's lunch? Does it include gross cash sales, or cash sales minus the cost of the papers? Here are the options. It could be: (a) $500, or (b) $502, or (c) $250, or (d) $252. The wording of Section 61 does not entirely clarify which answer is correct, does it?

This is where administrative authority comes in handy. You should first satisfy yourself that there are no definitions in the Internal Revenue Code for the terms used in Section 61. (There are not.) You should then turn to administrative authority for the answer, starting with the highest form of administrative authority—the regulations. If there were no regulations issued under Section 61, you might instead begin your search with

Sometimes Code sections are ambiguous and do not contain answers to specific questions.

After satisfying yourself that the answer is not contained in the Code, you should then turn to the highest form of administrative authority—the regulations.

the legislative committee reports that were issued when Section 61 was enacted. However, this is a very old section, and there are several interpretive regulations issued under Section 61.

Regulation Section 1.61-1 provides a general definition, and Regulation Section 1.61-3 tells what "gross income derived from business" means. Regulation Section 1.61-1 says in part:

> Gross income includes income realized in any form, whether in money, property, or services. Income may be realized, therefore, in the form of services, meals, accommodations, stock, or other property, as well as in cash.

Since the guy's lunch is property, the regulation says its value is included in Ed's gross income. That narrows down the answer to either (b) $502, or (d) $252.

Regulation Section 1.61-3 says in part:

> In a manufacturing, merchandising, or mining business, "gross income" means the total sales, less the cost of goods sold . . .

This regulation excludes the cost of sales from the term "gross income," thus giving us the correct answer to our question—$252 ($500 cash sales plus a $2 lunch less $250 for cost of papers sold). Note that the cost of sales is not a "deduction" like other normal costs of operating a business; it is an "exclusion," which is an amount that is never included in gross income in the first place.

We found some issues here that were not addressed in the Code section but were explained in the regulations. Other issues might not be discussed in the regulations but are found in revenue rulings or letter rulings. The answers provided by these documents are opinions of the IRS; *they are not the law.* Once in a while taxpayers disagree with the IRS and choose to have the courts decide who is right. The courts sometimes interpret the law differently than the regulations and rulings. That means it is important to consider judicial interpretation contained in the many volumes of opinions that have been handed down over the years.

## Judicial Authority

If you disagree with the amount of tax the IRS thinks is due from a client and you fail in your attempt to convince the IRS of its error, you should not tell the client to fork over whatever the IRS says to pay. That is what the judicial system is for—to settle disputes between the IRS and taxpayers. Sometimes the dispute relates to a *factual* issue, such as the amount a taxpayer has incurred for a business expense or the value of an art object donated to charity. Other times the argument relates to a *legal* issue, such as the proper interpretation of a particular Code section.

**Trial Courts** If a taxpayer and the IRS cannot come to some agreement during the administrative appeals process, a taxpayer has a choice of three judicial forums to begin litigation. They are the United States Tax Court, the United States Court of Federal Claims, and the United States district court for the district in which the taxpayer lives.

The U.S. Tax Court (Tax Court) is the court of choice for most taxpayers. It is a court of national jurisdiction, and it hears only tax cases. The judges are very knowledgeable in tax matters, so this court's opinions tend to be more highly regarded as precedent than decisions of the other two trial courts. Its decisions are appealable to the regional court of appeals having jurisdiction where the taxpayer lives, as will be discussed.

Tax Court decisions are divided into two categories. "Regular" decisions are published by the U.S. Government Printing Office in volumes called the *United States Tax Court Reports.* "Memorandum" decisions are not published by the government but are published by private tax publishers, such as Commerce Clearing House (CCH) and Research Institute of America (RIA), as a separate service. Memorandum decisions are just like regular decisions, but they are designated by the chief judge of the Tax Court as less precedential. This is because they either deal with factual issues or address questions that have been answered before by the Tax Court.

District courts are regional courts, and their judges hear an array of federal issues. There is at least one district court in each state, and the more populous states have more than one. Decisions from these courts are appealable to the regional court of appeals in the same manner as Tax Court decisions.

**Court of national jurisdiction:** A forum in which you can choose to litigate regardless of your place of residence.

**Courts of regional jurisdiction:** A court with authority over only those taxpayers who reside within its geographic boundaries.

The United States Court of Federal Claims (commonly called the Court of Claims) is a national court like the Tax Court. The difference is, the Court of Claims sits in Washington, D.C., while the Tax Court hears cases all over the country. This court hears most types of federal tax cases, in addition to other cases in which there is a claim against the federal government. The Court of Claims has its own appeals court; its decisions are appealable to the United States Court of Appeals for the Federal Circuit.

All federal tax cases, other than those from the Tax Court, are found in *United States Tax Cases* (*USTC*; published by CCH) and the *American Federal Tax Reporter* (*AFTR*; published by RIA). The "Citator" for each of these services provides an alphabetical index to the cases.

**Appellate Courts** The loser in the trial court, be it the taxpayer or the IRS, has the right to appeal the decision to an appellate court. A trial court decision can be appealed only to the appellate court that has jurisdiction over the case. If the trial court is the Tax Court or a district court, the case must be appealed to the regional appellate court having jurisdiction where the taxpayer lives. Cases from the Court of Claims can be appealed only to the Court of Appeals for the Federal Circuit.

With the exception of the Court of Appeals for the Federal Circuit, our federal appellate system is a territorial arrangement. It is made up of 12 courts of appeal, each having jurisdiction over a particular area of the country. For instance, if you happen to live in Texas, Louisiana, or Mississippi, you are under the jurisdiction of the Fifth Circuit Court of Appeals. If you live in Minnesota, North Dakota, South Dakota, Nebraska, Iowa, Missouri, or Arkansas, you are subject to the Eighth Circuit Court of Appeals. Each of these appellate courts is an independent jurisdiction, and they do not have to agree with one another. Consequently, a question con-

**Citator:** A reference of judicial decisions listed alphabetically, which provides the judicial history of each case and references subsequent cases that have referred to the case.

sidered by the Ninth Circuit Court of Appeals might be decided differently than the same question considered by the Second Circuit Court of Appeals. If an appellate court has issued an opinion on a particular issue, the trial courts whose decisions are appealable to that appellate court are obligated to follow the opinion. If an issue is handled differently by different circuit courts, the IRS will treat taxpayers in those jurisdictions accordingly. Taxpayers will not be treated uniformly in such cases unless the Supreme Court settles the dispute or Congress clarifies the law.

As an example, several years ago the singer Ethel Merman performed on Broadway for a little over two years in the musical *Gypsy*. During the run of the play on Broadway, Ethel lived in New York, but her permanent residence at the time was in Colorado. So she deducted her meals and lodging expenses while in New York as traveling expenses while "away from home" under the authority of Code Section 162(a). The IRS interpretation was that her tax home had become New York, so she was not away from home and her expenses were not deductible. Ethel took the issue to court in New York and, after being denied the deductions by the trial court, appealed the case to the Second Circuit Court of Appeals. The Second Circuit held that "home" means a taxpayer's permanent abode, and allowed Ethel the deductions because she was away from her home in Colorado.[5] In doing so, it created a rule that conflicted with the opinions of six other appellate courts.[6] For various reasons the government decided not to ask the Supreme Court to hear the case, so it represented a rule that applied differently to residents of the Second Circuit than to everyone else.

Our regional federal appellate court system creates a lack of certainty in tax cases, since the IRS can challenge any court ruling except one by the Supreme Court.

**Supreme Court** The U.S. Supreme Court is the only court that lays down precedent that must be followed by all of the lower courts. The IRS must also follow rulings of the Supreme Court as precedent. This single authority would clear up a lot of confusion in our tax laws except for a couple of problems.

First, the Supreme Court has complete discretion over whether it will hear a case. A party requests a hearing by Writ of Certiorari. If at least four members of the Court believe the issue is of sufficient importance to be heard by the Court, it will grant the Writ (*cert. Granted*). Most often, however, it will deny jurisdiction (*cert. Denied*). It is generally persuaded

Many tax issues are not clear cut and might have supporting authority on both sides of the question.

to hear a tax case only when there is a conflict on the issue among the appellate courts (that is, two or more appellate courts have decided the issue differently). Even then, sometimes the Supreme Court will not hear the case. Furthermore, even when the Supreme Court steps in and handles a tax case, its decision often has the effect of muddling the issues rather than clarifying them, leaving us even more confused and bewildered.

With all this in mind, you can see that often the answers to tax questions are not clear cut. Sometimes when the IRS says no, the courts say yes; or some courts say yes and other courts say no. Having an appreciation for this puts you at an advantage when dealing with the IRS. You should never submit to an IRS agent's adjustment on a client's return unless it is backed up by appropriate authoritative support. The next section tells you how to find the various sources of authority.

## WHERE TO FIND THIS STUFF

### *Free IRS Plain-Language Publications*

Many tax practitioners, especially those who specialize in providing low-end compliance services, do not even own a copy of the Internal Revenue Code. Nor do they have proprietary access to court decisions and IRS rulings. Some fulfill their tax research needs entirely with free IRS publications and instructions that accompany their tax preparation software.

The IRS offers publications written in plain, easy-to-understand language, on practically every tax topic. You can order one or more of these publications by calling the IRS at 1-800-TAX-FORM (1-800-829-3676). If you have access to TTY/TDD equipment, you can call 1-800-829-4059. The first publication you will want to ask for is Publication 910, *Guide to Free Tax Services*. It contains a list of available publications and an index of tax topics. It also describes other free tax information services. The publications take seven to 10 days to arrive by mail.

To download publications from the Internet, go to www.irs.gov. If you would like to get forms and instructions (not publications) by fax, dial 1-703-368-9694 to reach IRS Tax Fax. As an alternative to downloading files from the Internet, you can order *IRS Federal Tax Products* on CD-ROM. This CD includes over 2,000 tax products, including all of the above publications

> IRS publications are free, easy to read, and usually quite thorough, but they do not allow for creative and aggressive tax planning, because they do not describe court decisions that disagree with the IRS point of view.

and forms. It can be ordered by calling 1-800-233-6767. Also, Publication 3207, *Small Business Resource Guide*, is an interactive CD-ROM that contains information important to small businesses. It is available in mid-February. You can get one free copy by calling 1-800-829-3676.

While IRS publications contain information that is essentially complete and correct, they do not generally attribute the rules to a particular source. Therefore, when you are given a rule, you do not know if it is from the Code, regulation, IRS ruling, or court decision, and it is impossible to tell if there is an IRS slant on it. This can make research somewhat inefficient, as demonstrated by the example at the beginning of this chapter. It also does not afford sufficient precision for serious, aggressive, and creative tax planning. For that you need access to the sources of primary authority.

### Internal Revenue Code

The Internal Revenue Code is a basic element of most of the Internet and CD products to be discussed, but it is nice to have a hard copy of the Code for easy reference. It can be obtained in book form from law school and college bookstores, or it can be purchased directly from the publisher, either in book or CD form. The major publishers of the Code are CCH (800-248-3248; www.cch.com) and RIA (800-431-9025; www.riahome.com). The Code is also available in its entirety on the Internet at www.law.cornell.edu/uscode/26.

### Cases, Rulings, and Commentary

In order to obtain fast and accurate answers to your research questions, it is necessary to have a tax library with a keyword search mechanism that will find all of the relevant and up-to-date authority regarding your particular issue. Tax services by private publishers are multivolume references to Code sections that provide a keyword index to topics, commentary, and explanation. They are also updated regularly and refer you to the most recent cases and rulings affecting a particular subject.

> Tax services by private publishers have keyword indexes
> that lead you to the Code, committee reports, regulations,
> rulings, cases, and commentary on any given topic.

**Hard-Copy Tax Services Are a Thing of the Past** Only a few years ago, a tax library with a tax service and the full text of rulings and cases in book form required a start-up cost of $5,000 to $10,000. A popular tax service that is still available in book form is the *Standard Federal Tax Reporter* published by CCH. Another is the *United States Tax Reporter* by RIA. These volumes are organized by Code section and have a topical index. For each Code section you will find the law itself, regulations, selected "Committee Reports," a plain-language explanation by the publishers, and references to all the cases and rulings pertaining to that Code section. These services are available for reference in most business school and law school libraries.

In the past, in order to have direct access to the full text of court decisions and IRS rulings, it was necessary to also purchase them in book form. Both CCH and RIA reproduce federal court decisions dealing with tax issues. The cases are keyed in with citations to the tax services. Decisions of the United States Tax Court are published by the U.S. Government Printing Office, while memorandum decisions are published by CCH and RIA separately. The "Cumulative Bulletin," containing IRS rulings and announcements, is published by the government.

Since all of these volumes used to be purchased in hard copy, they took up a large amount of space. The tax services also required time-consuming filing to keep them up to date.

**Online and CD Resources** Today you can subscribe to a CD or Internet tax service for virtually no money up front and receive, for a relatively modest annual fee, all of the reference material just described. You can expand your virtual library, if you wish, with a vast array of commentary and practice aids in all specialty areas, including complete information on state tax issues. According to Douglas Fornberg, a sales representative for RIA, 90 percent of his sales are Internet based. Practitioners often still buy the Internal Revenue Code in hard copy for handy reference, according to Fornberg, even though it is available with the online service.

Following is a brief description of services from several publishers. Complete information on the products and their prices can be obtained by contacting the publishers from their Web sites. A great place to start

A CD or Internet-based tax service can provide you with a complete tax library for a modest cost.

for finding all sorts of online tax information is the "Tax and Accounting Sites Directory" at www.taxsites.com. This site, maintained by University of Northern Iowa professor Dennis Schmidt, will lead you to federal, state, and city tax resources as well as privately maintained Web sites.

### RIA
www.riatax.com
e-mail: info@riag.com
800-431-9025

RIA offers a complete line of Internet, CD, and print tax services and source documents that are as comprehensive as any in the industry. According to its brochure, which you can download from its Web site, RIA's *Checkpoint* Internet tax service is the most complete and authoritative tax research you can find. "In one centralized, integrated service, you get the entire spectrum of tax information you need: complete tax law, expert analysis, treatises, tax related news and cases, rulings, practical practice aids and more." Access to a thorough coverage of federal, state and local, and international issues is available. You can tailor your own service to your individual needs through a variety of price differentiated packages. According to Douglas Fornberg, an RIA sales representative, most tax practitioners get all the information they need for an annual cost of between $1,500 and $2,500. Call RIA to price a package that fits your needs.

### CCH
http://tax.cch.com
800-449-8114

CCH has a complete range of tax services available that are comparable to those offered by RIA. Its *TaxEssentials* is an easy-to-use Internet tax research and primary source library that provides everything you need to get fast answers to complicated tax issues. It includes the Internal Revenue Code, a vast array of administrative sources including regulations, revenue rulings, revenue procedures and letter rulings, as well as a full line of court cases. It also includes comprehensive and detailed explanations of hundreds of tax topics and issues relating to individuals, small businesses, estates and trusts, and many others. Access to the service is currently $495 per year.

CCH also offers the *CCH Internet Tax Research NetWork*, which allows you to choose from seven federal tax libraries that include CCH expert analyses and explanations as well as official source documents. Call CCH to price a package that fits your needs.

**Lexis**
www.lexis-nexis.com
e-mail: newsales@lexis-nexis.com
800-227-4908

The Lexis-Nexis Group offers databases from over 23,000 news, legal, business, and government sources, including a comprehensive tax database. Pricing plans are customized to accommodate the research needs of each firm or individual. Pricing can be based on a flat rate, hourly, or per-search contract. For specific pricing to meet your research needs, call Lexis-Nexis.

**Tax Analysts**
www.tax.org
e-mail: cservice@tax.org
800-955-3444

Tax Analysts is a not-for-profit organization that publishes tax information in print and electronic media and is dedicated to providing timely, comprehensive, and reliable information at a reasonable cost. One product offered is *OneDisc*, a Windows CD-ROM with all the basic documents that are essential for conducting tax research. According to the online literature, it features extensive linking to help you navigate easily between documents, the most advanced Folio search engine for superior search capabilities, and summaries of every document to help you understand key issues quickly. Besides all of the necessary source documents, the disc includes Tax Analysts' *Federal Tax Baedecker*—a plain-English explanation of key tax rules. The disc is currently priced at $99.95 for annual updates and $149.95 for monthly updates.

Tax Analysts also offers *TaxLibrary.com*, a Web-based tax research library offering everything available on *OneDisc* plus additional expert commentary. This service is currently available for $29.95 per month or $295.00 per year.

**BNA Tax Management Portfolios on the Web**
www.bnatax.com
800-223-7270

BNA Tax Management Portfolios are a less traditional tax service. BNA provides in-depth analysis of specific transactional issues by leading tax practitioners who are chosen for their expertise in a particular field. In addition to the detailed and comprehensive portfolios, you get completely searchable online versions of the Internal Revenue Code, the regulations, and other critical IRS documents such as revenue rulings and procedures, notices, and announcements. You will also find seamless links between the full text documents and related detailed analysis in the portfolios. BNA Portfolios are also available in print and on CD. Call BNA for information on pricing.

**Kleinrock Publishing**
www.kleinrock.com
800-890-1503

Kleinrock's *TaxExpert* is an affordable CD research product featuring in-depth explanation and analysis, a biweekly newsletter, comprehensive primary source material, and much more. You get:

✔ 19 volumes (on one CD) of expert analysis and explanation.

✔ A bi-weekly Federal Tax Bulletin.

✔ Complete, fully updated Code and regulations.

✔ A comprehensive library of 60,000 cases and rulings.

✔ IRS publications, audit guidelines, treaties, and more.

A monthly subscription is available for $395 while quarterly service is $295. Call Kleinrock Publishing for more details.

**CFS Income Tax**
www.taxtools.com
800-343-1157

CFS offers a CD with state-of-the-art research capability at an affordable price. Here are some of the features:

✔ Access to newly released documents at the CFS Web site and links to pertinent government sites.

✔ An advanced search engine that allows users to quickly search up to 15 tax database libraries at a time.

✔ The Internal Revenue Code cross-linked to regulations for easy reference.

✔ IRS regulations, including final, temporary, and proposed regulations cross-linked to the Internal Revenue Code for easy reference.

✔ IRS revenue rulings from 1990 to present.

✔ IRS revenue procedures from 1990 to present.

✔ IRS letter rulings and technical advice memos.

✔ Congressional committee reports.

✔ IRS announcements and notices.

✔ IRS penalties handbook providing instructions regarding IRS penalties.

✔ Social security information.

✔ U.S. tax treaties.

✔ Court opinions.

✔ Over 160 selected IRS publications.

✔ Circular 230, which is regulations governing practice of attorneys, CPAs, enrolled agents, enrolled actuaries, and appraisers before the IRS.

✔ Links to tax-related Web site set for all 50 states.

The CFS CD is currently priced at $99 for an annual renewal and $149 for a quarterly renewal.

These research products are used to determine the proper treatment of transactions and events for tax purposes but do not help with actually putting numbers on the tax forms. For that task, a completely different family of software is available. Tax preparation software is discussed next.

Tax research products do not help with filling out the tax forms. Tax preparation software is necessary for that task.

## WORKING WITH THE NUMBERS

When I began my career in the tax profession in the mid-1970s, practically all professionally prepared tax returns were done by hand. As you probably know from doing your own return by hand, one small mistake on a supplementary form or schedule can change all the calculations on the return and cause you to start all over again. I remember making those small mistakes on corporate returns that were two inches thick. Such were not times for small children and anyone else sensitive to expletives to be within earshot. In those days tax preparation firms reserved a large part of their budget for Wite-Out and antacid tablets.

Pioneering tax software firms were just getting started back then. But those were the days before the personal computer, and all of the input forms had to be filled out by hand and sent by mail to a processing center. It did not make the job appreciably easier. Additionally, the software tended to have numerous bugs, so detailed review of the finished forms was always advisable.

With the advent of the personal computer, tax software began an evolutionary process. Automatic calculation and recalculation of the numbers on a form or the entire return with the click of a mouse was a huge hit in the tax profession. The expedience of tax software has eliminated the need for Wite-Out, and drastically reduced budgets for antacid tablets.

The progress continues in software development. Virtually all vendors offer Windows-based programs, but you can still find DOS-based programs. The growing use of the Internet with user-friendly browsers has added a few new turns. The rapid advances in technology will soon produce conveniences in tax preparation that are beyond what we have today. The next section explains, in general terms, what you should expect from your current tax preparation software.

## Tax Software: Current Features and Capabilities

At a minimum, your software should properly calculate all the numbers on all forms and schedules that it supports or claims to support and print filing copies of those forms and schedules. I have encountered several frustrating bugs over the years in tax software, but recently vendors have been very quick to correct them. Most vendors allow updating for bugs and new features through their Web site, but some still distribute updating CDs during the filing season.

You should know what forms and schedules you anticipate using and be sure they are included in the software you choose. Data on federal forms should transfer to state forms that you choose to use. On each line of each form and schedule where a numerical amount is entered, you

Use of the Internet will likely produce greater conveniences in tax return preparation.

should be able to add supporting information, if you wish, by "drilling down" to a supporting schedule. You also should have the ability to flag a line for a recorded comment to yourself or a reviewer.

Help should be available for each line of the return at a click of the mouse, preferably in the form of official IRS instructions or, for state returns, state instructions. Some software also provides access to IRS publications. Those vendors that also market research software or maintain Web-based research databases generally provide accessibility from their tax preparation software, usually for an additional charge.

The software should include an organizer that you can print out and mail to your clients for them to record all the tax information you will need to complete their return. The following year, each client's organizer can then be customized with the information submitted the previous year. Some vendors now offer electronic organizers, to be completed by the client either online or from a file they receive by e-mail. When you receive the information back, you can load it into your software automatically, saving a great deal of input time.

Some software vendors offer electronic tax organizers that your clients can fill out with their return information, which you can then load into your tax preparation software automatically.

## Future Trends

Vendors are now beginning to offer Internet-based programs, allowing you to avoid loading software onto your computer. These programs can be instantly updated for corrections and new features and can be seamlessly integrated into a Web-based research database. You also have the option of storing all of your client data online with the vendor, pulling the information down at will for printing and revisions. Doing so allows a tax advisor to access client information from a laptop or any computer with Internet access.

The pace with which tax professionals accept this new technology will be linked to the universal availability of high-speed Internet access. Security is also a concern for some. Both of these obstacles are being conquered, however. High-speed communications—from cable to dedicated communication lines to direct satellite links—are becoming widespread and cheaper through competition. And although tax consultants remain cautious about jeopardizing the security of client tax data on the

There are large differences in prices and capabilities of tax preparation software, so shop around.

Internet, even those barriers are weakening as vendors adopt super-high-security measures.

Vendors still must account for the fact that technology is moving faster than many practitioners are able or willing to accept. That is why tax products are currently offered at both ends of the technological spectrum, from DOS-based software to Internet-based programs.

## Shopping Around

There are large differences in price among the various vendors that do not necessarily correlate with the capabilities and quality of the software. Many pricing packages are available. There are combinations of up-front charges for unlimited access to forms and per-return charges for forms that are used on a limited basis, such as foreign state forms. It pays to do extensive shopping and testing before you buy. All of the vendors allow you to test last year's version of their software at little or no charge. Some provide a demonstration on their Web site. The next section provides contact information for the vendors.

## Tax Software Vendors

Here is a list of the vendors of which I am aware, listed alphabetically by package name. To update their Web addresses and find any new vendors who come on the scene, go to Dennis Schmidt's tax directory at www.taxsites.com.

1040 Professional
Xpress Software
P.O. Box 280760
Columbia, SC 29228
800-285-1065
www.xpresssoftware.com

CrossLink Professional Tax Software
Petz Enterprises, Inc.
P.O. Box 611

Tracy, CA 95378
800-345-4337
www.petzent.com

**GoSystem Tax & GoSystem Tax RS**
RIA
395 Hudson Street
New York, NY 10014
877-467-8483
www.riahome.com

**IntelliTax SuperSystem**
Orrtax Software Inc.
13208 NE 20th Street
Bellevue, WA 98005
800-377-3337
www.orrtax.com

**Lacerte Individual 1040**
Lacerte Software Corporation
13155 Noel Road, 22nd Floor
Dallas, TX 75240
800-765-7777
www.lscsoft.com

**Package EX**
ExacTax
2301 W. Lincoln Avenue
Anaheim, CA 92801
800-583-3536
www.exactax.com

**The Professional Tax System**
TaascFORCE
6914 S. Yorktown Avenue
Tulsa, OK 74136
800-998-9990
www.taascforce.com

**ProSeries 1040**
Intuit
110 Juliad Court, Suite 107
Fredericksburg, VA 22406
800-934-1040
www.proseries.com

**ProSystem *fx* Tax 1040**
CCH Incorporated
21250 Hawthorne Boulevard
Torrance, CA 90503
800-739-9998
www.prosystemfx.com

**Saber 1040**
ATX
P.O. Box 1040
Caribou, ME 04736
800-944-8883
www.atxforms.com

**TaxACT Preparer's Edition**
2nd Story Software, Inc.
642 10th Street, Suite 202
Marion, IA 52302
800-573-4287
www.taxact.com

**TAX/PACK Professional**
Alpine Data, Inc.
737 S. Townsend Avenue
Montrose, CO 81401
800-525-1040
www.alpinedata.com

**Tax Preparer 2000**
HowardSoft
7852 Ivanhoe Avenue
La Jolla, CA 92037
858-454-0121
www.howardsoft.com

**Tax Relief 1040**
Micro Vision Software Inc.
140 Fell Court
Hauppauge, NY 11788
800-829-7354
www.mvsinc.com

**TaxSlayer Professional Tax Program**
RCS
3938 Washington Road
Martinez, GA 30907
888-420-1040
www.taxslayer.com

**Tax Solution for Windows & DOS**
Drake Software
235 East Palmer Street
Franklin, NC 28734
800-890-9500
www.drakesoftware.com

**TaxWise**
Universal Tax Systems, Inc.
6 Mathis Drive NW
Rome, GA 30165
800-755-9473
www.taxwise.com

**Taxworks 1040**
Laser Systems
350 North 400 West
Kaysville, UT 84037
800-230-2322
www.taxworks.com

**UltraTax**
Creative Solutions
7322 Newman Boulevard
Dexter, MI 48130
800-968-8900
www.creativesolutions.com

# Chapter 8

# Starting and Running a Part-Time Web-Based Tax Service

*Get ready, tax accountants, practically every aspect of the tax preparation field is changing. In fact, it's evolving into a totally new market and business.*

—Stanley Zarowin

In this chapter I describe my brief journey into the world of e-business. I do not profess to be an expert in this area, as my ride has only recently begun. I believe, however, that I have valuable advice to share. We all have a lot to learn, clinging tightly to the rails as technology steams all ahead full. As in the tax business, the ever-changing world of the Internet provides an environment for constantly updating our knowledge.

The experience has been fun so far and even exciting at times. It is kind of like being a modern-day pioneer. Think of being there during the great age of invention 100 years ago or so. Think of the tremendous opportunities that resulted, the huge industries that were born, the fortunes that were made, and the vast changes that took place. Welcome to the frontier days of cyberspace.

## MY MOTIVATION

I will begin with the basic motive for my venture, which, you may be disappointed to learn, is probably not the same as yours. However, divergent motives can arrive at the same end, so bear with me.

I have never considered starting a full-time tax practice for a couple of reasons. First, as a full-time instructor, it would necessitate a drastic reduction in my teaching schedule. That would mean a renegotiated contract with my employer and a significantly smaller salary. It would also require start-up costs, a great deal of hard work, and a reduced standard of living for the first few years while building my practice. Being quite risk averse and comfortable in my financial situation, these were not costs I was willing to incur at this stage of my career.

Second, I am a full-time instructor who likes his job. I left public accounting nearly 20 years ago because I wanted to teach and have been enjoying doing so ever since. I enjoy the lifestyle, the prestige, and the intellectual challenge. Those benefits are more important to me than the extra income I could make in public practice.

Having said that, I must also profess an entrepreneurial bent. I am like millions of others who want the simple safety of a steady job but who also yearn for the adventure and freedom of a business of their own. I have, therefore, always been on the lookout for opportunities, even though fully engaged in other fulfilling activities.

I ruled out the possibility of a traditional part-time tax practice early on for several reasons. First, I wanted the opportunity to conduct business around my own schedule. I wanted the ability to work when it was most convenient for me rather than when it was most convenient for clients. I wanted the option of working at 5:00 A.M. or at midnight, when the mood hit. This, I thought, was not possible to do with a tax practice. Yes, the work of return preparation and research can be done at any hour. But to successfully develop a traditional practice, it is necessary to be at the command of clients for consulting sessions and emergency situations.

I also wanted the ability to work out of my home office. My office at the university is unacceptable for conducting private business; and I was

I have never considered a full-time tax practice but have always been on the lookout for business opportunities.

> I wanted the perfect home-based business, and there was never a compulsion to pursue anything less than the ideal.

unwilling, at least in the early stages, to invest in outside office space. The convenience of my home office appeals to me. However, I thought about the prospect of opening my home to clients. I concluded that I wanted a more concrete barrier between the time spent with clients and the time set apart for course preparation, writing, and family activities. The bottom line was that I could see a tax business becoming more intrusive into my other activities than desired.

Having rejected the notion of a traditional tax practice, I was looking for the perfect home-based, part-time business, one in which I could choose my own hours to work and in which I was not required to meet with clients or conform to the demands of their schedules. One that made use of my background, knowledge, and talents. One that offered high prestige, was fun, and paid very well. Oh, yes—I was willing to spend plenty of time but not much capital to get started. Since I was fully satisfied with my current work, there was never a compulsion to pursue anything less than the ideal.

## INSPIRATION

What began as a purely voluntary activity on campus became the inspiration for my Web-based tax practice. As a tax professor at the University of Minnesota, I was approached several years ago by some advisors in the International Student Services Office. Their desire was for me to form a voluntary tax service for their international students, who are generally classified as nonresident aliens for tax purposes. At the time, I was unaware of the large number of international students we had on campus and that they were required to file a special tax return.

I eventually made contact with the Taxpayer Education Office of the IRS and worked with them to start a voluntary income tax assistance (VITA) site at the University of Minnesota for the benefit of international visitors. IRS personnel trained me and a few of my students in preparing nonresident alien returns that first year. Together with Accountability Minnesota, a nonprofit group of volunteer accountants, we began filling out tax returns for the international students and scholars on campus.

## Discovering a Demand for Nonresident Alien Tax Services

I was not truly cognizant of the need that existed for our services until we were literally overwhelmed that first year by clients. Each year the demand has grown with the ever-increasing number of international students and scholars who visit the University of Minnesota. Last year the volunteers at our VITA site prepared returns for nearly 800 taxpayers, generating tax refunds totaling about $500,000. This was accomplished by a group of between 10 and 12 volunteers working one night each week for three hours.

Adding to the demand for free help is the fact that practioners have avoided the area of the taxation of nonresident aliens like the Black Death. It is a very specialized area, with rules that do not apply to the general population of taxpayers. Tax practitioners do not see a sufficient client base of aliens to warrant educating themselves on the intricacies of the nonresident alien return.

Additionally, although the same rules apply to visiting researchers, professors, and other highly paid employees, most international visitors on campus are low-income students. This is not generally the type of client on which a tax professional chooses to focus.

We were, therefore, compelled to allow high-income nonresident aliens to use our VITA service, which is designed for low-income taxpayers. About the only alternative for them was to wander away and to try to figure out their return for themselves. We were so overburdened at the VITA site that such was the fate of a number. We could only do our best with the resources at hand.

As I became familiar with the rules for nonresident alien returns, I took over the training for our volunteers. I began to receive e-mail from international students and scholars throughout the year who were soliciting tax advice. I also began to get calls from payroll personnel at other colleges and universities seeking advice on withholding for nonresident aliens. In order to cut down on this intrusion into my time and to take some of the pressure off our VITA site, I decided it was time to disseminate some free information over the Web.

I discovered the huge demand for tax services by international students and scholars and that practitioners tend to avoid nonresident alien returns.

In order to reduce the intrusion on my time and to take pressure off our VITA site, I developed a Web site with free tax information for nonresident aliens.

I had begun using the Internet a few months earlier to provide course information for my students. I had taught myself how to design a crude Web page and to publish it. The University of Minnesota provides free Web space for faculty and students, as long as the site is not used for commercial gain. The Internet, I thought, would be a great way to provide basic tax information to nonresident aliens. This would allow many of them, who had simple returns, to complete them on their own. Consequently, they would be less dependent on our VITA site and would no longer need to contact me directly.

### Discovering the Utility of the Internet

It was 1997 when I first launched my Web site. I used Netscape Composer for this, which is now part of the Netscape Communicator browser. It can be downloaded for free from Netscape at www.netscape.com. I used the Netscape Help tutorial to learn how to create basic Web pages, how to format paragraphs and change the style of text. I learned about color and font, how to add lines, tables, images and links, and so on. You do not have to be very smart to do this, and it is not necessary to know HTML coding. I later purchased Microsoft's FrontPage 97 (now FrontPage 2000), which is a Web page creation program that offers features and capabilities more advanced than Netscape.

In order to spice up the site a bit, I taught myself how to manufacture some graphical headings, using Paint Shop Pro (www.jasc.com) for the graphics. A lot of graphics programs out there work well. In fact, Image Composer is the graphics program that comes packaged with FrontPage 2000. However, I like the functionality of Paint Shop Pro.

I bought a book that demonstrates many of the creative things you can do with Paint Shop Pro, *Creating Your Own Web Graphics with Paint Shop Pro.*[1] This book is out of print, but over a dozen Paint Shop Pro tutorial books show you neat things to do with the program. I also bought a book on Web page design (*Looking Good Online*[2]), which was very helpful for planning the navigation system and making the site user friendly. This book is out of print now, also, but numerous similar books are available. There is also a lot of online help available. For ex-

You can get Web page design tips at www.webreview.com and a free traffic tracker at www.extreme-dm.com.

ample, www.webreview.com is one of many places to go for tips on Web site design.

I signed up for a free tracker, which gave me a report of all of my visitors and where they came from, whenever I wanted it. A lot of trackers are available on the Web. For a list, go to http://server4.hypermart.net/freetrek/counterstrackers.htm. The one I used was Extreme Tracking (www.extreme-dm.com). I submitted my site to a few of the big search engines and made sure the people at the International Student Services office at the university knew about it. I was off and running.

In a couple of months, after my site had a chance to work its way into one or two of the major search engine directories, I began to get a few visitors, not just from the University of Minnesota but from all parts of the globe. It was fun to see that I was getting hits from Eastern Europe, Asia, and Australia, as well as Minneapolis. Soon other colleges and universities began to establish links to my site, through their payroll department Web sites, as a service to their own international students. I could trace the links with my Extreme Tracking tracker. The traffic to my site began to increase gradually with these links, but visitors still only numbered about 20 per day.

My motive of decreasing my e-mail from desperate international visitors backfired. E-mail inquiries about tax advice increased because international visitors (and those contemplating a visit) worldwide had access to my e-mail address through my Web site. Because basic tax information was available at the site, the questions became more sophisticated and detailed from people with more complex tax situations. Many of these were highly paid researchers, visiting professors, and workers on temporary visas who could not find help from local tax practitioners.

It was then that I began to contemplate the income potential of my volunteer venture. I was becoming overwhelmed by people who were desperate for tax advice and who could afford to pay for it. It was tax advice that I could dispense through e-mail according to my own schedule. I could just as easily prepare tax returns for these people, communicating

E-mail inquiries increased as traffic on my Web site picked up.

with them through e-mail and mailing them the return when completed. I would not have to interrupt my teaching schedule for this and would not have to maintain an office to meet with clients. Such a venture had all of the qualities of the part-time business I sought. *Was I nuts?* I had to get to work on a business plan.

## BUSINESS CONCEPT

A couple of key tasks should be performed before beginning a business, online or otherwise. First, a business idea—preferably a brilliant one— should be conceived. Next, research should be performed to see if anyone else has thought of the same or a similar idea and is employing it. If anyone is currently utilizing the idea in business, the perceived strengths and weaknesses of their operation should be studied. Can their methods be improved on? If not, are there enough potential clients to warrant entry into the market anyway? Only after I answered these questions would I be ready to contemplate and plan a detailed business strategy.

### My Idea

My brilliant idea, of course, was to offer online tax preparation services to international visitors who come to the United States on a temporary basis for work or study. Why was this idea so brilliant? The primary reason was that these are taxpayers who are being ignored by the vast majority of tax practitioners. In fact, I know of only a couple of firms in the Twin Cities area that have people willing to prepare nonresident alien returns and none that have special expertise in the particularly complex tax needs of international students and scholars. Additionally, these particular members of the taxpaying population are highly educated. They tend to have Internet savvy, and most have Internet access through their college, university, research institution, or employer.

English is typically a second language for them, and most can write in English better than they can speak it. The ability to communicate effectively in writing might be less intimidating for them. Many of them probably prefer the use of e-mail to engage and communicate with a tax

An online tax preparation service for international visitors had the qualities I was looking for in a part-time business.

consultant over using the phone or making a personal visit. For me, e-mail offers freedom from the phone and from a set schedule and normal business hours—just what I was looking for in a part-time business.

## Is My Target Niche Too Narrow?

The combination of the above factors makes international visitors ideal online customers, particularly for tax services, but they are a very small segment of the taxpaying population. Am I trying to focus on a market segment that is simply too small to support a business? Even before my survey of online tax services revealed virtually no competition, I concluded that there are plenty of potential clients to be served.

This year there are more than 4,000 international visitors on the University of Minnesota campus alone, according to its International Student Services Office. Nationally, there are nearly 500,000 international student visitors this year and another 200,000 or so visiting professors and researchers. There are also around 100,000 nonacademic temporary workers admitted to the United States on H-1b visas each year. Adding to this number are visitors on temporary business visas and temporary workers from Canada who can enter the United States without a visa. That brings the total of international visitors who are likely to be required to file a tax return to over 1 million.

Unlike residents of the United States, who must file a return only if their income is greater than a certain amount, all nonresident alien students and scholars must file a return if they have *any* income subject to tax. Additionally, the return they must file is so specialized that local tax services that cater to low- and medium-income taxpayers do not have the expertise to deal with it. I presumed, and subsequently verified through my online survey, that online preparers who offer their services to the general public are in the same situation.

## Why Such a Narrow Market Focus?

The Internet has broken down the traditional barriers to price competition, creating a vast, virtual auction house for products and services. It attracts shoppers of goods and services who are motivated by price. In the tax services market, this group tends to be low- and middle-income

My target niche includes about 1 million potential clients.

individuals. It is less likely that high-income individuals and businesses will surf the Web to look for a tax advisor, unless they are searching for a local consultant with whom they can establish personal contact. For these taxpayers, quality of service, expertise, and ready availability usually take precedence over price. My survey of online tax preparers confirmed that the target market for online firms is low- and middle-income individual taxpayers who have common and uncomplicated tax situations. My primary goal in entering the online market is to avoid a price war with more highly capitalized, general service competitors who service this market.

The virtual marketplace makes specialization the key to success. Even high-income taxpayers with unique tax situations will turn to the Web if they cannot find the expertise they desire among local practitioners. The advantage gained by online tax services that focus on niche markets is the same as in a traditional practice. However, with an online tax service the niche can be much more specialized because the market is not limited to the immediate geographic area. It is somewhat akin to the advantage international CPA firms have had over local shops. The client of an international firm can find tax expertise in virtually any field among the vast resources the firm has to offer. The downside, of course, is that the client must pay for that luxury while taking advantage of only a small segment of services available. If a client finds an independent practitioner who can offer as much expertise in a given field at a much lower fee, the independent practitioner will gain the advantage. The cheap global marketing provided by the Internet now permits clients to seek out independent experts online, regardless of their physical location.

On the other hand, it appears that the lower-end, mass-market practitioners are adversely affected by the Internet. The scramble for market share is causing heated and visible price competition among Web-based tax practitioners, which is pulling clients from traditional tax service providers. The bottom line is that a properly conceived and operated niche tax service will survive and prosper on the Internet, while a mass-market tax service must bear the brunt of intense price competition.

A tax practitioner servicing a niche market over the Internet gains a competitive advantage, while a general Web-based practitioner must overcome extreme price competition.

## Survey of Online Tax Preparers

According to an article written for CNET's News.com,[3] some 33.6 million U.S. taxpayers were expected to file online last year, with that number increasing at about 9 percent per year for the next five years. This is a surprisingly large segment of the taxpaying population, considering the fact that 50 percent of American households are not even connected to the Internet yet. That unconnected 50 percent is made up primarily of low- and middle-income households, which is the same group that online tax preparers focus upon. Think of how huge this market will become in the next few years when an Internet connection will become as commonplace as a car in the driveway.

I discovered ulterior motives contributing to the price wars among the larger firms. For some, the main purpose is not to make a profit from their online tax preparation services but to acquire clients for other services, such as financial planning, mortgage or refund anticipation loans, and live tax help. Smaller firms that promise not to sell client data or to solicit clients for other products or services could gain an edge. Such a privacy guarantee could be a highly visible selling feature, permitting a less competitive fee schedule.

As mentioned, of all the online tax preparation sites that I reviewed, I found none that offer services to nonresident aliens. For the benefit of you who wish to enter into the online tax preparation business, following is a sampling of what is currently out there.

> None of the online tax preparation sites that I reviewed offer tax services to nonresident alien individuals.

**Filing on the Cheap** Beginning with the ultra-cheap and even free do-it-yourself services, there is www.hrblock.com, www.turbotax.com, and www.hdvest.com, among others. At the H&R Block site, you can do your taxes online for $9.95, which includes electronic filing and printing of your return. Your state return is just $4.95, including free electronic filing. You can get an electronic refund advance of up to $5,000, which is actually a high-interest loan. The site also offers a mortgage center and an investment center as well as directions to the nearest H&R Block office if you get frustrated trying to fill out your own return.

The TurboTax site offers pretty much the same deal, with a bonus of free filing if your adjusted gross income is less than $20,000. TurboTax is owned by Intuit, which also sells the Quicken line of financial software. This is featured on its site, along with investment, mortgage, insurance, and banking services.

At the H. D. Vest site you get an even better deal. H. D. Vest is a financial services firm that lets you use its online tax software for free, regardless of your income level. You can then electronically file your return from this site for free. For this you become a willing prospect for its financial services and end up getting bugged incessantly by phone calls for the rest of your life.

**Professionally Prepared Returns** Some of the popular sites where a professional completes your return for you are e1040.com, Taxes4Less.com, Taxlogic.com, and Taxattack.com. The e1040.com site is run by Gilman & Ciocia, a tax preparation and financial planning company with offices in 17 states. It combines the convenience of Web data entry with the benefit of a live tax preparer. You fill in a questionnaire on the site that is immediately sent to a live preparer. The preparer, it is promised, will contact you within 20 minutes (during business hours) with any follow-up questions and then complete your return. The fee starts at $49.95 for a Form 1040. With the cost of electronic filing and a state return, the typical charge is around $85. This is comparable, if not cheaper, than walking into an H&R Block or Jackson Hewitt office. Gilman & Ciocia admittedly views its online tax service as a feed for its financial planning services.

At Taxes4Less.com, the primary focus is actually the provision of tax preparation services rather than attracting prospects for other services. However, the site does not promise to keep visitor data confidential, so you should not be surprised to find your name on a few mailing lists after having your tax return prepared. The procedure is basically the same as at e1040.com. You fill out an online questionnaire, at which point you see a detailed invoice showing the exact fee for your tax preparation services. A tax preparer will later call you to go over your information. Your return is reviewed and signed by a CPA before being returned to you within 36 hours. Prices start at around $35 for federal returns and $15 for state returns, with the addition of extra charges for supplemental forms and schedules.

At Taxlogic.com, the focus is on higher-end taxpayers. This site also relies on an online interview process and promises a professionally prepared return in about 48 hours with free electronic filing. The fee structure is simple. The cost is $75 for a federal individual return, $75 additional if you are self-employed, and $75 additional if you have rental income. State returns are $25 when accompanied by a federal return.

Taxattack.com is run by a New York–based CPA firm and also aims at the higher-end market. It also provides an online questionnaire and promises a phone call within 24 hours. Its fees average between $75 and $150.

These sites are a sampling of Internet tax help providers but probably account for the majority of tax returns prepared through online services. The sites offering professional tax help are similar in their procedures and have comparable fee structures. Those that offer a broader range of services tend to fall in the lower end of the price range. This accounts for the residual benefits they receive from their tax traffic.

**Who Is Filling the Niches?** All of the preceding sites compete in generally the same market—tax returns for resident individuals who are low-to middle-income taxpayers. This means large advertising budgets to maintain or increase market share. The only niche online tax preparer I found, other than myself, was www.clergytaxnet.com. Its specialty is pretty obvious from its name. Clerics are a good niche market because they are subject to special rules for both income tax and social security tax purposes.

This site provides an example of how a niche can expand. In addition to clergy tax preparation, it offers a tax newsletter for the clergy, a clergy tax law research center, mortgage loans for parsonage financing, a reference guide on clergy salary arrangements, and tax consulting packages for clergy members and church organizations.

This site has virtually no online competition, and its fee schedule, or lack thereof, appears to reflect that. Here is how the site literature explains its fees:

> There are no fee schedules common to this profession. Fees are based on time required to perform services, the type of services required, and the level of expertise and the complexity of the work. Different types of services command different rates because of the expertise level of the people who perform them. We can provide an estimate of any of our tax services. Cost is always an important factor to consider in addition to the value of the service.

This is typical of a high-end or specialized tax practice. Its tax organizer, which is what taxpayers must fill out to have their return prepared, costs $39 just to download or fill out online. This amount is subtracted from a client's fee if the organizer is sent in. Absent is any

Tax practitioners have barely begun to exploit niche markets over the Internet.

concern about charging more than the competition—a nice luxury when you are the only game in cyberspace. Of course, this site gets only a fraction of the traffic that the large general practitioner sites get, but it is a model for an independent tax consultant who does not want more traffic than is manageable.

## SUCCESS IS IN THE DETAILS

After my research, I was convinced that my business idea was sound and that I should proceed with the plan. I knew that the successful principles of engagement for a Web-based business owner are no different from what they have been for businesses throughout the ages. Sincere, honest, and trustworthy service and a money-back guarantee have always worked well.

But I could not present a smile and a handshake to a client in the brand-new business environment of cyberspace, nor could I establish the personal trust and confidence that come through tangible interaction. The technology that would make my business possible would produce impersonal clients—more demanding, more skeptical, and less trusting. They would be intolerant of small errors. They would be won over only by systematically efficient treatment, from their initial contact, throughout the return preparation process and receipt of their return, to follow-up questions and concerns. It would take great attention to detail. This, along with professional courtesy, would bring them back next year.

### Site Content and Design

A Web site visitor can be spookier than a brook trout, so keeping visitors around long enough to transform them into clients is a very delicate affair. Slow-loading pages and images, a poor color scheme, or inefficient navigation buttons can cause a visitor to dart off to another site.

First impressions are important, not only when meeting someone in person but also when introducing yourself and your business over the Internet. I knew that my site design would not only reflect my taste in color and style; to visitors, it would also reflect my intelligence and

A well-planned site that is easy to navigate with plenty of free, useful information will attract and hold visitors.

professional competence. For example, when you see typos, broken links, and confusing text on a Web site, what is your opinion of the author? If this person cannot even communicate effectively on a published Web page, is he or she someone with whom you would really want to do business?

My survey of online tax preparers revealed several ways to engage the client effectively with a variety of unique Web site designs. Most of the sites that I visited were quick to load, well laid out, and easy to navigate, and featured professionally designed graphics.

An additional element to consider was what it takes to prompt visitors to stop by in the first place, without any advertising or promotion. I was fortunate to have discovered through my informational site that free and useful information will attract visitors. I determined that the more useful information I could provide free of charge, the more potential clients I could attract.

**Bare Essentials** With this in mind, I took great pains to plan the transformation of my site from one that was purely informational to a proprietary virtual office. I pondered over how to lay the site out and the contents of each page. Following are the objectives that I wanted to achieve:

- ✔ The site must be loaded with information that potential clients need and want.
- ✔ The site must convey a professional image and be visually appealing.
- ✔ All pages and images must be fast loading in any Web browser.
- ✔ The site must be easy to read and understand.
- ✔ The tax services that I offer must be clearly and fully presented.
- ✔ The site must provide potential clients with the easiest and most convenient means to initiate an engagement.
- ✔ The site must be easy to navigate through, using any Web browser.
- ✔ The site must be error free, with no broken links, misspellings, or inaccurate information.

If you intend to start a business online, read *The Unofficial Guide to Starting a Business Online* before you begin.

These should be fundamental objectives for any Web-based tax practitioner. It is also fundamental that you learn, at least in general terms, the basics of Web site design and the business capabilities that the Internet currently has to offer. A good book on this is *The Unofficial Guide to Starting a Business Online.*[4] Read this book from cover to cover. If you decide to tackle the job on your own, it also contains some good resources to get you started.

**Keeping Pace with Trends and Technology** I mentioned previously that I used Microsoft's FrontPage 2000 to design my informational site. This software is easy to use and does not require you to learn a programming language. In fact, if you use Microsoft Office 2000 Premium—the Microsoft suite that includes Word, Excel, Publisher, and PowerPoint—you can publish Web pages in any of these applications with a few clicks of the mouse.

FrontPage 2000 offers templates for a variety of complete site designs with navigational buttons in place. These templates can be customized as much or as little as you desire. I opted not to take advantage of a template and to design my site from the ground up, simply because I was not enthralled with any of the template designs.

I have spent countless hours in preparing my site, from designing images to arranging content and planning the navigational structure. Today I have substantially achieved my goals on my site at www.thetaxguy.com. (Depending on when you read this, you may be viewing the old version or the new and improved one.) I have had compliments from visitors, primarily regarding my site content and ease of navigation.

I am concerned, however, that the site is not keeping pace with technology and what is considered "modern." In the early days of the Internet, the site would have been impressive; now it is merely functional. I am, after all, an amateur in Web design, and I believe my site reflects this. Many of today's Web visitors who perceive a site to be amateurish will leave and not consider doing business there.

Technology and the current Web fashion trends are moving at a speedy pace. The use of "splash screens" is popular now. For example, take a look at the site of the Big Five accounting firm of Arthur Ander-

In order to keep up with current trends and techniques, seek professional assistance for your Web site design and development or use a managed site.

sen at www.arthurandersen.com. If your computer is equipped for it, you will see a slick display of moving images and hear people talking in different languages before the home page is loaded. In the coming years, moving videos will become more functional and popular. Web site developers must be prepared to keep up with such trends by either continually updating their technical ability or employing professional help.

Although I have attempted to start and run my part-time tax practice as self-sufficiently and parsimoniously as possible, I have concluded that it is time to hire a professional Web site developer. I believe this to be the most economical path in the long run. I would recommend that anyone beginning a Web-based business today who is not a certified "geek" should either seek professional assistance for Web site design and development, or go with a managed site featuring standard packaged designs. Surf the Web and find sites that you like. Often the Web developer's credentials are listed. If they are not, e-mail the Webmaster, compliment the looks of the site, and inquire about the designer.

An alternative to hiring a developer is to find a ready designed and managed site. A feature that CCH offers is Execusite, which is a completely designed and functioning Web site for the small practitioner. It offers a dozen different designs that you can choose from and customize on your own. An Execusite package includes:

✔ A deluxe multipage Web site that creates a prestigious firm identity.

✔ CCH premium content, plain-language federal and state tax alerts that enhance your professional image.

✔ An interactive calendar that alerts clients to federal and state tax due dates.

✔ Your own unique Internet address.

✔ Free Web site hosting.

✔ Complete control of style and content.

✔ An online newsletter with informative articles.

✔ Interactive financial calculators and tools of interest to visitors.

✔ A firm contact page with address, phone numbers, and multiple e-mail links.

✔ Free search engine registration.

To find out more about Execusite, including its cost, visit the CCH Web site at www.tax.cch.execusite.

AccountantsWorld at www.accountantsworld.com also offers managed sites exclusively to accountants and tax practitioners. It too has several attractive layouts to choose from. Its package is free for the first year, then $50 per month thereafter.

Two sources of managed sites for tax practitioners are www.tax.cch.execusite and www.accountantsworld.com.

### *Choosing and Registering a Domain Name*

A domain name is the identity of your business on the Internet's World Wide Web. It should be easy to remember, easy to spell, and have a pleasing sound. It is a bonus if you make it clever and creative. The one I chose is thetaxguy.com.

Network Solutions, Inc. (www.networksolutions.com) had a monopoly on domain name registrations until it lost its government contract in 2000. Now more than 50 companies compete to register addresses, both new and old. You do not need a Web site in order to choose and reserve a domain name for future use. You can go to www.networksolutions.com, or one of the competing sites, to check to see if the one you want is available. If it is you can register it for $35 for immediate use. It costs a little more to "park" it for future use at Network Solutions. Some of the competing companies charge less.

There is also a secondary market in Web addresses, particularly those ending in ".com." Prices are soaring for the best generic and catchy domain names. Early in 2000 several domain names sold for astronomical amounts—business.com for $7.5 million, loans.com for $3 million, and beauty.com for $1 million.[5] Great Domains (www.greatdomains.com) is the major reseller and has over 1 million domain names for resale on its site. Another leading reseller is www.afternic.com, which has over 250,000.

A typical domain name, also called a uniform resource locator

(URL), looks like this: http://www.yourdomainname.com. There are three parts to it. The first part (http://www) is the part used by Web browsers to find pages on the World Wide Web. The second part (between the dots) is the part that you get to choose. The third part is the extension (for example, .com, .net, .edu, .gov, or .org). All Web site addresses end with some type of an extension. The common extension .com is used by commercial businesses and personal home pages. However, new extensions are being created, now that the Web has become an extremely busy place.

Web surfers locate a Web address by using a domain name. However, a string of numbers called the Internet Protocol (IP) is the actual address of your site, telling computers where your site can be found on the Internet. For example, the IP address for www.thetaxguy.com is 209.35.45.91. Typing in this IP address will also get you to my Web site.

As you begin to contemplate the perfect name for your online business, consider the following:

- ✔ You can use only letters, numbers, the hyphen, and the underscore in your domain name. Other punctuation marks and spaces are not allowed.

- ✔ Your name can be as long as 26 characters, but this includes the extension at the end.

- ✔ The domain name you choose must be unique and cannot already be registered by someone else. Domain names are not case sensitive, so capitalizing letters of a chosen name does not create a new name.

If you are considering an online business, even in the distant future, think about registering and parking a domain name now. Having a short, clever, easy-to-remember domain name that identifies your business can be a huge asset. A search of available .com domain names involving taxation at www.networksolutions.com will reveal that all of the really good ones have already been snapped up. The domain name www.irs.com, for example, was one that went early. Visitors think they are looking up the Internal Revenue Service with this name, so the site

Even if you are not planning on starting a business right away, try to find a clever domain name and park it for future use.

attracts thousands of visitors a day with no promotion whatsoever. To find out more about domain names, read the *Unofficial Guide to Starting a Business Online*.

### Choosing an Internet Service Provider

An Internet service provider (ISP) is your business's door to the Internet. Once you create your Web pages and choose a domain name, you must contract with an ISP to host your site on the Internet. To do this, all of your Web pages, images, and related files are uploaded to the ISP's server computer, where they will be made available to everyone with Web access.

Shopping for an ISP is something like searching for a remodeling contractor. There seem to be large differences in features and options and even larger variances in prices, which do not necessarily correlate with the features and options. Since I was using FrontPage 2000, I wanted to make sure the ISP offered FrontPage extensions and was otherwise compatible. Many of them, I found, were not.

The process I used to find a reliable ISP began with a look in the Yellow Pages. That is where I found the listing of local ISPs that cater to companies located in the Twin Cities and the surrounding areas. I was told that local ISPs might charge more than a national ISP but at the same time provide much more personalized service. However, I failed to find one that had someone live answering the telephone, and I received no responses to the messages I left. At that point I decided that perhaps the information I got was wrong, and it would be better to go national. Besides finding someone who would answer the phone, I also wanted to make sure the company was well established enough to be around for a while.

I did a Web search using "ISP" and "Web Hosting" and came up with a bunch of companies. I finally settled on Interland at www.interland.com (800-214-1460). This company provides FrontPage support, unlimited e-mail accounts, technical support available all the time, and all the space I needed for under $20 per month. If my traffic increases or I decide to do business directly online, I can always upgrade.

Shop around to find the ISP that will give you the best Web hosting deal. Do a Web search using "ISP" or "Web Hosting."

## Choosing How to Get Paid

I considered payment methods before going any further. This is actually something you should consider before choosing a plan at an ISP, in case you want the ability to process credit cards on your site. I thought about the hassle of trying to collect money by cash or check after having mailed the tax return to the client. Asking for payment for the service before mailing the tax return would probably discourage a large percentage of prospective users. Some of the online services use this method, but I wanted to make it as easy as possible for a client to do business with a stranger in cyberspace.

A typical arrangement in a traditional low-end tax practice is for the client to come to the preparer's office, review the return, and pay for it before leaving. More sophisticated tax work, such as planning and compliance performed by CPAs and attorneys, is generally billed to the client. In such cases, the practitioner has an ongoing relationship with the client, who lives or works in the same geographic area.

In the case of an online tax service, there would not be much compulsion for a client who lives on the other side of the world to send me a check once the tax return was in hand. Although most of them would, I thought bad accounts would be unacceptably high.

**Necessity of Accepting Credit Cards** I knew that to do business online, I could not deal with payments made by cash or check, and that the easiest way to accept payments would be by credit card. This would also be the most convenient method for the clients as long as they possessed a credit card. I was not sure whether international visitors tend to carry credit cards, so I distributed a small informal survey to the users of our VITA site. I asked them a few questions about the quality of their service, how much they considered the service to be worth, whether they would consider using an online tax service if our free service was not available, and whether they carried a credit card. I was pleased to discover that practically all of our visitors, even the low-income students, owned a credit card.

**Setting Up a Merchant Account** A merchant account for accepting credit cards can be obtained through a bank, financial institution, or independent service organization. There are several options for processing charges, and fee schedules vary widely. Obtaining the ability to accept credit cards through your Web site with real-time and automated processing is more costly than manual processing, so you must determine your ideal means of processing before you shop.

I did not need or desire the ability to process cards through my Web site. I did want the ability to authorize a charge before I started working on a tax return so I knew the client's account was good. I would then charge the card after the client had received the tax return and was satisfied with the work. I found that not all merchant services will offer this feature.

In evaluating merchant services firms, it is necessary to pay close attention not only to the fees but how quickly the funds will be available to you after the sale and what the steps are for processing transactions. Some plans require you to lease or purchase equipment, while others require you to purchase special software.

I contacted my bank to see if it offered merchant accounts, but its fees were unacceptably high. This is probably typical for a start-up business operating primarily on the Internet. I then did a Web search using "merchant account." This produced several dozen institutions offering credit card services. After all the searching, I finally found a local merchant services firm through the Yellow Pages that provided what I wanted at the best fees I could find. There was an application fee of about $700. There is also an ongoing monthly fee of $10 to maintain my merchant account, and a transaction fee of 2.5 percent or more of each sale, depending on the credit card the client uses. I also had to buy special software for processing the transactions. I chose this over buying or leasing an authorization terminal.

Accepting virtual checks is an optional supplement to credit cards. This is a system by which you can print client checks on your computer, and cash them as any other checks. Check out www.virtualpaymentsystems.com for information on this service.

> Accepting credit cards is the most efficient way to do business over the Internet.

## Determining the Fee Schedule

Now that I had figured out *how* to get paid, I had to decide how *much* to get paid. For most practitioners, this is a question of comparing their qualifications and services with those of their competitors, determining the market for their services on an hourly basis, and charging accordingly. For firms doing business over the Internet, however, simply quoting an hourly rate is not a viable option. A primary motive for tax-

> Potential clients who seek tax services over the Internet
> want to compare fees quickly and conveniently, so
> competition dictates having a stated fee schedule.

payers to seek tax services over the Internet is their ability to quickly and conveniently compare fees offered by competing firms. That is why all of the firms I surveyed that offer general tax services clearly state their fee schedule or promise to quote an exact fee prior to performing the service.

Even if a fee schedule is based on a stated dollar amount for each form and schedule required, an average hourly target rate must still be the goal. For example, in order to price Schedule A, the form for itemized deductions, you must estimate the average time it will take to complete Schedule A for all of your clients who require it. If you determine the average time to be 15 minutes, and if your target hourly rate is $100 per hour, your stated rate for Schedule A must be $25.

Some practitioners charge a low base fee for the basic Form 1040 and premium amounts for supplemental forms and schedules. Other practitioners charge a higher flat fee, which includes supplemental forms and schedules. It generally takes several years of experience to determine the fee schedule that works best and results in adequate compensation. If you are starting an online tax practice, it might be best to mimic the fee schedule of an experienced competitor initially.

In my case, I had no competitors and was uncertain of the market for my services, so I based my flat-fee structure on what I thought would earn me about $150 per hour. My fee structure is simple, but I reserve the option of increasing the fee once I have reviewed the information from clients. All clients, however, are provided an exact fee before I commence work, and I give them the option of having their material returned to them if the fee is not acceptable to them.

Being inexperienced in the amount of time it would take to process and package the tax returns for mailing, I underestimated the time requirements. Next filing season I will make appropriate adjustments.

> It may take several years to arrive at the appropriate fee
> schedule.

## Processing Tax Returns

Processing tax returns constitutes the bulk of a tax preparer's work during tax season. It begins with the gathering of information from clients sufficient to prepare the tax returns and coming to terms with clients regarding the work to be performed and the fee to be charged. Preparers provide clients with "client organizers," which constitute several pages of blank forms designed to help them organize all the information relating to tax returns. The clients then complete the organizers and submit them to the preparer before work can commence.

The tax returns (federal and state) are prepared using tax preparation software; during preparation time, the clients sometimes are consulted for clarifying information. The returns are then reviewed, printed, copied, signed, and packaged for either pick up or mailing. Clients then are consulted regarding necessary follow-up work and tax-planning suggestions.

These tasks are basically the same for an online tax practice as a traditional practice, with a couple of exceptions. First, with an online practice there are typically no physical meetings between clients and the practitioner. That means no need for well-furnished office facilities, with client waiting and meeting areas and convenient client parking. Consequently, there need not be a dress code for the practitioner or staff. I generally work in sweat pants, a T-shirt, and sneakers.

Second, clients submit information for return preparation either online, through e-mail, or by mail to an online preparer. If this information is received online, through a practitioner's Web-based organizer, it generally can be imported directly into the tax return preparation software. This process is very efficient, saving the practitioner a considerable amount of data processing time and expense. Information received through e-mail now can be handled the same way with the proper software.

For my first filing season, I wrote and published my own client organizers on my Web site for clients to print or download, primarily because the tax software I was using did not include organizers for nonresident aliens. My organizers were published in Adobe Acrobat, which is a universal format for printers. I also included access to the free Adobe reader on my site, for any clients who did not already have it loaded on their computers. The arrangement was then for clients to mail me the organizers, together with a copy of their W-2s, 1099s, and any other supporting information they considered necessary.

I rejected having clients input their data while online at my Web site. I was against this because it is not how I would prefer to submit my information were I to use an online tax service. It simply is not convenient for me to gather all of my receipts and income information and type it into a form while online at the computer. I would want to write comments, draw arrows, and include certain source documents with my information. I also would like to take my time and do the job in more than one sitting to make sure that I got everything right. If something was missing or not yet available, I would be concerned that I would not be able to save my data, log off, and get back in at a later date. Yes, filling out forms online is quick and easy for someone with a small amount of information to convey. But I thought it would be a source of confusion and frustration for those with more complex tax situations.

 I did not consider it convenient for clients to be required to submit tax return information online via my Web site.

Some online firms require clients to register and submit payment information before accessing the organizer. One firm even required payment just to fill out the organizer. This, I thought, would cause resistance from clients. The adequacy of security while inputting personal financial information over the Internet is also a concern for some and requires a more sophisticated and expensive Web hosting plan than I purchased.

I therefore decided that my system, with a paper organizer that can be accessed and printed from my Web site, would be the method of choice for many. The major drawback to my method is that client data must be typed into the software manually at my end, decreasing my efficiency significantly and adding time to each job.

Software firms are now beginning to offer interactive client organizers in files that can be downloaded from a Web site or e-mailed to clients for storage on their own computers. They can be filled out on-screen by clients at their leisure and stored for corrections or completion. Clients can then e-mail the completed organizers to the practitioner, who can input the data directly into the tax software. This method offers convenience to the client and a great deal of efficiency to the practitioner. It is not currently available in package form, however, for nonresident alien returns.

For my second tax season I have developed my own interactive client organizer. Such a document is easy to create with Adobe Acrobat

> My method of choice for the submission of tax information is to allow clients to download an organizer and fill it out at their leisure, then e-mail it back. This is not currently a packaged product for nonresident alien returns, however.

4.0. I have yet to conquer the transferring of client data from the organizer directly into my tax software.

## HOW DID MY FIRST YEAR GO?

Before I reveal how many paying clients I had my first year, I must provide a little preliminary information. First, I did not wish to be overwhelmed by clients and create ill will by not being able to handle the volume. I did not know how efficiently my system would work and was unfamiliar with my tax preparation software and credit card processing system. I therefore considered my first year a test year, during which I would learn the procedures and improve what I could.

I did not launch my proprietary site until late in 1999, which did not give it enough time to work its way to the top of the search engine lists before the 2000 filing season. My site therefore was attracting only about 20 visitors a day prior to tax season and averaged about 50 per day during tax season. This, I thought, was plenty of traffic to generate a sufficient number of clients to test the system. I did not promote the site in any other way.

My Webtrends reports showed me not only how many hits and visitors I had each day but also how many of my client organizers were being downloaded from the site. The average was about one organizer per day during the three-month filing season. This figure was a much better predictor of potential clients than the number of visitors per day. Had all of the downloaded organizers been mailed in with taxpayer information, I would have had nearly 100 clients that first filing season. As it turned out, only 30 of the organizers were mailed so my client total was 30 the first year.

I was challenged but not overly worked while maintaining a full-time teaching schedule, and I can honestly say that all of my clients were satisfied with their service. I learned my software well and developed efficiencies in my return preparation procedures. I considered Bob Lindgren's statement about attracting 55 clients his first year, while

> The first season of a Web-based tax practice should be considered a pilot run, during which business procedures and practices should be developed and refined, in order to ensure complete client satisfaction.

working 12 to 14 hours per day in his office. I also read an article about the founders of Taxes4Less.com, who reported 200 paying clients their first year on an advertising budget of $50,000.[6] Comparatively speaking, I did okay.

I am now several months from entering my second filing season, and the average number of visitors to my site is over 100 per day. I have recently entered into an alliance with a new Web site that caters to the needs of international student visitors (www.istudentcity.com). In exchange for writing short, periodic tax articles of interest to international student visitors, which are featured on the site, it has published a biography of me and has provided a link to my site. My goal is to develop banner exchanges with other Web sites that are of interest to international visitors. My advertising budget remains at zero.

Judging from the increased traffic volume at my site in the off season, I believe I will have enough clients to keep me as busy as I will want to be next year. If I get more clients than I can handle on my own, I have a ready pool of part-time help available in the volunteers I have trained for the VITA site.

> As with any business, it takes patience, endurance, and attention to detail and client satisfaction to build a successful online tax practice.

## FINDING YOUR NICHE

The niche market is wide open for tax services on the Internet. In fact, as stated earlier, I believe a niche market is the only way in which a small practitioner can successfully compete online.

A niche market is any population of taxpayers having similar tax service needs that require special knowledge or expertise. A niche can be based on the industry in which taxpayers work or focus on taxpayer

> For online niche tax services, the Internet is like free land, waiting to be claimed and cultivated.

lifestyle. For instance, ministers have tax advantages and disadvantages that set them apart from the general population of taxpayers. These differences have allowed the owners of www.clergytaxnet.com to build a successful niche practice. Ideas for lifestyle niches can be found in my book, *J.K. Lasser's Taxes Made Easy for Your Home-Based Business*, 4th edition (John Wiley & Sons, 2000), which describes the special rules for home office workers, and *J.K. Lasser's Gay Finances in a Straight World*, by Peter Berkery Jr. and Gregory Diggins (IDG Books Worldwide, 1998), which focuses on the tax and financial concerns of gays and lesbians. Both of these areas could generate online niche practices.

The best way to build a niche online is to provide useful information to the target audience. That information need not be limited to tax tips but could relate to the target population in many ways. For example, if you are an aspiring tax practitioner who is currently working or formerly worked in the real estate industry, your niche could be to provide tax services to real estate agents, investors, and developers. You could provide a wealth of information of interest to this group, including tax tips, real estate book reviews, and links to other pertinent sites. You could write articles on real estate taxation and even publish an online newsletter. The more useful information you provide, the more visitors you will attract and the more tax clients you will obtain.

Chapter

# Getting to Know the Internal Revenue Service

*The Internal Revenue Service shall review and restate its mission to place a greater emphasis on serving the public and meeting tax-payers' needs.*

—IRS Restructuring and Reform Act of 1998

In your role as a tax consultant, the IRS can be a formidable adversary when there is a difference of opinion regarding the application of a particular tax law or regulation. In most tax matters, however, the IRS serves as your partner and advisor by providing interpretations to complex statutes and helping you to meet your clients' tax responsibilities. It should be helpful in your practice to know as much as possible about the mission of the agency, its operating structure and procedures, and its initiative for electronic filing, which will affect all practitioners in coming years. This chapter presents a brief overview of the new customer-oriented direction the IRS is taking under Commissioner Charles O. Rossotti, much of which was called for by Congress in the Internal Revenue Service Restructuring and Reform Act of 1998 (RRA '98).

Congress established the office of the commissioner of Internal Revenue in 1862. The commissioner was given the power to assess, levy, and collect taxes and the right to enforce the tax laws through seizure of property and income and through prosecution. The commissioner's powers and authority remain very much the same today.

## MISSION, OLD AND NEW

Surveys indicate that the American public considers the IRS the most feared and despised of all government agencies. The Internal Revenue Service deals directly with more Americans than any other institution, private or public, and employs nearly 100,000 people. As the administrator and enforcer of our nation's federal tax laws, its ominous presence encourages most U.S. taxpayers to comply with their federal tax obligation honestly. As an example of its effectiveness, a majority of taxpayers recently surveyed indicated that they would prefer a mugging to an IRS audit.[1]

Its reputation alone has been a significant contributor to fulfilling the stated IRS mission for the past 40 years or so, which has been to "collect the proper amount of tax." The IRS has succeeded in its mission remarkably well. Roughly 98 percent of federal taxes collected are paid without active intervention by the IRS. Today it collects $1.7 trillion in revenue, more than the total gross domestic product of the United Kingdom and 26 times its collections in the early 1950s.

While meeting its stated goal, the IRS has been burdened with increasing demands. The volume and complexity of IRS operations expanded at a tremendous pace in the last half of the twentieth century. Since 1952, the number of tax returns filed has more than doubled, and the number of pages in the tax code has expanded from 812 to approximately 3,500.[2] There have been close to 10,000 changes in the Internal Revenue Code since the late 1980s alone, changes with which the IRS has been forced to keep pace.

In surveys, the IRS has ranked dead last among public and private institutions in public satisfaction.

The IRS stated mission from the early 1960s to 1998 was to "collect the proper amount of tax."

With its success in meeting its mission has come much study and criticism of the IRS in recent years. A presidential commission, several congressional committees, and Vice President Al Gore's National Partnership for Reinventing Government have been among the critics. These studies identified a wide range of problems, including inadequate technology and failure of modernization programs, poor service to taxpayers, violation of taxpayer rights, failure to follow established procedures, lack of adequate training and resources for IRS employees, and inappropriate use of enforcement statistics.

The IRS has clearly suffered from a public relations problem. Public and congressional discontent resulted in passage of RRA '98, by a margin of 402 to 8 in the House and 96 to 2 in the Senate. RRA '98 incorporated many of the recommendations from the studies that preceded it. The general focus of this legislation was to direct the IRS to do a better job in meeting the needs of taxpayers. A new mission statement for the IRS, as directed by RRA '98, reads as follows:

> Provide America's taxpayers top quality service by helping them understand and meet their tax responsibilities and by applying the tax law with integrity and fairness to all.

In its own words, "The public today has a legitimate expectation that the IRS will do its job in a manner that is no less effective than high-quality private and public sector organizations."[3] Its new mission statement reflects this attitude. The role of the IRS is to help the large majority of taxpayers who are willing to comply with the tax laws, while seeing to it that the minority who are not willing to comply are not allowed to burden their fellow taxpayers. The new mission of the IRS is to perform this role to a high standard, so that all of its services are seen by

A new mission statement was dictated by Congress with the overwhelming passage of an act to reform the IRS, RRA '98.

> The new IRS mission statement is consumer oriented, recognizing the responsibility of the IRS to provide the majority of taxpayers who comply with the law with high-quality service.

the people who receive them as comparable in quality to the best they get from other institutions.

Of course, the IRS is still committed to the obvious need to collect taxes. It is committed to be more effective in all aspects of its mission, which includes application of the law to those who are unwilling to comply voluntarily. Achieving its mission requires fundamental changes in many respects while retaining the essential elements that created its success in the past. These changes must take place while the IRS continues to administer a very large, complex, and dynamic tax system.

## SPECIFIC GOALS FOR IMPROVEMENT

The IRS has focused on three strategic goals as measurements of its success in meeting its new mission:

1. To provide top-quality service to each taxpayer.
2. To provide top-quality service to taxpayers as a whole.
3. To increase productivity throughout the agency through a high-quality work environment.

Many of its operational goals for parts of the agency can also be formulated in support of the achievement of these general goals.

### Top-Quality Service to Each Taxpayer

The only direct contact most taxpayers ever have with the IRS is over the phone, requesting forms or information on filing procedures. The IRS handles millions of these interactions with taxpayers each year. My personal inquiries over the years have generally been met with courtesy on the other end. Any frustration I have experienced has been largely due to lack of training or experience on the part of the IRS employee with whom I have dealt, rather than lack of patience or civility. It is obvious, however, that such has not been the fate of many who have sought help

In surveys, the IRS has consistently been ranked last in customer satisfaction when compared to other public and private institutions.

from the IRS. The University of Michigan has conducted a survey of people who have dealt with various public and private sector organizations for a number of years and has always ranked the IRS last in customer satisfaction.[4]

The IRS has begun to do something about its dismal service performance. It is committed to making the process of providing information to taxpayers easier and clearer and reducing the chances of error. In cases in which the IRS must perform an audit or collection action, it has pledged to treat taxpayers professionally and with full consideration of their rights.

Last filing season the agency expanded customer service operations nationwide. It opened 250 walk-in sites on Saturdays in shopping malls and other locations throughout the country and established longer office hours on weekdays. It staffed toll-free call-in centers around the clock, seven days a week. The agency also provided translators for those who use English as their second language. The IRS Web site has been extremely beneficial to taxpayers, providing immediate access to all forms and publications and answers to many tax questions. In 1999 the IRS Web site (www.irs.gov) had over 767 million "hits" during which taxpayers downloaded more than 57 million forms and publications.[5]

There is focused help for taxpayers in various stages of frustration with a long-standing collection or enforcement problem with the IRS. Problem Solving Days is an initiative begun in November of 1997. Through this ongoing program, the IRS provides taxpayers the opportunity to have face-to-face contact with an IRS employee who can assist them in resolving their problems.

The IRS has begun to measure success in achieving its service goals by conducting surveys of taxpayers relating to the quality of service they receive. These surveys will be summarized to measure the overall trend in taxpayer satisfaction with IRS service. Although overall IRS service is still rated low, more limited surveys of taxpayer satisfaction with particular IRS services, such as Problem Solving Days, show consistently high ratings, even when many taxpayers do not receive the outcome they seek.[6] According to the IRS, this is a clear indication that

> IRS service initiatives, such as Problem Solving Days, are beginning to show high ratings by the public and indicate that taxpayers appreciate quality service even if they do not receive the outcome they seek.

taxpayers tend to distinguish between the tax result and the quality of service they receive.

## Top Quality Service to All Taxpayers

The IRS is committed to applying the law with integrity and fairness to all, so that noncompliance is not an excessive burden on the vast majority of taxpayers who do comply. Our tax system will be jeopardized if those who voluntarily meet their tax obligations do not have confidence that their neighbors and competitors are also complying. When taxpayers do not voluntarily meet their tax obligation, the IRS will use its enforcement powers to collect the taxes that are due.

The overall measure of success in this goal is the total collection percentage, which is the percentage of taxes that are actually collected as compared to those that would be paid if everyone paid what was due. Studies suggest that noncompliance equated to about $195 billion in 1997, although reliable, up-to-date measures of overall noncompliance are not available. This figure works out to about $1,600 per individual return.

Since the passage of RRA '98, the number of IRS enforcement actions has declined substantially. For example, the fraction of individual returns audited in face-to-face audits has declined about 40 percent, and the number of collection cases closed has declined by a similar percentage.[7] The IRS denies that these significant declines in enforcement activity have been caused by reallocation of resources to customer service, since reallocations have amounted to less than 3 percent of compliance resources. Instead, the declines have resulted from continued reductions in staff due to budget constraints and the extra burden imposed on the IRS by the provisions of RRA '98. The IRS is committed to stabilizing the level of enforcement activity but claims it will require additional funding from Congress in order to increase its staff resources.

In the past, the IRS has placed great emphasis on direct enforce-

**IRS enforcement action:** The examination of returns by IRS auditors and the collection of previously assessed taxes by IRS collection agents.

Although enforcement actions have declined significantly since passage of RRA '98, the IRS is committed to reduce noncompliance through enforcement measures and other means.

ment revenue. Enforcement revenue is any tax, penalty, or interest gained from a specific taxpayer by an IRS enforcement action, usually an examination or a collection. The focus on enforcement revenue was due, in part, because it is precisely measurable and in part because it shows an indirect deterrent effect that increases compliance. However, this revenue is estimated to represent only 2 percent of the revenue collected by the IRS.

The IRS is now focusing on many other techniques that increase compliance, in addition to direct enforcement. Included are better and more targeted taxpayer education, voluntary agreements, improved regulations, and earlier intervention through notices and phone calls. Since about 98 percent of revenue is generated without IRS enforcement action, an increase of 1 percent in voluntary compliance would be roughly equivalent to a 50 percent increase in enforcement revenue.

Also, enforcement actions are costly because they are labor intensive and often lengthy, sometimes extending for years after the tax is due. Therefore, enforcement activity, while remaining a vital component of a strategy for achieving overall compliance, is not the only component on which the IRS focuses. Additionally, the IRS does not consider enforcement revenue a good measure of success in achieving the strategic goal of service to all taxpayers.

The IRS is now focusing its efforts on many techniques to increase compliance, including taxpayer education, improved regulations, and earlier intervention, in addition to direct enforcement.

## Productivity Through a Quality Work Environment

The third strategic goal of the IRS is to increase productivity by providing a higher-quality work environment for its employees. The IRS believes that the right work environment will help unlock employee potential. It will also help to recruit better skill-based staff. The IRS is committed to a workplace that is free of discrimination, does not tolerate artificial ceilings and barriers to advancements, affords equal opportunity, and recognizes employee performance and potential.

From 1993 through 1999 the economy grew in real terms by 23 percent, and the number of tax returns filed increased by 8.7 percent. Yet the number of IRS employees decreased from 115,000 to 98,000. If these numbers alone are considered, one might assume that the IRS is succeeding in achieving higher productivity. However, the IRS attributes the decrease in its personnel primarily to budget cuts. These cuts, it claims, have resulted in its failure to meet the public's service expectations, which has contributed to the concerted criticism leveled at the agency in recent years and an increase in noncompliance.

The IRS believes that it can handle the increased workload from a growing economy and improve performance on its other two service goals with only a slight increase in its workforce. To accomplish this, the agency believes investments will be required over the next several years for the replacement of equipment and facilities, training of personnel, and re-design of the organization and business practices.

The agency believes that it cannot succeed unless it achieves a high level of performance on all three of these goals. It cannot be successful if it collects taxes but does not provide top-quality service to each taxpayer, or neglects to respect taxpayer rights. At the same time, the agency cannot be successful if it provides good service but allows compliance to decline and thereby fails to collect taxes. If the IRS is able to achieve these strategic goals, the benefits to taxpayers and employees should be concrete and noticeable.

The decline in recent years in the IRS workforce has resulted from lack of funding rather than increased productivity, causing poor service and greater noncompliance.

# NEW MODERNIZED STRUCTURE
# OF THE INTERNAL REVENUE SERVICE

The organizational structure of the IRS is the vehicle through which decisions are made and actions are carried out, reflecting how the IRS interacts with taxpayers. The basic structure of the IRS, before its current transformation, was built around districts and service centers. It was established many years ago and has evolved over decades. It was organized into three tiers consisting of a multifunctional National Office, regional offices, and district offices. The agency was also divided into a number of geographic regions, each with its own regional commissioner, regional counsel, and regional director of appeals.

Within these geographic regions there were 33 district offices and 10 service centers. Each regional unit was charged with administering the entire tax law for every kind of taxpayer, large and small, in a defined geographical area. Consequently, every taxpayer was serviced by both a service center and a district. Within each unit, work was carried out by functional disciplines, principally Examination, Appeals, Collection, Criminal Investigation, Submission Processing, and Customer Service. Service centers and districts each performed in these functions for the same taxpayer, with the responsibility shifting depending on whether the work was done by phone, by mail, or in person.

Within this structure, there was little or no coordination of services for a given taxpayer. Also, there were eight intermediate levels of staff and line management between a front-line employee and the deputy commissioner, who was the only manager besides the commissioner who had responsibility over all aspects of service to any particular taxpayer.

Congress, through RRA '98, called for a restructuring of the IRS because it believed that its earlier structure was one of the factors contributing to its inability to serve taxpayers properly. The new IRS structure, which is being phased in over the next several years, is organized around taxpayer needs rather than the functional disciplines of the IRS. Looking

Under the old IRS organizational structure, operating units had no end-to-end responsibility for a given taxpayer. This cumbersome structure was the principal obstacle to high-quality service and productivity.

The new IRS structure, borrowing from the private sector, is organized around taxpayer attributes and needs.

to the private sector, the IRS recognized that many financial institutions have different divisions that serve retail customers, small to medium-size businesses, and large multinational businesses. The taxpayer base for IRS services falls naturally into similar groups. Table 9.1 provides a skeleton model of the new structure.

The modernized IRS is being built around organizational units with end-to-end responsibility. Each of the operating divisions will be structured in a way to most effectively meet the needs of the taxpayers it serves. By dedicating a separate unit with full end-to-end responsibility for serving each set of taxpayers, management will be better able to focus its efforts, resources, and staff to provide tailored products and services to help their market segment comply with the tax laws.

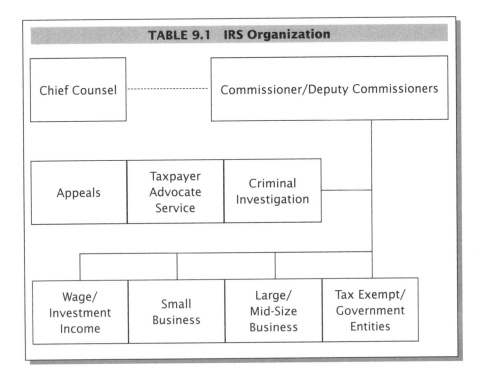

**TABLE 9.1    IRS Organization**

| Chief Counsel | Commissioner/Deputy Commissioners |

| Appeals | Taxpayer Advocate Service | Criminal Investigation |

| Wage/Investment Income | Small Business | Large/Mid-Size Business | Tax Exempt/Government Entities |

The focus of the Wage and Investment Income group will be on taxpayer education and assistance in the filing of returns.

## Wage and Investment Income Division

The Wage and Investment Income division will serve approximately 88 million filers, representing about 116 million individual taxpayers, including those who file jointly. These taxpayers will report wage and investment income only, almost all of which is reported to the IRS by third parties. These taxpayers typically deal with the IRS only once a year, when filing their returns, and most receive refunds. About 60 percent of these taxpayers file their own returns, depending directly on the IRS or volunteer groups for education and assistance. The focus of this division will be on taxpayer education and assistance and on helping taxpayers understand the law and to file correct returns.

## Small Business and Self-Employed Division

The Small Business and Self-Employed division will deal with individual taxpayers who are fully or partially self-employed and with small businesses. This includes about 45 million filers. This group of taxpayers tends to have much more complex dealings with the IRS than the wage and investment taxpayers. They pay the IRS about $915 billion annually, including personal and corporate income taxes, employment taxes, excise taxes, and withholdings for employees. This represents nearly 44 percent of the total revenue collected by the IRS. Because this division interacts more frequently with taxpayers on complex issues, it will have a compliance field organization including both examination and collections groups, reporting to a multifunctional manager.

The Small Business and Self-Employed division will be more involved in audit and collection actions.

## Large and Mid-Size Business Division

The Large and Mid-Size Business division will serve the approximately 210,000 filers who make up large and mid-size businesses, which are corporations with assets over $5 million. This group pays the IRS about $712 billion in taxes annually. Although collection issues are rare, many complex issues arise with this group involving the interpretation of tax law and tax accounting, some of which involve multinational questions. At least 20 percent of these taxpayers interact with IRS compliance functions each year, and the largest taxpayers deal with the IRS on a continuous basis. This division will be predominantly a field organization that will be structured into various industry groups.

## Tax-Exempt and Government Entities Division

The Tax-Exempt and Government Entities division will service pension plans, tax-exempt organizations, and government entities, representing a large economic sector with special needs. There are about 2.4 million filers in this sector, ranging from small local community organizations to major universities and huge pension funds. These organizations do not pay tax on their income, but they pay over $220 billion per year in employment taxes and income tax withholdings for employees. The IRS must administer complex provisions of the law that are generally not intended to raise revenue but to ensure that these entities stay within the policy guidelines that enabled them to maintain their tax exempt status.

Each of the four operating divisions will be reporting directly to the commissioner of Internal Revenue, working together as one executive management team. In order to ensure consistency of services, the IRS currently is studying ways to ensure communication and coordination among the divisions, such as establishing service-wide councils and setting up commissioner representative positions to focus on internal procedures that span operating divisions. Local field territory and

Local territory managers will have authority to make decisions that affect their local territory and will coordinate with the area manager for issues that cover a larger scope or geographic area, including all constituents in a geographic area.

area managers will assume responsibility for managing practitioner relationships and addressing systematic issues in the field.

## Role of the Chief Counsel, Appeals and Criminal Investigation

The new chief counsel organization maintains its traditional purpose—to assist the IRS in applying the law correctly and consistently for all taxpayers. The chief counsel will continue to maintain a centralized group of experts on particular subjects in the National Office. They will continue the chief counsel's traditional functions of drafting regulations and other published guidance, and issuing private letter rulings and technical advice. The chief counsel's field organization will be divided into specialized groups that are aligned with and are dedicated to the new IRS operating divisions. Both the National Office and the division counsel units will remain part of the office of chief counsel.

Appeals will remain an independent channel for taxpayers who have a dispute over a proposed adjustment by an IRS agent. Appeals staff will be aligned with and dedicated to the operating divisions, thereby allowing them to specialize in particular areas of the law. Taxpayers will likely be more satisfied with the service received from Appeals as a result of this specialization of staff. In addition, Appeals is currently working on improved procedures, such as "Fast Track Mediation," which seeks to expedite case resolution by resolving the case at the lowest level.

Criminal Investigation (CI) will become a line unit reporting directly to the commissioner and deputy commissioner, with 35 special agent in charge (SAIC) officers. This follows the recommendations of a study done by Judge William Webster. CI will closely coordinate its activities and strategies with the operating divisions.

The chief counsel's office assists the IRS in applying the law consistently for all taxpayers.

## Role of the Taxpayer Advocate

Taxpayers sometimes get caught in a continuous, frustrating loop with the IRS, especially under the agency's current (but disappearing) regional and functional structure. Other taxpayers may suffer a significant hardship because of the way the IRS is enforcing a particular tax law.

Taxpayers who cannot resolve issues with the IRS through normal channels can request help from the taxpayer advocate.

The office of the taxpayer advocate assists any taxpayer who has encountered a long-standing problem with the IRS or who has incurred or is facing a significant hardship as a result of an action taken or proposed by the IRS. The Taxpayer Advocate Service provides independent, objective assistance when resolving problems. The National Taxpayer Advocate also serves all taxpayers by submitting semiannual reports directly to Congress, updating Congress on the advocate's success at resolving taxpayer problems, and reporting any systemic issues that may be adversely affecting taxpayers.

Anyone facing such circumstances can get help from the Taxpayer Advocate Program, as long as they first attempt to use existing administrative or formal appeal procedures. Most problems are resolved through regular channels, but if any of the following seven circumstances apply to you or a client, you may ask for assistance from the Taxpayer Advocate Program:

1. You are suffering or about to suffer a significant hardship.
2. You are facing an immediate threat of adverse action.
3. You will incur significant costs if relief is not granted (including fees for professional representation).
4. You will suffer irreparable injury or long-term adverse impact if relief is not granted.
5. You have experienced a delay of more than 30 calendar days to resolve a tax-related problem or inquiry.
6. You have not received a response or resolution to your problem by the date promised.
7. A system(s) or procedure(s) has either failed to operate as intended or failed to resolve your problem or dispute within the IRS.

The taxpayer advocate may issue a taxpayer assistance order to suspend, delay, stop, or speed up IRS actions to relieve your hardship. The taxpayer advocate does not have the authority to override tax law but can help you deal with the IRS and make sure your rights are preserved. You may gain quick access to the Taxpayer Advocate Program by calling its toll-free number 1-877-777-4778.

The new Taxpayer Advocate Service is significantly different from the previous Problem Resolution Program employed by the IRS. Congress, through RRA '98, mandated a reorganization of the Taxpayer Advocate Service by dictating more independence from the IRS of both the National Taxpayer Advocate and the local advocate organizations. Two key changes were mandated that included:

1. An independent reporting structure for all taxpayer advocate employees.
2. Taxpayer advocate representation in every state.

Under the old IRS Problem Resolution Program, all Problem Resolution Program employees in the field reported to local IRS district directors rather than to the national program manager. Additionally, problem resolution officers were located in district offices and service centers, not necessarily in every state.[8]

## Time Frame for Restructuring

In an effort to keep disruptions in tax administration to a minimum, the IRS designed and implemented the new organization structure in phases. The designing and refining stage took place over several years, and the implementation phase was completed in 2000. The modernized four-division structure is now in place.

The Tax-Exempt and Government Entities division became operational in December of 1999. The Large and Mid-Size Business division began in March 2000, and the Wage and Investment and Small Business divisions became functional October 1, 2000.[9]

## Benefits of Restructuring to Taxpayers and Practitioners

The modernized IRS is committed to provide more focused customer service and enhanced accessibility to IRS information and personnel. This will help resolve issues more quickly and consistently. The structure is being built around specific taxpayer attributes and needs, enabling the IRS to more easily tailor products, services, and compliance strategies for particular taxpayer groups. In this way the IRS can develop a comprehensive and focused tax administration approach, allo-

The new organizational structure should help taxpayers and practitioners resolve disputes sooner.

cating the necessary resources to problem prevention and early intervention initiatives.

The reorganization will serve to coordinate audit philosophy and coverage through the elimination of regional management layers. Operating division commissioners, with line authority and end-to-end responsibility for serving the needs of taxpayers falling under their division, will be more likely to ensure the fair and consistent treatment of taxpayers.

The reorganization also promises to make the role of tax advisors easier and more efficient. A tax advisor representing a client in a dispute with the IRS should be able to arrive at a resolution with less administrative hassle, because a goal of the modernization effort is to move the decision-making process to the working level. Tax advisors will gain the goodwill of clients and have more time to devote to more productive activities, such as planning for future transactions.

## GOALS FOR ELECTRONIC TAX ADMINISTRATION

Currently individuals can file their annual tax returns electronically, online, or over the phone, as well as on paper. However, returns cannot be required to be filed in any form other than paper forms supplied by the IRS. Under the law prior to RRA '98, every return, statement, or document required by the Code had to be signed with a pen-to-paper signature, in accordance with regulations prescribed by the IRS. Each electronic return that was filed had to be accompanied by Form 8453, which had to be signed by the taxpayer and could not be transmitted electronically. These cumbersome procedures for transmitting signatures, together with the costs of implementing electronic filing as part of their practice, have discouraged many practitioners from taking part in this program.

Form 8453 is the taxpayer's declaration for electronic filing, which had to be signed by the taxpayer and mailed to the IRS.

Congress, through RRA '98, directed the IRS to streamline and expedite the electronic filing program. The 1998 act declared that:

✔ Paperless filing should be the preferred and most convenient means of filing federal tax and information returns.

✔ The IRS is to have the goal of having at least 80 percent of all such returns filed electronically by 2007.

✔ The IRS is to cooperate with and encourage the private sector by promoting competition to increase electronic filing of such returns.[10]

✔ The IRS is to develop procedures for accepting signatures in digital or other electronic form.[11]

The '98 Act further provided that the IRS must establish a "strategic plan" to eliminate barriers, provide incentives, and use competitive market forces to increase electronic filing gradually over 10 years. To the extent practical, the plan must provide that all returns *prepared* electronically (in other words, using some form of tax software), for tax years beginning after 2001, be *filed* electronically.

In order to ensure that the IRS receives input from the private sector in the development and implementation of the strategic plan, RRA '98 required the IRS to convene an Electronic Commerce Advisory Group. Congress required this advisory group to include representatives from small business; the tax practitioner, preparer, and computerized tax processor communities; and other representatives from the electronic filing industry. The chairperson of this group must make an annual report to Congress on the progress the IRS is making toward its mandated goals.

## Taxpayer Benefits of Electronic Tax Administration

Electronic tax administration will revolutionize how taxpayers transact and communicate with the IRS. Through growth of electronic tax administration, critical IRS resources can be shifted from processing paper to

Congress mandated that the IRS convene an Electronic Commerce Advisory Group from private industry to oversee the strategic plan.

The efficiencies of electronic filing will benefit the IRS, taxpayers, and tax practitioners alike.

providing customer service. The continuing reliance by the IRS on inefficient paper processing of taxpayer returns is costly for both the taxpaying public and the federal government. Within an increasingly constrained budget, these paperbound and error-prone processes divert critical resources from other areas of tax administration.

Both Congress and the IRS have recognized that bold and innovative steps must be taken to revolutionize how taxpayers transact and communicate with the IRS. Incremental approaches are no longer acceptable. Changes must be made in how taxpayers file their tax returns, pay what is owed, and receive the assistance and information that they need to comply with the tax laws. Tax practitioners must be ready and willing to partner with the IRS to make these changes, or they will lose significant ground in the competitive tax services industry.

## Progress to Date

The IRS issued the Electronic Tax Administration Strategic Plan required by RRA '98 in December of 1998. The short-term and long-term initiatives in this plan address the costs of electronic filing and changes to the program that may have discouraged practitioner participation in the past. In December 1999, an updated strategic plan was issued.

The IRS has entered into new partnerships with private sector companies to broaden the electronic services accessible through the IRS Web site. As part of these arrangements, the IRS established links from its Web site to the partners' Web sites. The partners' Web sites offered such services as free tax preparation software and free electronic filing to low-income individuals. These services became available during the 1999 filing season, and private sector partners are planning to expand their programs for providing free e-filing services in future years.

The number of electronic return originators (EROs) increased from 82,000 in 1998 to almost 90,000 in 1999. Some EROs charged taxpayers less to file electronic returns in 1999 than in previous years, and some offered free electronic filing to taxpayers who met certain criteria.

**ERO:** Electronic return originator. A tax practitioner who prepares returns for IRS e-filing and who e-files returns for taxpayers who have prepared their own returns.

The IRS continued to offer more forms and schedules that can be filed electronically in 1999 and will continue to expand the list, reducing the practitioner's costs of preparing and transmitting electronic returns.

In 1999 two pilot programs were conducted that allowed thousands of taxpayers to file paperless returns without the accompanying paper signature form. These pilot programs involved the use of personal identification numbers (PINs) as a taxpayer's signature, thus eliminating the need to file the paper form. Nearly 452,000 taxpayers participated in the online signature pilot program, in which the IRS distributed e-file customer numbers to taxpayers who prepare their own returns using tax preparation software to file from their home computers. Another 322,000 taxpayers participated in the practitioner signature pilot program, in which taxpayers filed through 8,100 participating practitioners using a PIN. This program is scheduled to expand in the coming years.

The IRS will continue to provide support to its Volunteer Income Tax Assistance sites that provide free electronic filing services to taxpayers. Last year 2,400 VITA and Tax Counseling for the Elderly sites provided electronic filing to over 400,000 taxpayers.

The IRS established the Electronic Tax Administration Advisory Committee (ETAAC) to provide an organized public forum for the discussion of Electronic Tax Administration issues, as required by RRA '98. The ETAAC is comprised of representatives from tax practitioners and preparers, transmitters of electronic returns, tax software developers, small and large businesses, employers and payroll service providers, individual taxpayers, state governments, and financial industry members. The committee provides continuing input into the development and implementation of the strategic plan for electronic tax administration.

## *Long-Range Plans*

The IRS will continue to encourage robust private sector competition while building on the alliance it has already forged with certain firms.

The IRS will continue to make electronic filing attractive to taxpayers and practitioners by reducing the costs and simplifying the procedures.

Competition among EROs will drive down the cost of electronic filing. The IRS also will continue to develop initiatives to make electronic filing paperless, thus reducing practitioners' costs, and will provide enhanced electronic services as loyalty incentives to those practitioners who offer free and/or low-cost e-filing services.[12] Many practitioners remain resistant because of the perceived costs and complexity of electronic filing. But as IRS marketing and simplification efforts attract more users, more practitioners will be forced to climb on board.

## CONCLUSION

Congress has prodded the IRS to become service oriented, to modernize its operating structure, and to efficiently utilize technology in its communications and transactions with taxpayers. IRS management seems to have accepted these challenges with enthusiasm, but most of the work remains. Transforming the culture of this behemoth agency might be akin to converting the Soviet Union to a free capitalist state, whereby a substantial period of floundering will ensue. Serving to keep the IRS focused on its goals, however, are the watchful and guiding eyes of oversight boards and committees, the impatient eyes of Congress, and the critical eyes of the public.

# Chapter 10

## Conversations with Six Tax Professionals

*I have loved this job from the day I started. I have a real passion for it.*

—Rita Benassi

hroughout this book I share with you the wisdom of many experienced and respected tax professionals. This chapter allows you to sit in on conversations I had with six of them. You can learn, from their own words, how they happened to choose a career in taxation, what their work day is like, what they like and dislike about it, and what advice they might have.

Allow me to introduce Rita Benassi, a tax partner with the international CPA firm Deloitte & Touche, who provides tax planning advice to some of the largest companies in the world. Craig Wilson, a self-employed CPA, is the tax and general business advisor to several successful start-up companies. Jay Zack is a former elementary school teacher who has risen to the top ranks of RSM McGladrey, Inc. Catherine Holtzclaw is a female entrepreneur with her own CPA firm, who does tax planning for other women entrepreneurs. Kevin Koehler is the son of a truck driver who always knew he wanted to be an accountant. He is a founding partner with a large regional CPA firm in the Twin Cities. Ed Ryan started out preparing tax returns for a regional firm in Chicago but was let go after his first tax season and was told that he should try sales. Ed is now the president of his own highly successful CPA firm. Each of these professionals has a unique and interesting story to tell.

**Rita Benassi, MBT, CPA, Partner, Deloitte & Touche LLP,
San Francisco, California**

**Gary:** First of all, how did you get interested in the tax business? What's the earliest time you can think of that you were thinking about being a tax person?

**Rita:** For me, it was high school, I guess. I took accounting classes in high school and knew that accounting was where I wanted to be. My dad was an accountant and so I had that sense growing up. He was in industry and so it's a little different. He also had a concentration in tax, even though he was an assistant controller. So it's what I knew—it's what I saw growing up. I also had an aptitude for it in high school and then went on to study it in college. So I guess I've always been one of those people that's very programmed, very driven, have this end point in sight, and just go get it. Whereas, for others accounting might have been the last thing that they thought about, and specifically tax.

**Gary:** Do you think you made the right choice—do you like your job?

**Rita:** I love my job. It's one of those things where my husband has agreed to quit his job of 12 years and move because of my career. . . . Obviously he doesn't "need" to work, because we make enough money in this profession that we don't "need" the two incomes. But it's one of those things he knows that, number one, I make a lot of money and, number two, I absolutely love what I do. So there was absolutely was no question when the opportunity to transfer came up that the answer was yes, of course we're going to do that. If I just made a lot of money, it's different. I mean, it's got to be both [income and job satisfaction]. But no, I have loved this job from the day I started. I have a real passion for it.

**Gary:** What do you like best about your job, Rita?

**Rita:** There's a lot of authority and responsibility. You know when I'm really busy, and under stress, and the adrenaline is pumping, that is a real rush. When I don't have that much to do like right now before the transfer—I'm in this true transition mode and I'm looking at stuff that needs to go to the vault and be filed, and just stuff that's not important. It's hard to get excited about coming in. I guess I'm the typical Type A stress-driven personality.

I think it's a very powerful position to be able to advise, in my case, from a corporate tax perspective, some of the top companies in the world. It's a power trip. And that's just being really honest about it, I guess.

I think it's a very powerful position to be able to advise, in my case, from a corporate tax perspective, some of the top companies in the world.

**Gary:** Now, you mentioned that it's hard to come in when you're doing really mundane things. What do you like least about the job?

**Rita:** The administration—time reports—expense reports.

**Gary:** So you *don't* like least the fact that you spend a great deal of time at work?

**Rita:** No. That comes with it. And if the adrenaline is driving you, it doesn't matter what hours you're working. But no, I hate time sheets, I hate expense reports, I hate billing, I hate anything to do with when you're done with the project and have to get the file put together, get it neat and tidy and put out somewhere. Now, I'm very much a perfectionist and a neatnik, so that's part of my problem because I want it [the project file] to be tidied—I want the bow to be wrapped before it goes somewhere. But yes, anything associated with administration—or having to do with calling to collect an invoice that's been outstanding for a while—none of that's fun.

**Gary:** What do you think it takes as far as qualities to make a good tax accountant?

**Rita:** First of all, top technical skills. Second, the ability to build strong relationships. Another thing, and I really haven't given this a lot of thought so you're just getting my off-the-top-of-my-head, but is to be a good listener. I think that one of the reasons I've been successful is something about the fact that I am able to really listen and have a good understanding. I don't know if it's a woman's intuition thing, and yet that's not to say that men aren't as good at this. I can read people, so I'll be sitting in a meeting and I can watch their body language and understand if we're not connecting. So I think that my skills in listening and intuition are consequential. You need to be really able to understand what somebody's needs are to be able to be a good consultant: If you don't sit back and listen to what a company's problems are, you're never going to be able to watch for solutions or opportunities for them.

> I think that one of the reasons I've been successful is
> something about the fact that I am able to really listen. . . .

**Gary:** That's very good advice.

**Rita:** Business today is so different from when I started. Companies don't call us anymore for the majority of our tax work. If we waited for companies to call we would be out of business.

**Gary:** What is your vision of employment opportunities in the future? During the next 10 years, let's say.

**Rita:** I'd say stronger than ever. I mean it [the business] is becoming very idea driven. Our client base is no longer just our attest clients, and I don't mean that in a negative way. I started with the firm, where it was pretty much this is the company that we do the audit work for and so we do their tax work. Now it's not that way. Our client base is anybody that's got tax issues.

**Gary:** Do you see a tax specialty that's growing faster than any others?

**Rita:** I think that international tax is still very strong. I think that international tax, as companies become increasingly globally located—that's a wave that we will continue to ride.

**Gary:** Do you encourage specialization?

**Rita:** Over time what we've done is we've publicized so much the opportunities in international tax, multistate tax, employee benefits, whatever, that all the best and the brightest (or more than a fair share) have gone into specialty areas. In other words, the message of the past has been "you've got to specialize in tax to be successful," so all our best people then go do that. Well, that was important to do as you're building the specialty areas. But once you have critical mass in those areas, you really have to step back and say, "But what about people like me?" and when I look at myself I say "Well what am I?" And this not an attractive term but a "generalist" is what I am—okay—a corporate generalist. And what's wrong with that? There's nothing wrong with that—in fact, that's tremendous. But over time we've told everybody that specialties are the place to be. And so what it's forced us to do is to go outside to hire people like me because we're not growing enough of them. "Generalist" is an important career track that I don't want to forget about and that's something that we're focusing on in our firm.

> [Being a corporate] "generalist" is an important career track that I don't want to forget about and that's something that we're focusing on in our firm.

**Gary:** So you're looking maybe for people with a broader view of things and people who can see more opportunities?

**Rita:** Yes, because what a generalist can grow up to be is what I do: It is what we call a lead tax partner role. What that means is, the buck stops here. I'm responsible for all tax services that we provide to one or more of our largest clients on a global basis. Now, I don't do that by myself. That means I bring in the best international tax expertise that we have in the firm, the best multistate tax experts, the best resources in France and Germany and all around, but I've become a quarterback or facilitator of sorts. And I'm responsible for the ultimate quality of the services that we provide even if I'm not necessarily doing the heavy lifting in each of the specialty areas. So, that's a career opportunity that I think has gotten short-shrifted, and I understand why it happened, but now we need to get that back on track. Corporate tax is a specialty.

**Gary:** Is it more difficult for women than men to become successful in the tax business?

**Rita:** That's a really hard question. Are you aware of what our firm has done on our initiative for the advancement of women? It is a critical initiative for which our firm has devoted a lot of time and effort.

**Gary:** I'm not real aware of what they've done.

**Rita:** Okay. Well, Deloitte & Touche has realized several years ago that when you get to the partner ranks, we did not have the same number of women as men, even though we were hiring 50/50. And they started studying to see why that was happening. And the assumption was that women were going off and having babies. But when they really looked at it they realized that women were not just going off and having babies. They were actually going off and doing something else, but continuing on in the workforce. And so we realized that was a tremendous cost for us because we spend a lot of money on our people. And if we hire 50 percent women and spend the money to train them, and then they leave, that's a bad business answer for the firm. So we started the Initiative for the Retention and Advancement of Women several years ago. We have found that this initiative has not only helped women over time since all of our statistics have improved, but also this initiative has ended up helping us retain men as well. There has been specific firm training, courses on men and women as colleagues, and monitoring key assignments to see if women are represented. Also, we're much more flexible as far as work arrangements, like part time, flex time, part year, and so on. I think we're much more flexible today.

> We started the Initiative for the Retention and Advancement of Women . . . [which] has ended up helping us retain men as well.

**Gary:** If you had the choice to make again would you make the same choice?

**Rita:** No question.

**Craig Wilson, MBT, CPA, Owner, Craig H. Wilson, CPA, Burnsville, Minnesota**

**Gary:** How did you decide to become a tax person? How did you decide to become an accountant?

**Craig:** That's a pretty interesting process. I was at the University of Minnesota, a junior in the College of Biological Sciences. I was talking about my future in that field and was given a lot of negative feedback as far as what the future opportunities were in the area of biological sciences. I was specifically interested in botany and met with my advisor. And she said, "Well, I've got a master's degree in botany and this is the best job I could get, talking to people like you."

So I did some reflection, thought maybe I did have a general interest in business and talked to somebody in the business department. That person said, "You know your grades are good enough, why don't you try accounting as a major?" And so it was on the strength of those conversations.

When I started in public accounting, I was in more of the audit area of our firm. I started with a fairly good-size local firm in Bloomington. I guess I always had more of a leaning toward tax. I thought it was an area that offered a couple of things. It offered you a real tangible way that you could quantify savings. And it also became pretty clear early on in my auditing days that there was a real different perception between what the tax people could offer and what the accounting people could offer. The auditors tended to be looked upon as a necessary evil by a lot of people, while the tax people were looked upon favorably—if they did a good job and could quantify some of those tax savings. They [tax people] were viewed with a little higher esteem in the eyes of the clients. Also with the clientele being closely held businesses that we dealt with, taxes were a very high priority for most of them. So from that standpoint I liked the idea of serving people and being able to see something that was of value to them. And so I had the opportunity after a couple of years in the audit side to change over to the tax department, and that got me started.

> The auditors tended to be looked upon as a necessary evil by a lot of people, while the tax people were looked upon favorably—if they did a good job and could quantify some of those tax savings.

**Gary:** Now, how long did you work for the local firm?

**Craig:** I actually spent two sessions with them. I was there for about three and a half years and then finished my master's degree in taxation. I then went off to teach for one year, at a school called Rockford College in Rockford, Illinois; I taught accounting. I decided to come back, so I called my former boss and he said sure, come on back. I joined them again and was there for about four years.

From there, I moved to being a tax manager with another firm in Minneapolis. In that transition things changed for me. I went from being pretty much a tax specialist into being much more of a generalist with a tax flavor, where I was actually operating more as the partner for my own clientele. And I became much more of a generalist again. In the process I was seeing a lot of the changes in technology and seeing that you could do a lot more yourself rather than what we used to do.

**Gary:** When did you decide to go out on your own?

**Craig:** The price of technology was getting cheaper and it became less and less necessary to have somebody else do your word processing. It was just as easy to type and correct your own graphs. So I realized a couple of things. First, I could afford to enter into this on my own. And secondly I had developed a fairly strong niche of small clients that didn't necessarily fit the bigger-firm mode. Moreover, I could easily deal with them from basically any place and deal with their issues on my own. It was at that point, not quite six years ago, that I decided to do this on my own.

**Gary:** So, you're more of a general small business practitioner. Do you audit these companies?

**Craig:** I don't do any audits. Primarily, the individual tax returns that I prepare are shareholders of the companies that I do work for. Other than that there are a few special-circumstance individuals. For example, I do business with a fair number of elderly clients. It's become kind of a hot practice development in the elder care services. I started this about 10 years ago even before I started off on my own. I had noticed that there were certain needs. Obviously they've got the ability to pay, but they may need extra services and time beyond what would be typical in your tax preparation services. I usually go and meet with people in their homes or wherever they are, make sure that checks are written in a decent way and provide hands on follow-up for quarterly filings, et cetera. I make sure that things are taken care of in that fashion.

**Gary:** What was your office arrangement when you first started?

**Craig:** I started my practice out of my home. Part of it was just from an economical standpoint, and part of it I wanted to have more time to be with my family. I don't think that if you're ever going to be in any kind of tax practice that you're going to totally avoid a busy-season–type crush. I thought that I'd be able to accomplish being able to at least work at home during those night hours rather than as before when I was working in downtown Minneapolis. Before, I'd virtually not see my children for five days a week, only a little bit on Saturday evenings and Sundays. Probably what prompted me more than anything else at that time to consider doing something different was something I remember my daughter said to me. One morning during the busy season I was still home when my youngest daughter (who at that time was three) got up extra early. As I was getting ready to go out the door she said "Oh, Daddy, you're going to work, aren't you?" I said, "Yes, I am." And she said, "That's where you live, isn't it?" And that hit me pretty hard. So I started to think, "Is there a different way I can do this?" And so that was probably the impetus for what got it all started in the first place. And so with the technical capability I thought I'd try doing this from home.

And so from home, I met a number of my individual clients there. They thought it was great just being around the dining room table to go through their tax information. Yet because of my locale, and because of the fact that it was my home— As far as my business clients, what happened is that it forced me when I met with them, out of my office to their office. By dumb luck if for no other reason I found that this is probably the best thing that ever could have happened, from a business-practice standpoint.

> As far as my business clients, [my home office] forced me . . . out of my office to their office. By dumb luck if for no other reason I found that this is probably the best thing that ever could have happened. . . .

**Gary:** Getting out to their office?

**Craig:** Getting out to their office rather than asking them to come to my office. It changed the dynamics of the relationships so that suddenly they didn't see me as this professional who held the keys to the relationship. You know, "We don't want to go down to that high-priced Craig unless we absolutely have to." It changed the perception that rather than me, they were the most important party in the relationship.

And I got to learn much more about what they do. From that standpoint two more things happened. One, they were given some better advice because I knew a lot more about their business than I ever did before. And secondly, I was able to become a much more critical player in their management. I shouldn't say management, but in their professional team I probably became their most key advisor in a lot of situations. And so out of that I've developed some very strong relationships with these business clients. It is that area that I have come to enjoy the most. I guess, too, the reason why it's probably the best part of the practice for me is that it makes you feel like you're doing something of real service or real value to these people.

As far as being home and being able to spend some time with family, that worked out well. I did have a real flexible situation. Recall the daughter who earlier I had talked about who was three years old. I remember before she even went into kindergarten and even afterward, when during busy season I'd be downstairs working. I had this large desk where there was a room under it. A lot of days she'd spend time down there with me while I was working. She had this little fort that she set up under the desk and would pass notes up to me to talk and communicate with me. It had become a real fun thing. I'd always be able to take a break to have dinner with my family and take a break when the older kids would get home from school, to find out how their day went. So rather than those breaks being around the water cooler with the other people in the office, they became part of the family ritual. As a result, I did get a lot closer to the family.

> [With my home office] I'd always be able to take a break to have dinner with my family. . . . So rather than those breaks being around the water cooler with the other people in the office, they became part of the family ritual.

**Gary:** Now are you still working out of your home?

**Craig:** Probably 70 percent of my time is still out of the home. I've got this office arrangement here in Edina that for right now it's kind of the best of both worlds. I do get to spend time at home when I want to spend the time at home. You'll find that if you've got your home office, there are a couple of things that happen. One, your office tends expand and expand, and you're trying to take over more areas of the house. It can become somewhat of a conflict to control that. The second issue is that there are times when it's good to have the office setting to provide some boundaries. I've found that there were times (and there are still times) when I wouldn't be in the office on purpose. I was doing some personal things. I would get people that would call the office number and not get me. Since they knew what my home number was, they'd call me on the home line. I really didn't want to be answering business calls right at that time. And so the office outside of the home actually provides some boundaries for that.

> There are times when it's good to have the office [outside the home] setting to provide some boundaries.

**Gary:** What have you done in the area of marketing? Have you actively marketed your services?

**Craig:** I wasn't even in the phone book for probably the first two and one-half years of my practice. I guess my belief is that your marketing is going to come primarily from your current clients and secondly I guess I'd also try to get a strong subsidiary referral base from other professionals. I've got a person that's in the computer software applications business. I've referred business to her and she's referred business to me, and it's been a really good fit that way. I've got somebody in the financial services area who I have a lot of respect for. I've referred business to that person and they've referred business back to me.

**Gary:** How about your fees? Are your fees strictly hourly, and how do you go about determining what your fees should be?

**Craig:** My fees now are strictly hourly. When I first started I also thought I could try to do some things on more of a monthly fee arrangement. I looked at the client's history and we came up with what we thought would be a fair fee. It smoothed out my cash flow, and it smoothed out their cash flow because there weren't the big bills at certain times of the year and nothing in between. I've found that to be a very unworkable situation. Because what tends to happen is over time if you call it a retainer, it's difficult to keep them a priority because that deal is set. And then you've got this other one sitting here which is a live file that if you get this project done you know it's $450 of extra billing. And so it becomes a very difficult process to balance that act to keep the client that's paying on a monthly basis at a right level of service that they deserve. So because of that I've done away with that element. As far as the hourly rate goes, I generally check around a little and find out what other people are doing. My hourly fee is $125 per hour, which is at the higher end for most sole practitioners.

> A monthly fee arrangement becomes a very difficult process to balance . . . to keep the client that's paying on a monthly basis at a right level of service that they deserve.

**Gary:** What types of personality traits do you believe best fit this business?

**Craig:** Obviously you have to have some communication skills to deal with clients face to face. Additionally, at least for starting out you have to have a great deal of flexibility. When I say flexibility, understand that there are a given amount of uncertainties that are going to arise—those that you're not going to plan out—and you need to be flexible in how you're going to deal with them.

**Gary:** Did you ever borrow money or have the need to borrow money to stay in business?

**Craig:** No. I basically capitalized my business. I spent perhaps about $7,500 to get started.

**Gary:** Was the start-up cost mainly for hardware and software?

**Craig:** Out of my home, I had set up for that as a bare-bones office arrangement to get me going. Over the course of the time I have since spent quite a bit of money in making the office more to my liking and more usable and serviceable. I've probably put another $10,000 into the home office just to make it more of a professional office.

### Jay Zack, CPA, Partner, McGladrey & Pullen, LLP; Managing Director, RSM McGladrey, Inc., Minneapolis, Minnesota

**Gary:** What is your background?

**Jay:** Well my first degree was in education. I taught at an elementary school for six years and realized that it wasn't going to be a real moneymaker for me. Not that money was everything I wanted, but I wanted more of a challenge. So I started back to school after about three years of teaching. I was going to the University of Minnesota at night. After six years, I left teaching. I went out and interviewed with businesspeople to try and figure out where I wanted to go. Then I went back to school full time for one year, to get enough credits to sit for the CPA exam. I interned at McGladrey during the time I was going to school and never left. I've been here ever since.

**Gary:** When did you first decide that this was the route to go?

**Jay:** You mean having taught school and then going into the business world? As I went out and spent that summer interviewing with people, Gary, people were literally offering me jobs. Offers were just based on, I think, having enough guts to go out and do what I was doing. I read some of the books such as the *What Color Is Your Parachute* books, that were in their first printings back then. I determined that it would be nice to have a technical background in whatever I went into. So whether it was sales, marketing, communication, or some general business field, if there was a technical piece you always fell back on it. I enjoyed the accounting classes I took at the U at night and thought, Well, why not just go this route?

**Gary:** And were you directed into the tax area?

**Jay:** I was directed into the tax area by an opening to do part-time tax preparation in the winter of 1978. It was what I needed, and I enjoyed that. As I interned I found that the skill base that I had brought from teaching school was so different than the skills of people that were coming out of school in those days. Those people were still a little bit of the "green-eyeshade"–type individuals who wanted something technical, enjoyed the technical work, and enjoyed working by themselves.

That was during the late seventies, which was kind of the beginning of the change for the accounting profession. The expectations were changing, of types of skills required in a career of public accounting. The people side of the business was much more prominent than before. Everybody had to sell, deal with clients, build a team, work with peers, and so on. I already had that part, as the communication was simple for me. Writing a business letter was also easy for me. I taught people how to write business letters. So that whole communication piece was easy and helped my transition to the business world.

> The expectations were changing, of types of skills required in a career of public accounting. The people side of the business was much more prominent than before.

**Gary:** When you recruit new employees, what personality traits are you considering?

**Jay:** It's still critical to have the technical expertise. It's nice to know that people understand accounting. I don't personally believe there's a real high correlation in grades and ability and technical ability. But somehow you have to feel that when you interview someone, they've got down the technical basics that they should have learned in school.

**Gary:** Do you like for people to have taken a couple tax courses at the undergraduate level?

**Jay:** Yes, at a minimum, because we still hire directly for our tax group and always have. I like the schools now that offer two tax courses, as opposed to just one when I was there. They didn't have the variety that they have today.

The other critical thing is the personality of people and if they can talk and walk and function and if they can present themselves, both verbally and in writing. It's real difficult to interview on their writing skills and how legible they may write; now with computers, everybody prints beautifully. All of the communication skills are more important today than they ever were. Yet that's the one thing that really the students in college aren't spending a lot of time on. So we do some training of communication skills when they get here. Also it is the ability to present an idea so that they know the client understands what they're saying and to know when the client doesn't understand.

> All of the communication skills are more important today than they ever were. Yet that's the one thing that really the students in college aren't spending a lot of time on.

**Gary:** Are there nonbusiness courses, such as communications, that you like to see people have?

**Jay:** The communications are all great. I'd hope that after 150 hours [the new credit requirement to sit for the CPA exam] you would start to get into some of those things. Internally we're starting to do some sales training, networking training, even at about the two-year level and above.

**Gary:** Now, in this firm, what is the career path that a person would take?

**Jay:** In the tax consulting area, we'll very often hire people as interns. Like the other shops in town, when we go out and look for interns we're looking for full-time people. We want people that will intern with us, learn the business, like what they see, and want to come back again in the summer or fall as a full-time employee. That initial staff position is typically a two-year position before they're up for a senior position on our staff. The senior is another roughly two years to a supervisor level, which is a two-year shift to a manager. So here it is about a six-year staff progression. Manager is running at about three years if there is a standard, so you're at nine years in your career until you get to senior manager, and senior manager to partner is typically a two- to three-year step. So in getting to partner it's a total of 11 to 12 years. When I started it was eight years. But today it would be a rare occurrence to have a staff person become a partner in eight years. They'd have to come in with maybe a legal background or something like that. (We have a few attorneys on our staff.)

**Gary:** In your firm is it up or out (i.e., either get promoted or asked to leave)?

**Jay:** I'd say 10 years ago it was up or out. Today we have full-time senior manager positions, full-time manager positions, and full-time paraprofessional positions, quite a few of those. But for the staff and senior staff levels we have few people that do not become managers but stay full time. Typically the first six years [to manager level] is pretty much up or out, unless you're going to be content with a fixed salary and limited duties of preparing returns or reviewing individual returns. However, we would have a place for someone like that.

**Gary:** Do you have a dual track in compliance and consulting, like some of the other firms?

**Jay:** No we haven't figured out how you successfully switch that. We use our compliance as a little bit of our training ground for the consulting. We still think you can teach through the compliance. Yet at the supervisor level and above, hopefully we can get more out of compliance. I push my compliance down to managers so the fewer returns I have to sign, the fewer forms I have to worry about. Then I can deal with the acquisition, disposition, whatever comes up in the everyday tax world of our clients, which is more fun.

In our firm we're working to develop tax consultants as opposed to tax compliance people. In some of our offices we still have partners doing a fair amount of review, getting a lot of chargeable hours in the busy season. Sure, my chargeable hours go up in the busy season because issues come up at that time. But they're much flatter across the board than those of many other partners. So our goal is to get our tax manager group into 60 to 70 percent of their time doing consulting as opposed to compliance. And our senior managers up toward 80 percent and our good partners 80 to 90 percent of their time doing consulting. Right now our good partners are hovering around 70 percent, so it's a continuing move away from compliance and more into the things that you need all the communication skills to do.

We still think you can teach through the compliance.

> In our firm we're working to develop tax consultants as opposed to tax compliance people.

**Gary:** Now, what would you tell someone about how much money you might make in this business?

**Jay:** Now starting salaries are either side of $40,000 with a college degree. Advanced degrees can get more than that. Our managers are into the upper 50s and probably go up to $75,000 or $80,000. Senior managers go from probably $75,000 to $120,000. Some of our full-time senior managers are at the low hundreds and then partner compensation can be probably double or two and one-half times that. For us probably $250,000 is the top end. At the partner level, our average compensation is $170,000 maybe. It's not as high as some people think, and it's not as low as some people think.

> Now [in Minneapolis] starting salaries are either side of $40,000 with a college degree. Advanced degrees can get more than that. Our managers are into the upper 50s and probably go up to $75,000 or $80,000.

**Gary:** In advising someone who is considering a career in tax, how would you view the future of this industry? Is it a growing industry? Or are there dangers of it not growing or even shrinking?

**Jay:** I still think it's a growing industry because if you follow Congress, even if they start over, you're going to have to know the old rules to transition, and the new rules aren't going to be any easier. There's going to be a tax system of some sort. Also, it's just great preparation for almost any other accounting/financial area you may want to go into, consulting-wise.

I always tell people that I've always been working a couple inches over my head from the day I started here, when I didn't know what I was doing. Even up until a half-hour ago before I started this interview, I was still doing things that I've never done. It's been like that for me for 20 years.

**Gary:** Every day you come in and learn something new.

**Jay:** Yes. It's kind of amazing.

**Catherine Holtzclaw, MBT, CPA, Owner, Holtzclaw & Associates, LLC, St. Paul, Minnesota**

**Gary:** How did you first get interested in tax work? How did you know that you wanted to be an accountant?

**Cathy:** I started out in a very traditional way for a woman. I started my college career in elementary education, and that really wasn't ringing my chimes. So I began taking business classes. I took my first accounting class, really enjoyed it, and decided that that was what I wanted to do. I began my career with a public accounting firm in central Illinois with the environment very different from what it is now. This was back in (I will admit) 1967. And it was very different than it is now. Things are really quite a bit more open now for women. I started there while my children were small. I worked in tax primarily. I had a personal loss. I lost my first husband in an automobile accident. I then went back to school and got my master's in business taxation.

**Gary:** So that's after you had been in the accounting business for a while.

**Cathy:** Yes. Before I had my children I had a number of years in public accounting, sat for the CPA exam, and was certified. I was also a controller of a community college, and I taught accounting in a community college. Then I enrolled in the MBA program but then felt that the MBT course work would meet my needs more, and I really got hooked on tax. I had a lot of accountant friends tell me that tax was the worst class they ever took and they didn't like it. Tax seems to be the kind of discipline that either you like it or you don't like it.

> The MBT (Master of Business Taxation) course work would meet my needs more, and I really got hooked on tax.

**Gary:** That's right.

**Cathy:** I really like it. After I received my master's at the University of Minnesota [Master of Business Taxation, MBT] I went to work for a large international CPA firm in downtown Minneapolis and worked there for three or four years. Then I went to work for a fair-sized local CPA firm and then 15 years ago I joined a gentleman in his practice—I bought into his practice. And that's kind of how I started.

**Gary:** What prompted you to go out on your own?

> I got tired of hitting the glass ceiling, and I knew that in the traditional environment I wasn't going to be a partner. . . .

**Cathy:** Frankly, I got tired of hitting the glass ceiling, and I knew that in the traditional environment I wasn't going to be a partner, and I am just a very ambitious person. I had started to develop a practice of my own. I had a client following, but not enough to support myself. That's what motivated me to join someone and buy into his practice.

**Gary:** Now, was this a person who was near retirement?

**Cathy:** No, but he had a practice that was too large for him. He had gotten to the point that tax season was just totally driving him crazy and he realized that he needed to bring someone in.

**Gary:** So did you actually buy accounts or did you just join up with this fellow?

**Cathy:** No, I bought accounts. I established myself and then my practice grew. I have since terminated the relationship with this gentleman and my practice is a good-sized practice. I have three permanent employees. Two of them are accountants, one an office administrator. During tax season I take on other temporary employees to make it through the crunch.

**Gary:** Are you primarily tax, and do your employees then do primarily tax work?

**Cathy:** Yes. Primarily tax work. We work with a lot of small closely held businesses. We do a certain amount of compilation work to get us to the point of actually doing the tax return, but the thrust of a lot of my planning and so on is tax planning, which of course is for the small closely held businesses. I do a lot of individuals. I do 500 individuals and I probably have 100 business clients. But primarily we do tax.

**Gary:** How does your time break down between doing compliance-type work and doing consulting work?

**Cathy:** I'd say maybe 60 percent compliance. It kind of depends upon what you consider consulting, because we do work with a lot of businesses, helping them get set up on Quick Books, etc., so I guess that's kind of consulting. There are a lot of meetings concerning entity selection with people who are thinking about getting into business. But a lot of the individual work is compliance.

**Gary:** When you first started out, did you have a target of a particular type of client that you wanted to work with?

**Cathy:** I could see that my best market was small businesses, one-owner, two-owner kinds of businesses. My clients maybe at most have up to 25 employees. I would say a large percentage of my business owners are women, but that kind of goes with the demographics of who is starting businesses nowadays. Many women are starting businesses. There's still kind of a niche in the fact that you're not going to find very many CPA firms that have women as partners, and a lot of women who are entrepreneurs like to do business with other women.

> You're not going to find very many CPA firms that have women as partners, and a lot of women entrepreneurs like to do business with other women.

**Gary:** Did you ever work out of your home?

**Cathy:** No. I have always worked in an [outside] office. I feel a bit more of the pressure of having a professional presence and not being discounted. Maybe this comes by being a woman. I think some people think that if they go to somebody who is working out of their home and particularly if it's a woman working out of her home, they're going to get a cheap price. I'm here year around. I feel as though a professional image is important.

> I think some people think that if they go to somebody who is working out of their home and particularly if it's a woman working out of her home, they're going to get a cheap price.

Gary: What type of marketing have you done?

Cathy: I advertise some, which is kind of targeted to St. Anthony Park, which is right in the neighborhood. Mostly I do networking. I work in organizations. I work a lot in the neighborhood that my business is in. I'm very active in a local business association and have been on some boards. Also I am in the *Women's Press*. I'm very active in the Midway Chamber of Commerce and have been on the board for the last five years as the treasurer, et cetera. The best networking for me is with other professionals—lawyers, bankers, and somewhat with brokers.

> Mostly I do networking. I work in organizations. I work a lot in the neighborhood that my business is in.

Gary: Your fee schedule is strictly hourly? What do you charge?

Cathy: Right now I am at $130 an hour for my own services. I charge $60 an hour for my specialists.

Gary: What would you say you like best about your work?

Cathy: Working with people and having a continual relationship with them. Some of these people I've worked with for 20 years. It's not like you talk to them all the time. But you have that continuity of watching their families grow and get involved with a lot of their life. Their parents pass away and then you do their parents' estate, and if their kids are in college you do that planning.

Gary: What do you like least?

Cathy: Tax season. It's very difficult when you're pressed to do that much of your work in such a small period of time. In running a business it's very difficult because of your staffing. It's incredible to try to get to people. That's probably the biggest challenge is to try to even out your year a little bit, but it's always going to be deadlines of March 15 and April 15.

Gary: You seem to remain pretty busy during the off season.

Cathy: Yes, although during the off season our offices are open only four days a week. I've worked for too many firms who thought you came out of tax season and then still you drop back to 50 hours a week or something. There's too much in life. I know it would be very easy to get sucked into working all the time. Also I'm pretty committed to the balance and to taking vacations. That's kind of why I just came back from a vacation. And I'm getting ready to go on a vacation. But this is a good time for my husband to leave.

> I've worked for too many firms who thought you came out of tax season and then still you drop back to 50 hours a week or something. There's too much in life.

**Gary:** Now, I'm going to have a little section in this book on purchasing accounts. Do you have any kind of rules of thumb since I think you're the only one I've talked to that has actually bought into a practice?

**Cathy:** I bought into a practice initially and I have now bought part of my former partner's business. We have bought various parts of practices. Typically the way I would be willing to do it would be on a percentage of actual collections over a period of time. I would never buy a practice with money up front, because you never know how much you're going to get. We bought a practice several years ago and it was basically over a three-year time period on the collections that we actually had.

**Gary:** What's a typical percentage?

**Cathy:** In my mind business clients are worth more than individual clients. I would say between 15 and 25 percent [of billings] each year for those first three years. I wouldn't pay 100 percent in those years. At a maximum I would pay 75 percent, but not unless I get it. For each client, you get them into your computer system and then send out a personalized organizer, but you're out money and they could just go somewhere else.

**Gary:** If you were going to sit down with someone who was thinking about entering the tax business, what would you tell that person as far as how long they should work for someone else?

**Cathy:** I think that what you should do is to use the period of time that you're working for someone else to get out there and start networking. I would say that my previous employers did encourage me a lot even though I felt as though I'd never be partner with them and was hitting the glass ceiling. You can't wait until you are going to start a practice. You can't go to a luncheon meeting and get a client. You have to go and participate and join a committee and meet people. People have to trust you before they're going to refer you business. It's a lot of work. When you're working for someone else, you may get no recognition or maybe not even any support for that, but if your ultimate goal is to start your own practice, you have to have your network. And if it's a cause or whatever, it's got to be something you're interested in. If you have the passion for whatever the activity is, that obviously shows. If you're going to do something, do it well. Don't be in 10 organizations, be in two organizations and participate.

Also, you have to have the [tax] experience, and you have to know what you're doing. It's wonderful that I had a master's degree, but it was after I really got down in the trenches and was doing things and doing research and spotting the issues that I learned the business.

> I think that what you should do is to use the period of time that you're working for someone else to get out there and start networking.

### Kevin Koehler, MBT, CPA, Partner, Lund Koehler Cox & Arkema, LLP, Minnetonka, Minnesota

**Gary:** How did you get attracted to the tax profession?

**Kevin:** Oddly enough, when I was in eighth grade we had a Social Studies class and we read *The Professions*. I read *The Accountant*. I was going to be an accountant. So I've always known I was going to be an accountant.

**Gary:** So there was no mentor?

**Kevin:** No. I never knew any accountants. I just read it and said, "That's what I do!" When I got to college I scheduled out all of my four years, including my internship, and I stuck to it all through it. So I've been lucky. I've always known what I wanted to do.

**Gary:** So you think you made the right choice.

**Kevin:** Oh, yes. I can't imagine I'd do anything else. I could do different aspects of the profession, but who I am is an accountant.

**Gary:** And so you wanted to be an accountant. Now, how did you get into the tax area?

**Kevin:** Just client-driven, client needs. In our practice we started out as a sole firm. Lund was the sole practitioner. I knew him from Larson Allen and joined him.

**Gary:** Where did you first start working as an accountant?

**Kevin:** I interned at Deloitte, did that route, and was offered a job. I knew I was going to work at Honeywell for the next three years [doing their audit]. I said, no, I don't want to work on that.

So I went to Larson Allen, because I wanted a smaller firm. Back then there were about 50 people. I just liked one of the partners who were recruiting. So that's how I went to Larson Allen. I was there for three years and then I went with one of my clients as a controller, but later we were acquired by another firm. Kurt Lund, who was another LAWCO [Larson Allen] partner, had since gone on his own. He heard about it and since we kind of knew each other we hooked up. The practice grew until we were about maybe 10 people. We knew we needed a tax person so we went out and interviewed people.

**Gary:** At this point all you're doing is audit stuff?

**Kevin:** I'm doing everything. Compilation, review, audit, tax, I do everything. As a typical small-firm generalist, you do everything. We knew we were growing pretty rapidly, and getting more complex clients, and larger clients because of the referral network. We knew we needed to develop a tax department. So we set out trying to hire somebody and did some interviewing. We came to the conclusion we'd never be able to hire the right person. I decided I had the most interest in tax and most of my practice was tax-driven. I went back and got my MBT degree and I was going to form the tax department. So that's what I did six years ago. I've only been exclusively tax for really the last five years, but I would guess I've practiced tax for 20 years.

**Gary:** How many people do you have now?

**Kevin:** About 55, counting our technology group.

**Gary:** As far as the market is concerned, what if somebody wants to be a tax professional?

**Kevin:** There's a tremendous demand.

**Gary:** Do you see any end to that?

**Kevin:** No, because I think there's a shortage of generalist people going into accounting and further divide that into the tax area. I think the tax area is more demanding from their perception, so it scares off some of the potential people that would go into the area.

**Gary:** When you hire someone, what kind of personality traits are you looking for and what are you least wanting in a candidate?

**Kevin:** Well, first of all you have to have a core competency. Once you have the core competency, the number-one attribute is to be able to manage a client. So you can do what we call taking an ownership of the client, where the client will look to you for their primary tax advisor and maybe in other areas also. That's what we're really looking for—the ability to manage a relationship by taking an ownership of the client. It's somebody who can talk, communicate, and listen.

> Once you have the core competency, the number-one attribute is to be able to manage a client. . . . It's somebody who can talk, communicate, and listen.

**Gary:** Now, if you've got somebody that's just decided they want to be a tax person, let's say an undergraduate, and they're in the tax department, how early do they get client contact?

**Kevin:** In our practice, because they're going to do a little bit of everything, they'll probably do some fieldwork right away. From a tax point of view, the way they get the most client contact is just by simply calling clients with questions. However, the way we try to get them involved in the process is to have them go to client meetings. Early on a lot of times they may be just sitting in a corner, not literally but figuratively, and not doing a lot other than being introduced and saying hi. I may ask them questions so we get them in the process. We think that's our best way to get people familiar with the consulting practice.

**Gary:** And what is the career path once they've decided to move into the tax area for your firm?

**Kevin:** I think our path here is: Senior is two to three years, manager is six years, and partner probably 10. In today's world it's really how fast you can progress. A lot of times it becomes a maturity issue. People have different levels of maturity. Some people at 24 are just not going to have the client's confidence no matter what they do and no matter how well they do it. So initial maturity is a factor. Usually starting in the 30s they'd be partner-level material. Our new partners are 32 to 33, so it's been 10 years. I think that's a good path. But frankly client contact and having complete client control would be at three years.

> Senior is two to three years, manager is six years, and partner probably ten. In today's world it's really how fast you can progress.

**Gary:** What would you tell someone who was wondering how much money they could make in this business, as far as the first couple years, then five years, then 10 years?

**Kevin:** Maybe we should just jump to the middle. At about five years you'd probably be somewhere between $60,000 and $75,000, which would be a good level in today's market. After that partnership just depends on how good a partnership you're in. I would say partner compensation would be $75,000 to $300,000. That would be a range, which is a really wide range because it really depends on the firm you're in. I can't imagine a tax partner being at less than $150,000 with a firm of any size at all.

**Gary:** What do you see as the hottest areas in tax, the biggest growth areas?

**Kevin:** Some of the areas are growth areas and some of the areas keep me awake at night. Mergers and acquisitions is always hot and especially big in the consulting area, because there's a lot of activity on the market with businesses being sold. Now sales tax is a big area. Clients used to be geographically located and worked in that geographical area, so if you had a Minnesota client you did Minnesota taxes. When I started 20 years ago I did very little out-of-state work. A typical client was located in Minnesota, where maybe sometimes I did some of the border states. Now almost all clients are in almost all states and are getting to be international. With state taxes it's not so much the income tax that becomes the issue, because that's kind of just who between the states gets the piece of the pie. Rather it's the sales tax issues. The clients don't think about it [sales tax] but it's an area that keeps me awake at night.

International is becoming a huge area in a lot of different ways. Talent-wise it's especially big in the software industry, which itself is a big area. A lot of the people coming over are foreigners, so we're getting a lot into that aspect. So international is another hot tax area.

Obviously estate and trust tax are now a growing area with the wealth transfer. Certainly the stock market has been a big part of that. Long-term tax planning for your high-net-worth clients is now a big area, and we have started to do that.

Mergers and acquisitions is always hot and especially big in the consulting area, because there's a lot of activity on the market with businesses being sold.

**Gary:** Now, within your group, do you have employees who specialize in particular areas?

**Kevin:** Now we're starting to. Again, the size and the growth of the firm is dictating that. We're all generalists, but we are all starting to a certain degree to find our areas. We know that we need to specialize even more. We have one fellow that has a very narrow niche practice in doing cost segregation studies. This involves breaking out the costs on buildings into shorter lives. That's a very specific tax consulting area that Jim, one of our tax partners, has carved out. He's spending a good deal of time there, and he also does mergers and acquisitions. He's a tax partner that's really developed kind of a market niche and doesn't do general service work. When I think of general service I think of general planning and compliance. He is really doing all planning and doesn't do really any compliance work.

We have one fellow that has a very narrow niche practice in doing cost segregation studies.

**Gary:** Getting back, if you were going to interview a new candidate, what personal attributes are you really excited about and what personality traits are you trying to avoid? Assume you're going interview a tax person, an MBT graduate.

**Kevin:** Well, things that impress me are one, just the presence a person has. Even in tax work it is really sales work. You may have a great idea or a great answer, but the client is the one that really makes the decision whether they think it's a great answer. It's the ability to effectively communicate, to portray a confidence. You can almost get that feeling when you walk into a room and you meet somebody. A first impression is usually a pretty good one. Confidence is certainly a strong attribute. Accounting is always a tough business and it is long hours. I think I'd be lying to

... the ability to juggle the work and the time lines, and the clients and their expectations is an absolute must.

say you're going to have a nice 40-hour week. It's a demanding job. The ability to work hard and not wear out is still a character trait that you really need. Another one is the ability to juggle the work and the time lines, and the clients and their expectations is an absolute must. You could be the smartest guy in the world but if you can't handle 12 clients that are all asking for their stuff tomorrow and somehow juggle that and keep them all happy, you're not what we are looking for. That's an ability that I don't know how to articulate but you can't survive unless you could do that. It's like when I tell somebody yes, we're working on it. Sometimes I'm not working on it at that time, and the client may know that but he or she knows I'll get it done.

Also important I think is honesty and the ability to face up to clients and have their trust. When you do screw up you can say "Hey, I goofed," and most clients will let you get away with it unless it's a massive mistake. Most clients are pretty forgiving in a lot of areas. Character traits that don't work are just the opposite. You can take the characteristics that are desirable and take the ones that aren't. For example, can't manage clients, wears out, can't manage multiple databases are some of those.

Also important I think is honesty and the ability to face up to clients and have their trust.

**Gary:** Some of the larger firms have alternative tracks say for working parents. Do you have something like that?

**Kevin:** One of our tax partners is an MBT out of De Paul. I think she works 40 hours a week, but she is considered part time. At times she works far more than that. If full time she would be at 70 hours per week. What dictates her schedule is her kids and that her husband travels. She tries to work three days a week during the off season and full time during busy season with some limitations on that amount. That's the reality to get talent.

**Gary:** With respect to courses and educational background other than the MBT, are you looking for certain areas that people might have?

**Kevin:** I think writing is always the biggest. I'm not a very good writer. I write a lot of tax appeals and I write some that are very informal. I wish my writing skills were a lot better. I have the advantage that my wife writes appeals for the county so I usually write it and she just rips it.

**Gary:** What is your favorite aspect of the job?

**Kevin:** Well, I think a good client relationship is the most satisfying, and the intellectual stimulation. Figuring stuff out is still fun to me. It's fun being an expert. It's kind of fun to look at something and know it, which is second nature to me.

**Gary:** Well, you're a pretty big firm now.

**Kevin:** Yes. I never realized that but we probably are. We just hired an outside consulting firm to help us try to focus. A lot of firms operate as a bunch of sole practitioners formed in a group. We're trying to be operating as a firm and focus our resources on what we should be working on. It is really much harder to do than you'd think it would be.

**Gary:** Interesting, but a fun thing to work on.

**Kevin:** I like what I do. I'm proud of the firm.


**Edward M. Ryan, MBT, CPA, CFP, PFS, President, Edward M. Ryan, CPA, Minneapolis, Minnesota**

**Gary:** How did you become interested in tax, Ed?

**Ed:** It goes back to the time I spent in Chicago. That is when I had my first public accounting experience. I was assigned to the tax department of a major regional company and I spent my first tax season filling out forms, Fast Tax forms. At the same time I dislocated my shoulder while playing hockey, so that was really fun playing tax man while shuffling around forms with one hand. What interested me about taxation was the fact it was logical, there were rules and laws, and it was interesting applying those rules to daily life. That's what got me initially interested. Then I moved to the Twin Cities and joined a very small firm, a one-man firm. I was assigned the responsibility of running an office my first year. That year we prepared about 500 individual tax returns, all done by hand.

**Gary:** How did you get interested in accounting?

**Ed:** I started my college career in pre-med, which was a mistake because I wasn't cut out for medicine. After a year of attempting biology, and zoology, and chemistry and physics and all that good stuff, I had to find a second career. Of course, naturally it would be accounting. I took a variety of courses. I took some history, some English, and some accounting. When I took the accounting course there was a certain logic to it. Math is something that I had always enjoyed, and it made sense. Accounting made sense. It was a good fit for my way of thinking and I continue to have that interest. I graduated from St. Norbert College in Green Bay, Wisconsin.

**Gary:** Then you came to Minneapolis and went to work for a small firm. Now, what brought you here?

**Ed:** I was let go by the firm in Chicago after the first tax season. And they told me, "You know, you should be in sales." I said, "Well, I'm not really interested in sales. I like accounting. I like tax."

**Gary:** These days they'd be wanting you because you should be in sales.

**Ed:** Right. Every job is sales anyway. I interviewed here in the Twin Cities. I came here because I went to school here for a year at St. John's in Collegeville. It was a nice town, it was a sizable town, and it was good for a change. About two or three years after I first joined the practitioner here I wanted to do more on the business side. I signed up for a new program at the University of Minnesota. It was called a Master's in Business Taxation, an MBT. I think it was up and running about a year or maybe two, not many. I was very interested in getting to know the technical side of incentive compensation, profit-sharing, estates, gifting, income taxes, partnership, corporations, and so forth so that the clientele that I served could be served better. And so I did that between 1980 and 1985.

> I signed up for a new program at the University of Minnesota. It was called a master's in business taxation, an MBT.

**Gary:** How long were you with the other fellow?

**Ed:** I was with the other fellow for about seven years, one as an employee and six as a partner. In 1986 I started my own firm. I started with myself and a secretary and away we went.

**Gary:** So you wanted to broaden your base a little bit?

**Ed:** I really did. I really had more of an interest in the planning than I did in the compliance, while his interest was in compliance. Not that we don't do compliance, but the fun is in the planning. It makes you more accountable because now you have a target you have to hit. It's a lot more fun because there's more of a reward that you're able to share with your clients. Tax and planning provides a great opportunity to really assist families in the management of their financial affairs. It's very self-fulfilling because you can see the results and they're reoccurring.

> Tax and planning provides a great opportunity to really assist families in the management of their financial affairs. It's very self-fulfilling because you can see the results and they're reoccurring.

**Gary:** What do you like the best and what do you like the least about what you're doing today?

**Ed:** Well, the best thing is delivering the goods, if you will. Meaning, giving families an opportunity to manage their financial affairs confidently. They're in a position where they're more knowledgeable, they understand what's going on, and they're now able to implement the plan. So a lot of it is really education. They're educating me about their family lifestyle and I'm educating them about tax and planning opportunities. So that's very rewarding. That's the reason you get up every day.

What is the one thing I'd like not to be able to do? Let's see. I think some of the technical compliance requirements tend to get overbearing from time to time.

They're educating me about their family lifestyle and I'm educating them about tax and planning opportunities. . . . That's the reason you get up every day.

In our industry there's a lot of checkmarking required, in regard to financial accounting and of course in regard to tax as well.

**Gary:** When you first started out, did you focus on a particular niche or a particular type of client?

**Ed:** I think when we started we saw a probable need in executive planning. Executives at that time weren't really thinking about tax aspects, for example, of stock options, deferred compensation, or maybe executing some acceleration in regards to the deductibility of items. They weren't really clued into that. When we started, we developed these tax plans that would go for a year or two, or three, and place their income and their expenses on this. That plan would be the platform or the vehicle we would use to implement and discuss strategy that they might be interested in.

Executives at that time weren't really thinking about tax aspects . . . of stock options, deferred compensation, or . . . acceleration in regards to the deductibility of items. They weren't really clued into that.

**Gary:** So you are a Certified Financial Planner?

**Ed:** Yes I am. I'm also a PFS [Personal Financial Specialist], which is the AICPA's designation. The concepts of financial planning apply themselves very easily, not only to the family, but to the business. So, when we do tax and planning we're really doing it from the perspective of cash flow, succession, individual income tax issues, maybe retirement issues, but their concepts are all the same. You basically have an engine that's the cash flow, whether it be the personal cash flow or the business cash flow. You also have the output or the assets that are the accumulation on the business side or the accumulation on the personal side. The idea is to convert labor to capital.

To take the PFS exam, a candidate must hold a valid CPA certificate. Candidates for the PFS designation must have completed an experience requirement before they register for the examination. The PFS designation is intended to identify CPAs with expertise and experience in personal financial planning, not those who want to enter this field.

**Gary:** Now, did you have a marketing program for attracting this type of client?

**Ed:** Yes. A lot of what we did would be through our relationships with other professionals. That was probably number one. We did do some marketing. We sent out some brochures to various locations in the Twin Cities. But the primary growth of the business happened through (as it does today) a one-on-one relationship with a referral source. We have a group of folks that we've known for a number of years. Whether they be in insurance or investment or legal or the banking industry, they are familiar with what we do. It's through those relationships that we see the most fruit from.

> . . . the primary growth of the business happened through . . . a one-on-one relationship with a referral source.

**Gary:** In the financial planning area, do you sell any products in your firm?

**Ed:** No, we don't. We've had the opportunity to do so. We've been solicited many times, but our approach is that we want to stay in our niche, where we are very comfortable and we have been successful. We like what we do. We like tax and planning. We want our relationship with a client to be independent in fact and in appearance, and that's important to us. So, we don't have plans to nor we are presently considering anything but a fee-based firm.

**Gary:** What's your hourly fee?

**Ed:** My stated rate is $250. My realization is less than that.

**Gary:** Now, Ed, you've grown substantially. Do you have a business plan for the size that you'd like to see your firm at or any kind of strategic plan that you've put together?

**Ed:** No. We don't have a structured financial plan for the firm. But we do have a very sharp focus as to what we want to accomplish, and we will continue to hire until we do. The sharp focus that we have is that we feel we're in a position uniquely in terms of our client relationships and trust—whereby our objective is not really to meet a client's needs, but rather we want to anticipate their needs because of the experience that we have. We will continue to invest in our employees and new employees until such time as we feel that we've accomplished that. And we're not there yet. So I really don't have a vision of five or 50 or 500. We really have more of a vision of anticipating client needs, and that's the high ground that we want to accomplish. That's where we want to be. And we're getting there, but we're not there yet.

> . . . we do have a very sharp focus as to what we want to accomplish, and we will continue to hire until we do.

Gary: If you were going to sit down with someone who was interested in entering the tax profession, what would you say about the number of years that they should work for someone before launching out on their own?

Ed: It really depends on the person. I think two to five years would give you some real confidence and solidity in, most importantly, how to engage. Meaning, we're in such a technical field. The tax and planning field is very technical. You need to have the ability to convert the tax and planning language (what I like to call Greek) to English for the client. That takes a while to sort of master the technical side and then to enunciate that or to identify that clearly, so that the client can actually act on it. It really does depend on the person. I've seen folks in the past who are very focused, very sharp, very engaging, and have an easy time of it. At the same time there are those who have a lot more difficulty.

> You need to have the ability to convert the tax and planning language (what I like to call Greek) to English for the client.

Gary: Again it relates to your last answer. What personality traits do you think are most valuable for someone in the tax consulting area?

Ed: Well, there are a lot of good technicians out there. There are a lot of folks who can tumble the numbers and are mathematicians or are theoreticians, they're very good at that. But I don't think there are as many folks who are really willing to share themselves in a way in which the transmission of value has occurred. Meaning if the client really senses and realizes that you really care about their situation and you are willing and able to solicit, offer, and recommend scenarios and options that would be helpful, that is what it's all about. It is also if you can solicit the goodwill of your clients, and what that really means is that you have to personally invest yourself. You can't do it by sitting on the bench. You're going to have to risk something. People understand that, and people know that—if you're really in it or not. If you are, then you are going to be a lot more successful.

# Resource Guide

## TAX-RELATED WEB SITES

| *Organization* | *Web Site Address* |
|---|---|
| Accreditation Council for Accountancy and Taxation | www.acatcredentials.org |
| American Bar Association Section of Taxation | www.abanet.org/tax/ |
| American Institute of CPAs | www.aicpa.org |
| Bureau of National Affairs Tax Portfolios on the Web | www.bnatax.com |
| CFS Income Tax | www.taxtools.com |
| Commerce Clearing House | www.cch.com |
| Econotax Franchises | www.econotax.com/ |
| Emory University School of Law Tax Page | tax.law.emory.edu |
| Internal Revenue Service | www.irs.gov |
| Jackson Hewitt Tax Service (franchisor) | www.jacksonhewitt.com |
| Kleinrock Publishing | www.kleinrock.com |
| LawSchool.Com | www.lawschool.com |
| Lexis-Nexis | www.lexis-nexis.com |

| | |
|---|---|
| Liberty Tax Service (franchisor) | www.libertytax.com |
| National Association of Enrolled Agents | www.naea.org |
| National Association of Tax Practitioners | www.natptax.com |
| National Society of Accountants | www.nsacct.org |
| National Society of Tax Professionals | www.nstp.org |
| Peoples Income Tax Service (franchisor) | www.peoplesinc.com |
| Professor Tax, Inc. (franchisor) | www.professortax.com |
| Research Institute of America | www.riahome.com |
| Tax Analysts | www.tax.org |
| Tax Search, Incorporated | www.taxsearchinc.com |
| Tax Sites Directory (comprehensive directory) | www.taxsites.com |
| Tax-Jobs.Com | www.tax-jobs.com |
| The Internal Revenue Code Online | www.law.cornell.edu/uscode/26 |
| U.S. House of Representatives | www.house.gov/ |

## BOOKS

Adams, Bob. *Complete Business Plan* (Adams Streetwise Publication, 1998).

Dugan, Ann, ed. *Franchising 101: The Complete Guide to Evaluating, Buying and Growing Your Franchise Business* (Upstart Publishing, 1998).

Rich, Jason R. *The Unofficial Guide to Starting a Business Online* (IDG Books Worldwide, 2000).

# ORGANIZATIONS

## *CPA Review Courses*

Here is a partial list of professional CPA review courses available to candidates. Many colleges and universities also offer CPA review courses.

Becker CPA Review
15760 Ventura Blvd.
Encino, CA 91436
818-981-3233

Convisor-Duffy CPA Review
176 West Adams, #2100
Chicago, IL 60603
312-782-5170

Kaplan CPA Review
888 Seventh Avenue
New York, NY 10106
800-KAP-TEST
www.kaplan.com/accounting

Gleim CPA Review
P.O. Box 12848
Gainesville, FL 32604
800-87-GLEIM
sales@gleim.com

Lambers CPA Review
790 Turnpike Street, Suite 203
North Andover, MA 01845
800-272-0707
978-685-5002
www.lamberscpa.com

Logicat, Inc.
18 West 27th Street
New York, NY 10001
212-529-1840

MicroMash CPA Review
6402 S. Troy Circle
Englewood, CO 80111
800-CPA-PASS
www.MicroMash.com/learning
MicroMash@aol.com

Person/Wolinsky CPA Review
4 Roosevelt Avenue
Port Jefferson Station, NY 11776
888-CPA-PREP
www.cpareview.com

Rigos CPA Review
1326 Fifth Avenue, #230
Seattle, WA 98101
800-636-0716
206-624-0716
www.rigosrev.com

Totaltape CPA Review
9417 Princess Palm Avenue
Tampa, FL 33619
www.cpaexam.com
bisk@bisk.com

Wiley CPA Review
605 Third Avenue
New York, NY 10158-0012
800-272-2100 (orders only)
www.wiley.com/cpa.html
cpa@wiley.com

Wise Guides, Inc.
1061 Fraternity Circle
Kent, OH 44240
800-713-2098
216-673-1616

## *Tax Organizations*

National Association of Enrolled Agents
200 Orchard Ridge Drive, Suite 302
Gaithersburg, MD 20878
301-212-9608
301-990-1611 (fax)
www.naea.org

National Society of Tax Professionals
P.O. Box 2575
Vancouver, WA 98668-2575
360-695-8309
360-695-7115 (fax)
ATTN: EA Exam Department
www.nstp.org

National Association of Tax
Practitioners
720 Association Drive
Appleton, WI 54914-1483
800-558-3402 (U.S.)
800-242-3430 (WI)
800-747-0001 (fax)
www.natptax.com

# Notes

## Chapter 1   The Role of a Tax Consultant

1. See IRS Publication 947, "Practice Before the IRS and Power of Attorney."
2. IRC §6694.
3. This is an actual Tax Court case, accurately represented. TC Memo 1993-323.
4. IRC §7433.
5. IRC §7811.
6. Form 1040 Instructions, p. 4.

## Chapter 2   Enduring Demand for Tax Services

1. "Demand for Tax Pros Hits an All-Time High," http://careers.wsj.com, April 4, 2000.
2. Testimony Before the House Committee on Ways and Means, Hearing on Fundamental Tax Reform, Statement of Frank Luntz, Ph.D., President and CEO, Luntz Research Companies, April 13, 2000.
3. 158 U.S. 601 (1895).
4. 240 U.S. 1 (1916).
5. Jeffery L. Yablon, "As Certain As Death—Quotations about Taxes (Expanded 2000 Edition)," 86 *Tax Notes* 231 (January 10, 2000).
6. Michael J. Graetz, "The U.S. Income Tax: Should It Survive the Millennium?" 85 *Tax Notes* 1197 (November 29, 1999).
7. Yablon, "As Certain As Death—Quotations about Taxes."
8. Susan Page and William M. Welch, "Things-to-Do 1998: Tax Reform Tops List," *USA Today*, December 22, 1997 (reporting results of *USA Today*/CNN/Gallup Poll, that 5 percent of those surveyed consider the current system "basically fine" and 95 percent want change); Ann Reilly Dowd, "Get the Facts on Tax Reform," *Money*, January 1998, at 86 (reporting result of November 1997 *Money*/ICR Research poll, in which two out of three respondents favored Dick Armey's version of the flat tax).
9. Robert Hall and Alvin Rabushka, *The Flat Tax*, 2nd ed. (Hoover Institution Press, January 1995).
10. See www.flattax.gov.
11. USA Tax Act of 1995, S. 722, 104th Cong. (1995).
12. "Testimony Before the House Committee on Ways and Means, Hearing on Fundamental Tax Reform," Statement of Jefrey Pollock, President, Global Strategy Group, Inc., April 13, 2000.
13. See www.house.gov/tauzin/cvr.htm.
14. Gene Steuerle, "Cutting Taxes—Why the Limited Enthusiasm?" 87 *Tax Notes* 1275 (May 29, 2000).
15. Bruce Bartlett, *Washington Times*, October 18, 1999, p. A16.

16. "Treasury Report on Simplification and Reform," U.S. Treasury, November 27, 1984.
17. Graetz, "The U.S. Income Tax."

## Chapter 3   Self-Assessment and Education

1. Herb Cohen, *You Can Negotiate Anything* (Bantam Books, 1982), p. 15.
2. David Leonhardt, "Battle of the Graduate Schools," *New York Times*, July 5, 2000.

## Chapter 4   Your Business Plan

1. Albert S. Williams, *On Your Own! How to Start Your Own CPA Firm*, (American Institute of Certified Public Accountants, 1990).
2. D. Timothy Bates, "Franchise Startups: Low Profitability and High Failure Rates," *EGII News* (December 1993), p. 9.
3. Ann Dugan, ed., *Franchising 101: The Complete Guide to Evaluating, Buying and Growing Your Franchise Business* (Upstart Publishing, 1998).
4. Bob Adams, *Complete Business Plan* (Adams Streetwise Publication, 1998).
5. *AICPA Management of an Accounting Practice Handbook* (American Institute of Certified Public Accountants, 2000).

## Chapter 5   Choices for Business Organization

1. Frank Zaffino, "Projections of Returns to Be Filed in Calendar Years 1999–2005," 18 *SOI Bulletin* 178, 184 Table 1, 179 fig. A (No. 3, 1999).
2. Donald C. Alexander, "The Questionable Continued Flourishing of S Corporations," 87 *Tax Notes* 577 (April 24, 2000).

## Chapter 6   A Little about Taxes, Permits, and Record Keeping

1. Gary W. Carter, *J.K. Lasser's Taxes Made Easy for Your Home-Based Business*, 4th ed. (New York: John Wiley & Sons, 2000).

## Chapter 7   Tax Research and the Tools of the Trade

1. The rule is in §7805 of the Code.
2. See Rev. Proc. 2000-3, 2000-1 I.R.B. 103, for the latest list of areas in which the IRS will not issue advance rulings.
3. See Rev. Proc. 2000-1, 2000-1 I.R.B. 4, for these rules.
4. Rev. Proc. 99-42, 1999-46 I.R.B. 1, shows what these amounts are for 2000.
5. *Robert F. Six and Ethel Merman Six v. United States*, 450 F 66 (2d Cir. 1971).
6. *Coerver v. Commissioner*, 297 F.2d 837 (3d Cir. 1962); *Bercaw v. Commissioner*, 165 F.2d 521 (4th Cir. 1948); *Commissioner v. Mooneyman*, 404 F.2d 522 (6th Cir. 1968); *England v. United States*, 345 F.2d 414 (7th Cir. 1965); *Jenkins v. Commissioner*, 418 F.2d 1292 (8th Cir. 1969); *Wills v. Commissioner*, 411 F.2d 357 (9th Cir. 1969); and *York v. Commissioner*, 160 F.2d 385 (D.C. Cir. 1947).

## Chapter 8  Starting and Running a Part-Time Web-Based Tax Service

1. Andy Shafran and Dick Oliver, *Creating Your Own Web Graphics with Paint Shop Pro* (Que Corporation, 1996).
2. Steve Bain and Daniel Gray, *Looking Good Online: The Ultimate Resource for Creating Effective Web Designs* (Ventana Communications Group, 1996).
3. Greg Sandoval, "Small Tax Web Sites Angle for Big Bite," CNET News.com, April 13, 2000.
4. Jason R. Rich, *The Unofficial Guide to Starting a Business Online* (IDG Books Worldwide, 2000).
5. "Dot-Com Name Shortage Yields Many New Companies," *New York Times*, August 28, 2000.
6. "Web Tax Preparers Take on the Big Guys," *Los Angeles Times*, March 8, 2000.

## Chapter 9  Getting to Know the Internal Revenue Service

1. Testimony Before the House Committee on Ways and Means, Hearing on Fundamental Tax Reform, Statement of Frank Luntz, Ph.D., President and CEO, Luntz Research Companies, April 13, 2000.
2. IRS Publication 3349, "Modernizing America's Tax Agency."
3. Ibid.
4. Ibid.
5. Ibid.
6. Ibid.
7. Ibid.
8. "IRS Modernization," www.irs.gov/prod/news/mod-faq4.html#Q8.
9. "IRS Modernization," www.irs.gov/prod/news/irs-mod.html.
10. IRS Restructuring and Reform Act of 1998, §2001(a).
11. IRS Restructuring and Reform Act of 1998, §2003.
12. "FY 1999 National Taxpayer Advocate's Annual Report to Congress," www.irs.gov/prod/ind_info/rpt99-prob19.html.

# Index